Far Above Rubies

The Women Uncommemorated
by the Church of England

To

Alison Adcock

But for whose efforts even fewer women would be
commemorated by the Church of England

Far Above Rubies

The Women Uncommemorated by the Church of England

Richard Symonds

'*Who can find a virtuous woman? For her price is far above rubies.*'

Proverbs, 31, 10

First Published in 1993
Gracewing
Fowler Wright Books
Southern Avenue, Leominster
Herefordshire HR6 0QF

Gracewing Books are distributed

In New Zealand by	*In Australia by*
Catholic Supplies Ltd	Charles Paine Pty
80 Adelaide Rd	8 Ferris Street
Wellington	North Parramatta
New Zealand	NSW 2151 Australia

In U.S.A. by	*In Canada by*
Morehouse Publishing	Meakin & Associates
P.O. Box 1321	Unit 17, 81 Auriga Drive
Harrisburg	Nepean, Ontario, KZE 7Y5
PA 17105	Canada
U.S.A.	

The right of Richard Symonds to be identified as the author of this work has been asserted in accordance with the Copyright, Designs and Patents Act, 1988

ISBN 0 85244 244 0

Typesetting by Action Typesetting Ltd, Gloucester

Printed in Great Britain by Loader Jackson, Arlesey.

Contents

List of Plates

Preface and Acknowledgements

In 1988 a book by me was published as *Alternative Saints –
The Post Reformation People Commemorated by the Church
of England*. In this the lives were discussed of those British
people who lived in the Church's own lifetime and who each
have been allotted an annual day in the list of Lesser Festivals and Commemorations in the Calendar of the Alternative
Service Book (1980). In seeking to understand why each of
these was chosen whilst others were excluded, the question
arose of why so little attention had been given to the claims of
women. Among the twenty post Reformation British people,
only one woman, Josephine Butler, was reluctantly included.
The reason given for this disparity by the Chair of the responsible Committee was that conduct which was regarded as
sanctity in men had traditionally been regarded as insanity
in women.

The implication that no other women worthy of commemoration could be found presented a challenge which this book
has been written to meet.

The Alternative Service Book (1980) is licensed until the year
2000. When its extension or revision is considered, there seems
little doubt that the list of those who are allotted days in its
Calendar will be expanded. Under a convention by which no
one is included who has not been dead for 50 years, a number
of people will in any case become eligible in 2000 who were not
in 1980; it appears likely that not only the claims of these but
of others who lived earlier, but were previously overlooked,
will be considered. It would be surprising at a time when there
has been so much discussion of ordination of women if there
is not also strong interest in the inclusion of more women in
the Church's Calendar.

Lord Longford, in reviewing *Alternative Saints* in *The
Tablet*, said that 'One of its merits is to leave us with a
delightful parlour game' in the discussion of who deserved to

be commemorated. I hope that the present book also will contribute to a debate at various levels which will help to ensure that the future selection is made in a less hurried and better informed manner than was the case in the ASB (1980).

The book is self contained and assumes no knowledge of *Alternative Saints*.

I am grateful to several friends who have read and criticized the book in draft and above all to Mrs Alison Adcock who was the eloquent champion of the claims of women to commemoration during the discussions of the ASB in the General Synod and its Revision Committee in 1978. She has furnished me with lists of possible candidates which have been invaluable. Canon A.M. Allchin, Director of the St Theosevia Centre in Oxford, has generously shared with me his knowledge of the history of saints and of Anglican Sisterhoods and has persuaded me to include a chapter on Mother Harriet Monsell. Canon Geoffrey Rowell and Rev. William Pickering have also kindly read and commented on the draft.

I should like to thank the following for assistance on particular aspects:

Sister Mary Eleanor of the Community of the Resurrection of Our Lord, London, for access to unpublished material on Mother Cecile.

The Reverend Mother Superior of the Community of St John Baptist and its historian, Mrs Valerie Bonham, for help with Mother Harriet Monsell.

Dr Carl Bridge of Armidale, N.S.W., and George Ivan Smith for help with Caroline Chisholm.

Mr and Mrs Lionel Jebb for allowing me access to the papers of Eglantyne Jebb at her childhood home at Ellesmere, and for saving me from various errors in writing about her.

Professor Aparna Basu of New Delhi for criticizing the chapter on Pandita Ramabai.

Ms Janice Murray of the McManus Galleries in Dundee and the staff of the Dundee Central Library for access to unpublished letters and memoirs of Mary Slessor.

The staff of the Walsall Local History Library for access to materials on Sister Dora.

Lady Laura Easthaugh and Dr Grace Brame for help with Evelyn Underhill.

Major Jenty Fairbank of the Salvation Army for material on Catherine Booth.

I wish to thank the following for permission to reproduce illustrations: The National Portrait Gallery, London, Mr. Lionel Jebb, The State Library of New South Wales, Kings' College, London, Mrs. Valerie Bonham, The Community of the Resurrection of Our Lord, The Walsall Local History Collection, The Dundee Art Gallery and Museum, The Salvation Army International Heritage Centre and The Community of St. John Baptist, Clewer.

Finally, I should like to thank my wife, Ann Spokes Symonds for constant encouragement and valuable advice.

Because lists of books for further reading are listed at the end of the chapters about individual women, no bibliography has been thought necessary; one book which I have found generally valuable, though, alas, out of print, is Katherine Moore's *She for God*, (Allison and Busby, London, 1978).

Oxford   Richard Symonds

Introduction

In 1978 the General Synod of the Church of England met to approve the final version of its Alternative Service Book (ASB) which was to be its first new prayer book for 300 years. In the Calendar of the new book the saints of the Apostolic period appeared under the heading 'Festivals and Greater Holy Days', but in addition there was a section of 'Lesser Festivals and Commemorations' in which were included people who had lived not only before the Reformation but after it, within the Church of England's own lifetime.

The list of the people proposed for inclusion in the new section had emerged from a long process of consultation by the Liturgical Commission, followed by a review by the Revision Committee which was responsible for producing the final draft of the ASB. Compromise and balancing were evident. Thus Thomas More was included together with both Cranmer, who took part in the examination which led to his execution, and Tyndale who More when Lord Chancellor would probably have caused to be condemned to death if he had laid hands on him. Charles I was confronted by Bunyan, who served in Cromwell's army. Many of the venerated figures who established the Church's Middle Way were there — Hooker, Andrewes, George Herbert, Nicholas Ferrar and Jeremy Taylor. The High Church was well represented by Ken, Keble and Edward King; the Evangelicals by the Wesleys, Simeon, and Wilberforce. William Law represented the mystic tradition and James Hannington the missionary martyrs. Yet one lobby seemed to have been strangely inactive or unsuccessful. Among the names which came to the General Synod for approval in 1978 there were no British women who had lived since the Reformation. Even Elizabeth Fry and Florence Nightingale, who had been proposed earlier by the Liturgical Commission, had been deleted. Few women who had lived since biblical times indeed appeared at all.

1

The Chairman of the Revision Committee, Dr Margaret Hewitt, was aware that there might be criticisms on this account, for in introducing the draft, she stated bluntly:

> 'There can be no doubt that, in the present day, any suggestion that women are discriminated against gives rise to unease and concern. The Revision Committee, however, was not concerned with the operation of the Equal Opportunities Act, since it was concerned with sanctity, not equality ... We did not feel able to accede to the view that women should have any greater claim to our support than men, simply because they were women.'

It was not surprising, she added, 'that women appear in relatively small numbers in the ranks of the sanctified, since up to very recent times in the West, it was more difficult, and certainly less acceptable, for women than men to distinguish themselves in society without attracting odium. Hence it was arguable that behaviour which was held to imply sanctity in men only appeared as insanity when engaged in by women and was recorded as such by their contemporaries.'[1]

There was one member of the General Synod, Mrs Alison Adcock, the wife of an Oxfordshire vicar, who firmly refused to accept this explanation. In the General Synod debate she protested that the number, range and variety of women in the draft Calendar were inadequate and that there were lamentable gaps. Of the six post-biblical women included, she pointed out, three were nuns, and little was known about the lives of the three others, of whom two, Saint Felicity and Saint Perpetua, were young martyrs. 'We Christian wives, mothers, widows and spinsters,' she declared, 'need women Christian heroines and saints to look up to and take as our examples. We cannot look to men to show us how to fulfil these vocations, but all Christians need the reminder afforded by such saints of the breadth of the spectrum of Christian excellence and how brightly it can shine in home and family.'[2]

Pertinaciously she put forward a series of amendments. Two, proposing Catherine of Siena and Queen Margaret of Scotland, were carried. Two, suggesting Lady Margaret Beaufort and Saint Jane Chantal, were defeated. The fifth amendment, proposing Josephine Butler, was defeated by 3 votes in the General Synod. The Bishop of Derby, Dr C.W.J. Bowles, however, prompted by the indomitable Mrs Adcock, persuaded the House of Bishops by one vote to reverse this decision and to include Mrs Butler, not only for her own virtues but in recognition of the contribution made to the Church by parsons' wives. With some grumbling, the General Synod accepted the amendment, which could not have been deleted at this stage without throwing out the whole Draft Calendar. Josephine Butler thus scraped into the ASB as the only British post-Reformation woman, along with 19 men.[3] One other woman, St Teresa of Avila, found a place among five post-Reformation Continental Roman Catholics, the others being St Francis de Sales, St Vincent de Paul, St Francis Xavier and St John of the Cross.

The purpose of this book is to suggest that a much more equitable representation of women could be achieved in the list of those people who are commemorated by the Church of England. It is also hoped that the lives of those considered may have a more general interest, for several of them are not well known and all were pioneers in various ways.

In the process of selection the question immediately arises of the criteria which should be applied. How the Church came to decide to honour later Heroes of the Faith is described briefly in the appendix of this book and at more length in the present writer's earlier book *Alternative Saints*.[4] The Church of England does not make saints, though it inherited saints from the Roman Catholic Church at the Reformation and included them in its Book of Common Prayer. The only post-Reformation person whom it ever commemorated before 1980 was King Charles I, for the anniversary of whose death services were prescribed in 1662 but were deleted from the Prayer Book in 1859. The Roman Catholic Church has specific criteria for recognizing saints: the three theological virtues of faith, hope and charity and the four cardinal virtues of prudence, justice, fortitude and temperance must have been shown to a heroic degree and confirmed after death; and miracles must be proved. However the Church of England's criteria for commemoration are much less precise. In circulating a list of candidates in 1969 the Liturgical Commission declared 'We do not make saints. What may be said about each of the people whose names are recorded in this list is that their life and example excite us to holiness.' Those listed were not, it said, to be regarded as mere representative figures, chosen to represent a geographical area, a period in the Church's history or to reflect some aspects of its life. 'They are individual men and women whose lives have excited others to sanctity.'[5]

In light of this somewhat general guidance, it is difficult to understand the failure of the Church of England to identify women from within its own history who deserve to be remembered. The Roman Catholic Church, after all, has experienced no difficulty in finding women saints in all periods, whether before or after the Reformation. Although Nonconformists, do not make saints, many articles about the lives of their saintly women members can be found in the publications of Methodists, Presbyterians and Quakers. Has the Church of England alone no women worthy of commemoration? It hardly seems so, as one reads through the journals of Missionary Societies and the biographies and the little Sunday School books about its heroines, as well as unpublished letters by and about them. The candidates exist if there is a will to find them, at least in the 19th and 20th centuries. In the quest for them far more have been found than can be fitted into this book.

The list of the people at present commemorated may not only be criticized for its neglect of women. It appears unbalanced in several other ways. Although Roman Catholics as well as Anglicans are included, members of other denominations such as George Fox, Elizabeth Fry and Isaac Watts, who were considered at various stages, were finally omitted. John Bunyan, who was included, had been baptized in the Church of England, as of course were the Wesleys who remained Anglicans throughout their lives. Bunyan however was described as an author rather than a pastor. In light of the warmer relations which have developed between the Church of England and other churches in recent years it might have seemed fitting to commemorate some recent heroes and heroines of other denominations. It could also have been helpful to include representatives of the Anglican Communion overseas, particularly those who worked in some of the countries of origin of Britain's immigrants. Further, in the ASB the 19th and early 20th centuries are so sparsely represented that the erroneous impression could be given that Anglicans as a whole, clergy and laity, were oblivious of the social injustices of the Industrial Revolution. In fact this was a time both of spiritual renewal and heroic activity after the Church's cynicism, selfishness and neglect of Christian responsibilities in the 18th century.

All the women to whom individual chapters are devoted in this book lived in the 19th and early 20th centuries. It is interesting to note that the American Episcopal Church has moved along similar lines. Its book of Lesser Feasts and Fasts, published in 1980, the same year as the ASB, commemorated no post-Reformation women. The edition of 1988 however contains a number of women, all of whom were Anglicans or Episcopalians born in the 19th century, namely Florence Nightingale, Evelyn Underhill, Queen Emma of Hawaii, the missionary organizer Julia Emery, and four Sisters who died of the plague whilst nursing in Memphis in 1878.[6]

Before considering the 19th and 20th century heroines, a brief look may be taken at the scope for British women to lead lives of sanctity in earlier times.

The Anglo Saxon Abbesses

There seems small doubt that there were better opportunities for women to earn reputations for holiness before the Reformation than for many years after it. In very early, legendary, times medieval chroniclers maintained that St Helena, who was mother of the Emperor Constantine and discovered the True Cross in Jerusalem, was born in York in the third century. They also claimed that her contemporary, St Ursula, who was martyred by the Huns with her 11,000 virgin companions in Cologne, was the daughter of a British Christian king. Then there are recorded the rather more authentic lives of Anglo Saxon women saints, such as St Edburga, St Ethelburga and St Sexburga. Most were queens who persuaded their husbands to make Christianity the religion of their realm or royal widows or daughters who became abbesses of convents, cared for the

sick and poor, and encouraged education. Some were martyred by pagan Danish invaders. A number were holy virgins,
such as the Abbess St Winifrede of Wales who miraculously
caused the hand of a pursuing prince to drop off; in similar
circumstances St Frideswyde, Patron Saint of Oxford and still
commemorated in the Cathedral there, struck her pursuer
blind, but restored his sight when he repented. Several of
these Anglo Saxon ladies were described as having miraculous
powers over animals. Serpents were turned into stones; wolves
were chastened; wild geese were charmed into ceasing to
devour the abbey crops and to allow themselves to be rounded
up. They could be stern when required; St Edburga, when a
thief denied his guilt, caused his entrails to fall out.

It is remarkable that several of the saintly Anglo Saxon
abbesses ruled over double monasteries of men and women.
This also happened among the Celts. Saint Brigid in Ireland,
who was not a princess but a slave girl, rose to become an
abbess who even had authority over bishops and priests.

The abbess-saints are portrayed by chroniclers as encour-
aging learning and spending much of their days and nights in
prayer. They lived simply. Saint Bega, though the daughter of
a King, cooked dinners and carried them to the workers who
were building her monastery in Northumberland, in order to
speed up the work. Saint Brigid washed the sores of lepers.
The kindly Saint Walburga even after her death cured gluttons
of indigestion and obesity.

Two of the most interesting Anglo Saxon women saints,
both of whom are already included in the ASB, are St Hilda
of Whitby and Queen Margaret of Scotland. St Hilda, Abbess
of Whitby (614–80), was related to the royal families of both
Northumbria and East Anglia and was an adult when baptized. Not only did she promote the founding of abbeys, the
instruction of clerics in Latin and the education of laymen in
the vernacular, but her piety and wisdom were so renowned
that rulers and common people would bring every kind of
problem to her for her advice.

Queen Margaret of Scotland (1046–93) was a member of
the Royal Anglo Saxon family of England; she took refuge
at the Scottish Court after the Norman Conquest, later marrying King Malcolm III. As Queen she had a leading part

in the reform of the Scottish Church and the foundation of churches and monasteries. Her private life was devoted to prayer, reading and almsgiving. She was a civilizing influence on a rough husband, and mother of two Kings. She was can-onized in 1249 when an indulgence of 40 days was granted for visiting her shrine at Dunfermline. After the Reformation, when relics were at a discount in Calvinist Scotland, her body was exported to Madrid and her head acquired by the Jesuits at Douai.

Queen Margaret's daughter Matilda carried into the twelfth century the noble Anglo Saxon tradition. Married to King Henry I of England, she encouraged learning and was a friend of Archbishop Anselm. She founded the Hospital of St Giles in London, where she would wash the feet of lepers and kiss them; when her brother, King David of Scotland pro-tested, she said that she was kissing the feet of the Eternal King. After Queen Matilda it was to be many years before another similarly influential Christian Englishwoman would emerge.

The Middle Ages

The Normans were a warlike people who tended to allow a lower place to women than the Anglo Saxons. After the Con-quest of 1066, convents were seldom ruled by an independent abbess but usually by a prioress who was responsible to an abbot. Educational standards in convents probably declined; in the late middle ages few nuns appear to have understood the Latin which they chanted.[7]

Pious ladies however were still eminent among the ruling class as promoters of learning. The Countesses of Pembroke and Clare founded the colleges at Cambridge which were named after them. Devorguila, the wife of the Scottish John of Balliol, and herself a descendant of both Scottish and Anglo Saxon Kings, founded Balliol College Oxford, together with her husband, in expiation of the latter's sins. Lady Margaret Beaufort, mother of King Henry VII, founded not only St John's and Christ's Colleges, Cambridge, but professorships of Divinity at both Oxford and Cambridge.

The cult of virginity and chastity remained strong. In the 12th century Christina of Markyate, from a family of Anglo Saxon nobles, was forced by her parents to marry, in spite of having made a vow to remain a virgin. She kept her unfortunate husband at arms length until the marriage was annulled and then founded a community of nuns.[8] The wealthy Margery Kempe of Lynn in the 15th century, on the other hand, had twelve children before she persuaded her husband that they should live chastely, on condition that she paid his debts. She then spent several years visiting Rome, Jerusalem, Santiago and other holy places before returning to nurse him in his old age. The case of Margery Kempe was indeed one of sanctity or insanity. Some of her contemporaries regarded her as a saint and admired the way in which she rebuked Bishops and even Archbishops. Others were driven to distraction by her 'boisterous weeping and sobbing' both in Church and at table, and said she was a hypocrite.[9]

After Hilda of Whitby and Margaret of Scotland, the third of the British women from the Middle Ages, to be included in the ASB is Dame Julian of Norwich (1343 – ?). She is particularly dear to Christian feminists because she related how in her visions she saw 'the deep wisdom of our Trinity as our Mother.' She spent most of her life as an anchoress in a cell attached to the Church of St Julian in Norwich, pondering on the lessons of the visions which had come to her for only a few days in her thirtieth year. Out of this came her book *Revelations of Divine Love*, full of the divine humanity of Christ and of the charity of God for the people in the street outside her cell. These would come to consult her through a grating; among them was Margery Kempe to whom Dame Julian gave sound advice about how to test whether her revelations came from God.

The Reformation

At the Reformation monasteries and nunneries were ruthlessly dissolved and the traditional ways in which women could lead holy and reflective lives, or exercise considerable power as abbesses or prioresses, disappeared. The first generation after the Reformation however produced remarkable aristocratic ladies who were inspired by the new learning as well as by the new religion, and were tutored by some of the greatest scholars of the age. Erasmus noticed how in noble houses and at court damsels had continuously in their hands psalms, homilies and other meditations. Among the greatest prodigies were the unfortunate Lady Jane Grey and Sir Anthony Cooke's four daughters, one of whom married Lord Burghley and another of whom became mother of Francis Bacon.[10]

Somewhat lower in the social scale there were early opportunities for heroic virtues to be demonstrated in public. In Foxe's *Book of Martyrs*, first published in 1563, the death and sufferings of many women on behalf of the Protestant faith were recorded, mainly in the previous reign of the Roman Catholic Queen Mary. For the most part they were wives, widows and daughters of quite humble men in south east England — shoemakers, pewterers, cutlers or weavers, even of husbandmen and ploughmen. They were sentenced for denying the real presence of Christ in the Sacrament, for describing the Mass as an idolatry, refusing to come to Church, and for disputing the efficacy of Confession and Absolution and the authority of the Pope.

Some accompanied their husbands to the stake; others left the homes of their families who had conformed. In the records of their trials some appear simply and humbly asserting that they have found in the Bible all that was necessary for salvation. Others however answered their accusers with spirit, crying out that 'your priests are the children of perdition and your Sacrament a naughty and abominable idol' or that they 'believed not the Holy Church to be their mother, but the Father of Heaven to be their father.' Groups of women met their deaths together, singing psalms and clapping their hands amidst the flames. Joyce Lewes, a gentlewoman of Lichfield, whose husband had submitted, prayed so movingly before her execution that God would abolish the idolatrous Mass and save the kingdom from idolatry that the people and sheriff shouted Amen. A particularly pathetic case was that of Joan Waste of Derby, aged 22 and blind from birth, who had paid neighbours to read the New Testament to her and from her attentive listening came to believe the Sacrament only to be a memory or representation of Christ's body. On trial, she promised that she would conform if the Bishop who was examining her would answer for her at the Last Judgement; the Bishop would have agreed, but his Chancellor was shocked and told him he could not take responsibility, so the blind girl was led to the flames.[11]

In the later years of the following reign Roman Catholics in their turn were severely persecuted. This was not however on the same scale and was principally motivated by suspicion that they were plotting the murder of Queen Elizabeth, which was encouraged by the Pope, or of harbouring others who were doing so. One of these martyrs was Margaret Clitheroe of York, a well-to-do butcher's wife who separated from her husband and family when she became a Roman Catholic. Accused of harbouring Jesuits and seminary priests, she refused to plead and in 1586 was crushed to death by the cruel Peine Forte et Dure. Her two sons became Roman Catholic priests abroad, and her daughter a nun. Margaret Clitheroe, with many of her British contemporaries, has recently been canonized by the Roman Catholic Church. The Church of England in its Calendar commemorates on October 31 'Saints and Martyrs of the Reformation Era,' a graciously comprehensive phrase by which both Protestants and Roman Catholics may be remembered.

The Seventeenth Century

Among 17th century Roman Catholics no one has more claim to the admiration of Christian feminists than Mary Ward (1585–1645). Born into a Yorkshire family who had suffered much for their faith, she was inspired to see her vocation as the founding of an order whose task would be the education of girls and in particular the daughters of the persecuted English Roman Catholics. To do this its members could not lead enclosed lives and when in England must often wear lay clothes to avoid arrest. She founded houses not only in

England, but on the Continent, where they were mostly attended by English exiles; she adopted a constitution similar to that of the Jesuits, by which the Superior was directly responsible to the Pope.

The freedom and authority which her system gave to women, at a time when all nuns were required to be enclosed and to wear habits, offended conservatives in the Vatican. Although her constitution had been approved by an earlier Pope, her houses were dissolved; she was declared a heretic and imprisoned in a convent. The vows of her nuns were cancelled and the exiled English ladies were thrown on the streets. The patience with which she submitted, the holiness of her life and the many petitions on her behalf eventually caused Pope Urban VIII to summon her to Rome, where he told her that her sufferings had been intended as a trial of her virtue, and allowed her to resume her work. She went to London, once more in secular dress, to spend her last years in educating and instructing Roman Catholic girls in the Faith; the outbreak of the Civil War obliged her to retreat to Yorkshire, where her adventurous life had started, and where she died in 1645.[12]

In the 17th century women became more prominent in the sects which separated from the Church of England than inside it. Thus Catherine Chidley (1590–1667) formed the 'Old Brownist' Church with her husband and organized the Leveller women. A group of women in Bedford took the initiative in setting up the church which Bunyan joined. The prophetess Elizabeth Poole was given an extensive hearing at the Whitehall Debates of Cromwell's armies, as they pondered how to settle the problems which arose from the Civil War. The Quaker Anna Trapnel fell into a trance which lasted 12 days whilst attending the examination by the Council of State in 1654 of a Baptist preacher. Mary Vere (1581–1670) was a patron and confidante of Puritan Divines and Elizabeth Warren a religious pamphleteer.

A number of the women sectaries, especially the Baptists, left memoirs giving an account of their conversion and how they came to be numbered among the elect. These often follow a fixed pattern of doubt, false security, renewed and often agonized doubt and eventual true assurance.[13]

Margaret Fell

From its beginning the Society of Friends recognized the ministry of women on an equal footing to that of men. Among Quaker ministers, missionaries and writers in the 17th century were Elizabeth Horton, Rebecca Travers and Barbara Blaugdon. The tradition was set by Margaret Fell (1614–1702), who might be considered almost as worthy of commemoration in the ASB as Elizabeth Fry if a Quaker were to be included. When George Fox started the movement she persuaded her husband Judge Fell to allow their house in Lancashire to become the virtual headquarters of the Friends. Here she copied and circulated Fox's letters, and coordinated the travels of Quaker missionaries, providing them with shoes and breeches and Hebrew and Greek dictionaries; she visited them when in jail and raised a fund to maintain their families. Despite all these activities she was successful in rearing eight of her nine children to maturity, a quite unusual proportion in her time.

She was herself imprisoned for four years after the Restoration for holding Meetings for Worship in her house and refusing on principle to take the Oath of Allegiance. When freed however she charmed Charles II and James II into releasing other Quakers from jail and dispensing them from taking oaths, though she seized the occasion at the same time to rebuke the Royal Stuarts for their wanton ways.

After the death of Judge Fell she married George Fox but considerably outlived him, becoming known as the 'nursing mother' of the Society. She was an inspiring leader as well as an energetic and wise administrator. She has a not insignificant niche in feminist religious history as author of *Women's Speaking Justified*. This not only reminds her readers of the role of women in the Old and New Testaments, but shows remarkable historical sense in relating St Paul's advice to the Corinthians about the position of women in the Church to the particular circumstances of Corinth, with its lax morals and centres of prostitution, and arguing that this was not representative of his views elsewhere.

Good sense was her greatest quality. In her old age she struggled – though in vain – to prevent Friends from adopting a uniform dress and thus isolating the community, reminding them shrewdly of Christ's rebuke to the Pharisees, and declaring 'Let us beware of separating or looking upon ourselves to be more worthy than we are.'[14]

Whilst English women were active in various ways in the sects, their role in the Church of England in the 17th and indeed until late in the 18th century, was more restricted. There were still pious benefactresses of learning such as the Countess of Sussex who founded a College at Cambridge at the end of the 16th century in the name of her husband, and Dorothy Wadham who did the same at Oxford early in the 17th century. Devoted wives, too, kept Anglican traditions alive in families and estates during and after the Civil Wars, when their husbands were killed, absent, or imprisoned. One such was Lady Carbery, for whom, and in memory of whom, Jeremy Taylor wrote his *Holy Living* and *Holy Dying*. John Donne in 1637 preached a well known sermon commemorating Lady Danvers, mother of George Herbert. Thomas Ken's eulogy for Lady Margaret Mainard in 1682 has also been preserved. But the style of these and similar 17th century sermons is so governed by convention that the personalities of the ladies whose piety and domestic virtues are praised hardly emerge. A notable writer of devotional works in the 17th century was Susanna Hopton who became a Roman Catholic, but was restored to the Church of England by reading Laud and Chillingworth.

The Women of Little Gidding

There were Anglican women in the 17th century who would have liked to lead formal religious lives as virgins. Nicholas Ferrar's nieces, Mary and Anne Collett, who were members of his Little Gidding Community, went to the Bishop of Lincoln, John Williams, to ask him to receive their vows. He refused, warning them of the wrongfulness and unwisdom of such vows, and that they should learn 'not to think of human nature above that which it is, a sea of flowings and ebbings, and of all manner of inconstancy.' They never married however. As Mary later described the purpose of their lives,

'Let us not blame either our sex or our condition as disabled for the advancement of God's kingdom. We have a talent and a great one committed to us, if we be careful to employ it. Not in the tongue, no, that belongs to the Ministry, but in the hands and feet ... We may tread out the way to Heaven and we may lead by good works, though we cannot teach by words.'[15]

Margaret Godolphin

Quite as determined as the Ferrar girls to live a life of devotion, but in much more difficult circumstances, was Margaret Godolphin (1652–1677) whose life was piously and movingly recorded by John Evelyn who was almost an adopted father to her. Her own father, Thomas Blagge, had been Groom of the Bedchamber to Charles I and a colonel in his army. He died when she was a child and she was sent to the court of the exiled Queen Henrietta Maria in France where she resisted pressure to convert her to Rome – 'Rudely treated and menaced, almost a martyr before the age of seven,' says Evelyn. At the Restoration she became Maid of Honour to the Duchess of York and then to the Queen. Her virtue, beauty and wit at the lascivious court, according to her biographer, made her looked upon as 'a little miracle.' She was torn between her love for Sidney Godolphin and her desire to devote her life to prayer, contemplation and good works. She leaned towards the latter, preferring 'wholly to wait on God, night and day, avoiding impertinencies and ceremonies of visits, formal meals etc.'; but Evelyn urged her to marry Godolphin. An active life, he said, was preferable to a contemplative one; as a wife 'you could be hospitable to strangers, institute your children, give instruction to your servants.' 'All the decencies of her sex and custom of the nation, the honour of the condition and want of monasteries and pious recesses,' he argued, 'obliged her to marry.' Visiting Paris with relatives, she found her dislike of the Roman Catholic Church confirmed, but wrote wistfully, 'Their nunneries seem holy institutions.'

At the age of twenty three she eventually married Godolphin. Her husband gave her disposal over the substantial marriage portion which she brought and she was able 'to relieve many indigent people and poor housekeepers,' to adopt a poor orphan girl and engage in many other charities. She died in childbirth after only two years of marriage.[16]

Mary Astell

The difficulties for Anglican women in leading devout and useful lives after the Restoration led Mary Astell to write her celebrated book *A Serious Proposal to the Ladies* in 1694. In this she deplored both the lack of education of, and lack of vocations for, unmarried upper and middle class women. She proposed that a number of them should pool their resources and set up an institution which would have the character of a women's college or a convent without vows. The residents would keep all the fasts and vigils of the Church of England and attend church each day. Some of them would be semi-permanent and live retired lives; for others it would be a place of preparation for marriage, or a secure home for heiresses and 'daughters of gentlemen who had fallen into decay.' The proposal aroused much interest and it was rumoured that the Princess (and future Queen) Anne would provide £10,000 for the scheme; but the influential Whig Bishop Burnet killed the project by declaring that it smacked of popery. Mary Astell was a somewhat intolerant High Church woman who wrote fiercely against Dissenters. She is more significant in the history of feminism than in that of the Church.[17]

Hannah More

In the 18th century only among the Quakers, and for a brief period among the Methodists, did women exercise a ministry. The Anglican attitude was expressed with characteristic bluntness by Samuel Johnson. A woman preaching, he said, was like a dog standing on its hind legs. She did not do it well, but it was remarkable that she did it at all. Towards the end of the century however, as evangelicalism spread from the Wesleyans, an increasing number of Anglican women, particularly spinsters, found an outlet for the expression of their religion in visiting and exhorting the poor to whom they distributed food, clothing and pious literature. A transitional character was Hannah More (1745–1833) whose life fell into two distinct parts. Daughters of the Master of a charity school near Bristol, she and her four sisters were taught by him the same curriculum as that of his schoolboys. The sisters then set up a highly successful girls' school in Bristol. Hannah was liberated from the life of a school mistress in an unusual way. She became engaged to be married to an older man who turned out to be such a confirmed bachelor that he was too nervous to appear at the wedding; full of remorse, he settled a pension on her in compensation. Now financially independent, she went up to London at the age of 28 with one of her sisters in search of a literary career. Here she had a succession of triumphs. She wrote a play which was produced by Garrick. Dr Samuel Johnson described her as 'the most powerful versificatrix in the English language.' Sir Joshua Reynolds read aloud to his friends her poem addressed to Garrick's dog Dragon. Burke and Gibbon were among her admirers, though she sternly described *The Decline and Fall of the Roman Empire* as 'a mass of impiety and bad taste. Horace Walpole wrote to her as 'Dear Holy Hannah' who might 'be one of the cleverest of women, if you did not prefer being one of the best.'

She became however uneasy with the fashionable life she was leading, resolved never again to enter a theatre, and withdrew to a cottage at Cowslip Green in Somerset where she wrote improving and successful works such as *Thoughts on the Importance of the Manners of the Great to General Society*, and *Strictures on the Modern System of Female Education with a View to the Principles and Conduct of Women of Rank and Fortune*. Here William Wilberforce visited her one day and, dismayed at the moral and spiritual condition of the Mendip villages, implored Hannah and her sisters to set up schools for the children of the poor. Financed by him, the sisters waded or rode pillion through muddy lanes and set up a dozen schools where, according to Hannah, 'They learn of weekdays such coarse works as may fit them for servants. I allow of no writing. My object has not been to teach dogmas and opinions, but to form the lower class to habits of industry and virtue'. Despite this, the schools were strongly, sometimes violently, opposed by farmers who feared that their miserably paid and housed labourers would demand better wages if they were educated, and also by lazy and non-resident Church of England parsons whose neglect of their parishes was exposed. In the winters physical conditions were so bad that the sisters retired to Bath where Hannah at the request of the Government wrote a number of cheap books for the poor as a counter to literature which was sympathetic to the French Revolution. In these she declared that the distress caused by bad harvests was due to the atheism and sedition of the times. The sisters distributed food and clothing to the poor, but Hannah took the occasion to point out how an all wise and all gracious providence had used the scarcity to show the poor how dependent they were on the rich, as well as the advantages which they derived from the Government and Constitution of their country.

In her later years Hannah lived in retirement and wrote a great number of books and essays popularizing Evangelicalism and earning her more than £30,000, a fortune for those times.

Overpraised in her lifetime, her reputation as a writer sank very low in the age of the Romantics and, as a rather crude Evangelical, her doctrines were found rigid and narrow by Tractarians and Anglo Catholics. Allegations of hypocrisy were however unfair. She was a woman of integrity, piety and moral courage: on the other hand she was a snob and suffered from spiritual vanity. In the later part of her life she tended more and more to divorce piety from intellect, and even one of her warm admirers referred to the 'fat complacency which she used in speaking of the Evangelical faith.'[18]

It has to be admitted that from the Reformation to the end of the 18th century Dr Hewitt's observations prove generally valid. It is hard to find Anglican women whose names can confidently be put forward for commemoration. Insofar as candidates can be found, either too much or too little is known about them. Even Holy Hannah, so charmingly pious as a girl, becomes insufferable later in life, and perhaps the only woman who might deserve commemoration is the Quaker Margaret Fell. The position in the 19th century was to be very different.

The Nineteenth Century

Many developments now combined to allow Anglican and other Christian women more varied opportunities for expression of their religion than had ever existed before. The Industrial Revolution created a well-to-do middle class whose daughters, widows and, eventually, wives sometimes acquired private incomes and thus freedom. A first step in freedom in conservative families was sometimes unchaperoned attendance at the 8 a.m. Communion Services introduced under the influence of the Tractarians and Anglo Catholics. Anglican girls of the middle class, who in the 18th century had even less access to secondary and higher education than their Non-Conformist contemporaries, now had their own schools with increasingly high standards, and later in the century gained access to universities and to a few professions. Travel and communication became much easier with the advent of railways and steamships, the postal service and telegrams.

Missionary societies came to recognize that the effective way to conversions led through the harem, which only women missionaries could penetrate. The Tractarians revived the monastic tradition within the Church of England and encouraged the establishment of sisterhoods. Evangelical, and later Anglo Catholic, fervour not only swept into religious practice, but stirred up conscience and action about social conditions in Britain and its Empire. A supply of educated recruits for sisterhoods, missions and social work was at hand, for the 19th century censuses showed that the number of females in Britain considerably exceeded the number of men.

Each of the following chapters is devoted to the life of a woman with a strong claim to official commemoration. Eight of these were Anglicans: of the others Caroline Chisholm was born an Anglican but became a Roman Catholic on marriage. Mary Slessor was a Presbyterian. Six of the women spent most of their lives in Britain. The others worked in India, Africa and Australia.

The individuals fall into four groups. Octavia Hill, Pandita Ramabai, Eglantyne Jebb and Caroline Chisholm were inspired by their religion to work for great social causes; many more in this category can be found among the newly liberated women of the 19th century. Christina Rossetti and Evelyn Underhill represent the contemplatives and mystics, less seldom found or recognized in the Church of England than by Rome. Mother Harriet Monsell and Mother Cecile are two of the foundresses of the Anglican Sisterhoods which were established in the 19th century for the first time since the Reformation and which combined spiritual life with care of those abandoned by the laissez-faire state. The work of Sister Dora and Mary Slessor was carried out at a local level, where they are already regarded almost as saints; if commemoration of such as these were raised to the national level a medieval practice of the Church would be revived. Mary Slessor also represents that remarkable body of women missionaries, few of whose lives have been written compared to the many biographies of their male counterparts.

The next three women to be discussed, Elizabeth Fry, Florence Nightingale and Catherine Booth, were more famous in their time than any of those who are put forward in the previous chapters. Their reputations now however are more controversial. The 19th century produced so many devoted and remarkable women of various kinds that a further chapter deals briefly with a number of others who might be considered by some to be as deserving of commemoration as those whom the writer has selected. The last chapter contains some reflections on the qualities shared by the women who have been suggested for commemoration and on how these compare with those of the men who are already included.

The Alternative Service Book is licensed until the year 2000 and will be revised before that date. A convention has been established that no one is considered for commemoration until they have been dead for fifty years. No one therefore who died after 1950 is discussed in this book as a possible candidate for inclusion in the revised version.

Notes

1.   General Synod, *Report of Proceedings*, 1978, Vol. 1, p. 146.
2.   *Ibid.*, p. 174 ff.
3.   *Ibid.*, p. 442 ff.
4.   Richard Symonds, *Alternative Saints — The Post Reformation British People Commemorated by the Church of England*, London & New York, 1988.
5.   *The Calendar and Lessons for the Church's Year*, Report of the Church of England Liturgical Commission (London, 1969), p. 14.
6.   *Lesser Feasts and Fasts*, 3rd edition, New York, 1980; 4th edition, New York, 1988, published by Church Hymnal Corporation.
7.   K. Moore, *She for God*, London, 1978, p. 31.
8.   C.H. Talbot (ed.), *The Life of Christina of Markyate*, Oxford, 1959.
9.   W. Butler-Bowden, *The Book of Margery Kempe*, London, 1936.
10.   K. Moore, *op. cit.*, p. 79 ff.
11.   Accounts of all these are in volumes 5, 6 and 7 of J. Foxe, *Acts and Monument*, (London 1877; first published 1563).
12.   *Life of Mary Ward*, compiled from various sources, London 1909.
13.   E. Graham *et al.*, *Her Own Life*, London 1989, p. 3.
14.   Isabel Ross, *Margaret Fell, Mother of Quakerism*, London, 1949.
15.   A.M. Williams, *Conversations at Little Gidding*, Cambridge 1970, p. LXXVII.
16.   John Evelyn, *Life of Mrs Godolphin*, ed. Samuel Wilberforce, London 1847.
17.   Ruth Perry, *The Celebrated Mary Astell*, Chicago, 1986.
18.   Lady Chatterton, quoted in M.C. Jones, *Hannah More*, Cambridge 1952, p. 235.

PART I
CAUSES

1

Octavia Hill and the Slums (1838–1912)

*'It is by the small graciousness, by the thoroughness of
the out of sight detail that God will judge our spirit and
our love.'*

Octavia Hill

At Queen Victoria's Jubilee in 1887 the three women who
were considered to have done most for the country during
her reign were invited to the service in Westminster Abbey.
Florence Nightingale, the heroine of the Crimea, and Anne
Clough, the first Principal of Newnham College, Cambridge,
were in their late sixties and at the end of their active careers:
Octavia Hill, still only 48, had long been famous, for she had
started to work at the age of 13. The roots of her achievement
can be traced to her family background and the influence on
her of three very different men: first her grandfather, Dr
Southwood Smith, then F.D. Maurice and John Ruskin. Her
father, James Hill, was a banker and merchant in Wisbech,
Cambridgeshire: a strong and impulsive Radical, he purchased
a newspaper in which he campaigned against Church rates and
municipal corruption; he also founded an elementary school,
a Mechanics Institute and a lending library. He was three
times married. When his first wife died, leaving him two
daughters, he contracted a 'marriage' with her sister which
was at that time illegal.[1] She also died, leaving him with
three more girls and a boy. Seeking a governess to care
for his children, James Hill was impressed by some articles
written by Caroline Southwood Smith, which advocated an
educational system under which children's bodies as well as
their minds should be cared for. He first employed and then
married her. They had five children, all girls. Octavia was born
in 1838. Two years later James Hill's bank crashed. He was
declared bankrupt, suffered a nervous collapse, and was never
able to work again.

Caroline Hill's father, Dr Thomas Southwood Smith, came to her rescue and that of her children, installing them in a cottage in what was then the village of Finchley, close to his own house. Southwood Smith, who was both a Unitarian Minister and a Doctor of Medicine, was one of the great sanitary reformers of the 19th century. In the face of strong opposition from vested interests he had disproved the prevalent belief that cholera and typhoid were spread by contagion, and had shown that they were due to the insanitary conditions in which the poor lived. This led to the first Public Health Act of 1848 and the construction of sewerage systems in the British cities. He had campaigned for the better ventilation of slum houses and alleys and had caused 'model dwellings' to be built in areas where fevers were frequent. His bust in the National Portrait Gallery carried an inscription by Leigh Hunt,

'Ages shall honour, in their Hearts enshrined,
Thee, Southwood Smith, Physician of Mankind,
Bringer of Air, Light, Health into the Home
Of the rich poor of happier times to come'.[2]

It was indeed to the 'rich poor of happier times to come' that his granddaughter was to devote her life. He became her guardian, and years later she would quote from reports on sanitary reforms which she had copied out for him. Octavia and her sisters were allowed to listen to the talk of the distinguished visitors who came to discuss the social questions of the day. Robert Browning, who had been among them, recollected how another guest had said to him 'Those are wonderful children, you can talk to them about anything'.[3]

Despite Dr Southwood Smith's help, the family were too poor to employ a servant. Caroline Hill, a Unitarian like her husband and father, made a virtue of this and brought up the children to look after themselves. She taught them to read and write but would not let them read books which would enlighten them about the sin and evil and misery in the world. She read the classics with them, but mainly encouraged them to educate themselves. Thus they set up a school for their dolls and learnt French, History and Geography in order to teach them. As her daughter Miranda recalled, their mother seldom gave a distinct order or made a rule, but it was clearly understood that if a thing was right it must be done, and she seemed to live continually in the presence of God.[4] On their birthdays the children were encouraged to give, as well as to receive, presents.

Caroline Hill was determined not to remain dependent on her father, and decided to earn her own living, as she had done before her marriage. In 1851 she moved to London to become Manager of the Ladies Cooperative Guild which had been formed under the inspiration of Christian Socialists to enable ladies in distressed circumstances to earn their living by designing and painting on glass. The children were able to live with their mother at the Guild's offices in Russell Place. There was no money for their education. At first Octavia, then aged 13, studied painting on glass and looked after the stores; a year later she was given more responsible work when she was placed in charge of a toy-making department which had been started in order to employ ragged school children. She had to choose the shape and colour of each piece of toy furniture, assign tasks to individual children, price the articles, supervise packing and keep the accounts. She organised meals for the children at which they were persuaded to share out the food which they brought, and took them on visits to the country houses of patrons of the Guild.

About this time she came to know the two men who, with her grandfather, were to have the greatest influence on her life. Her Unitarian mother had taught her a system of ethics rather than a formal religion. It was from F. D. Maurice, then Chaplain of Lincoln's Inn, that she learnt the doctrines of the Church of England, into which she was now baptised and confirmed. 'It was Mr Maurice', she wrote, 'who showed me a life in the Creeds, the services and the Bible; who interpreted for me much that was dark and puzzling in life ... that I might believe not only that God was manifesting Himself to each man in the inward consciousness of light and beauty ... but that a real person had come among us, whose will had been brought into harmony with His ... that He had declared that we might have life, that life was knowledge of God'.[5]

Maurice was a social as well as a religious teacher. Octavia attended not only his sermons but his lectures, as well as those of Charles Kingsley, Tom Hughes and other Christian

Socialists. 'Reading a Socialist book', she wrote to a friend when she was 14, 'is one of the greatest happinesses anyone can have'.[6] Shaken by the misery of the London slums after her gentle village life, she was in danger of becoming a prig. 'I have renounced parties', she wrote, 'the love of show is detestable'.

Shortly before her fifteenth birthday her other great teacher entered her life. John Ruskin at the age of 34 was already famous as the author of *The Stones of Venice* and of the first volume of *Modern Painters*. Visiting the work room of the Guild to inspect its handicrafts, he was impressed by Octavia's artistic talent, and he set her to work copying pictures for *Modern Painters*. For the next ten years she continued to spend part of her time helping and being trained by Ruskin. His marriage had recently broken up, and he would often pay a social call on the amiable Mrs Hill and her intellectually lively daughters. It was not only art which came under discussion. Ruskin had become indignant at the robbery of beauty from the lives of the poor and this was leading him to write about social problems and to attack the soulless policies of laissez-faire economics.

In 1855 Maurice published an essay which challenged the concept of eternal punishment, and was called upon to resign his Chair at London University. The controversy spread to the Ladies Guild where he had offered to take a Bible class for Octavia's toy-making children. The Managers of the Guild, afraid of losing financial support from a wealthy Evangelical subscriber, asked Maurice to withdraw. Caroline Hill resigned on principle. Octavia, though vehemently resenting the affront to Maurice and all that he stood for, felt unable to leave her children, but shortly afterwards the Guild came to an end. The family now moved into a house in Nottingham Place and set up a private school for the daughters of their friends. As well as teaching there, Octavia was employed by Maurice as secretary to the classes for women when these were started at his Working Men's College. She not only organised the classes and kept the books, but had to give lectures if any of the volunteer ladies failed to turn up.

Her duties for Ruskin, for the Working Men's College, and in the family school, as well as the additional private teaching which she undertook in order to earn money to pay off her father's debts, imposed a considerable strain; sometimes she reproached herself for impatience – 'O, it is easy to work early and late, to keep accounts and to manage housekeeping etc., but the gentle voice, the loving word, the Ministry, the true tender spirit – these are the great gifts and will endure when the others have perished'.[7]

She pondered whether art or social work was to be her main occupation in life. Sometimes the two seemed to come together, and Ruskin warned that in her drawing 'If you devote yourself to human expression, I know how it will be, you will watch it more and more and there will be an end of art for you. You will say "*Hang* drawing. I must go to help people"'. But he told her that she would not make an income as an artist and advised her 'Never let drawing interfere with any other thing you may feel to be wanted. You have infinite sympathy and power of teaching and helping people: use it. Feel it to be as much work for me as any other'.[8]

After the toy-making enterprise closed, Octavia continued to keep in touch with and help the children, and she was thus familiar with the appalling homes in which most of them lived. The Hills also held informal classes in the kitchen of their school for working class women of the Marylebone district to help them to make clothes for their children. On one of these evenings a young mother collapsed. Octavia accompanied her to her home which turned out to be in a damp unhealthy basement. She searched in vain all over Marylebone for a landlord who would take in the family at a price which they could afford. At about this time she listened to a remarkable address by Charles Kingsley to the Ladies Sanitary Association whom he told that the deaths of four out of five children were unnecessary. They could be prevented, not by legislation, but only by direct personal influence on both landlords and tenants. 'It is in the power', he declared, 'of every woman in this room to save three or four lives in the next six months'.[9]

Some years later in the spring of 1864, Octavia called on Ruskin. He talked of the dreariness of his life: 'I take my mother for a drive; I paint or answer letters', he said, 'but one longs to *do* something'. Octavia replied that she knew very well what she would do, if she had Ruskin's resources. 'Well what would you be doing?' he asked. 'Something to provide better homes for the poor', she replied. Ruskin immediately asked her for a plan.[10]

She had indeed a plan, which was not to build new housing, but to obtain possession of one of the tenements where the poorest classes lived and, by substituting a firm but sympathetic landlady for a slum owner, to transform both the property and the tenants. Ruskin, who on the death of his father had become a rich man, gladly agreed to purchase a suitable property, which Octavia would manage, on the understanding that he would receive 5% interest on his investment. This was less than the rate paid on most slum properties at the time but would be sufficient to prove that the experiment was financially sound and not just a work of charity.

Octavia now bought with Ruskin's money three houses in Paradise Place in Marylebone. This was a 'court', several houses crowded round a small common place, with only one narrow access from the street. No water was laid on; there were no dustbins, and refuse was thrown on to the stairways or cobbled yards. Inside, each ill-ventilated room was occupied by a whole family; most windows were broken; plaster and paper were falling from ceiling and walls; fireplaces were in disrepair. The landlord of such slum properties was usually someone of slender means who had bought them as an investment and meant to make as much as possible out of them, but either had not the capital or the will to carry out repairs. His dealings with tenants were often inconsistent, sometimes harsh, sometimes lenient, and arrears of rent were frequently large. One landlord, who was an undertaker, told Octavia, 'Yes, Miss, of course there's plenty of bad debts. It's not the rents I look to, but the deaths I get out of the houses'.[11]

The principles which Octavia now applied were described by her in an article in the *Fortnightly Review* in 1866, in which she explained her conviction that 'the spiritual elevation of a large class depended to a considerable extent on sanitary reform' and that sanitary reform itself depended upon educational work among grown-up people; the latter 'must be urged to rouse themselves from the lethargy and indolent habits into which they have fallen, and freed from all that hinders them from doing so. I further believe that any lady who would help them to obtain such things, the need of which they felt themselves, and would sympathise with them in their desire for such, would soon find them eager to learn her view of what was best for them; that whether this was true or not, her duty was to keep alive their own best hopes and intentions, which come at rare intervals, but fade too often for want of encouragement. I desired to be in a condition to free a few poor people from the tyranny and influence of a low class of landlords and landladies; from the corrupting effect of continual forced communication with very degraded fellow lodgers; from the heavy incubus of accumulated dirt, so that the never dying hope, which I find characteristic of the poor, might have leave to spring'.[12]

Octavia's approach to her project was clearly thought out and systematic. It was no use improving housing unless the behaviour of tenants was improved at the same time. As a manager therefore she needed to be in direct touch with the tenants; she dispensed with middlemen and made a weekly visit to collect the rent in the daytime when it was handed over by the wives, whilst the men were out at work. She won their friendship and confidence also by inviting the women to the domestic classes held in her family's house and school.

Although, Octavia related, the houses 'were in a dreadful state of dirt and neglect, the repairs required were mainly of a superficial character; slight in regard to expense – vital as to health and comfort. The place swarmed with vermin; the papers, black with dirt, hung in long strips from the walls; the drains were stopped, the water supply out of order'.

These things were rapidly put right, but no new appliances of any kind were added until the tenants had shown that they were capable of looking after them. A regular sum was set aside for repairs: if any of it remained at the end of the quarter, each tenant decided in turn how the surplus should be spent. This brought about a remarkable decrease in the losses from carelessness.[13]

Once the houses in Paradise Place were put in order, more of Ruskin's money was used to buy a row of cottages nearby. These were in very bad condition but had the great merit of providing an open space for a playground.

The well-to-do girls from the Hill family's school in Nottingham Place helped enthusiastically in the work, taking children off the hands of harassed mothers, teaching them to play and mending their clothes. One of the shops in the second property was turned into a Club Room. Classes were arranged there for children, and a savings bank was operated in it, but its main purpose was social, a place where tenants could chat and find themselves to be members of a community. Octavia took great care not to be seen as a Lady Bountiful. The relationship with the tenants was one of 'perfect respectfulness'. 'I should treat them with the same courtesy as I should show to my other personal friends; there would be no interference, no entering their rooms uninvited, no offer of money or the necessaries of life. But when occasion presented itself I might offer ... help and counsel in their difficulties, introductions that might be useful, a loan of books, a bunch of flowers'.[14]

At the end of two years Ruskin had not only received his 5%, but £48 of the capital had been repaid. Overcrowding had been reduced; sets of two rooms had been let for little more than the rent of one. Although Octavia received no remuneration, the usual percentage was set aside for this, to prove that the scheme was realistic.

The success had been achieved, she related in her article, through 'extreme punctuality and diligence in collecting rents, and a strict determination that they should be paid regularly'. 'Yet', she continued, 'nothing has impressed me more than the people's perception of an underlying current of sympathy throughout all dealings that have seemed harsh. Somehow, love and care have made themselves felt'.[15]

She had helped the tenants to pay the rent in two ways: she had provided a simple system by which they could save money, and she had provided work in slack seasons. The men were paid to do odd jobs on the houses and the girls to do the cleaning which was the landlord's responsibility.

She concluded by thanking 'her poorer friends' for what she had learned from them, 'their energy and hope amid overwhelming difficulties have made me ashamed of my own laziness and despair'.[16]

She had started out on the modest work which was to make her famous 'with an almost awed sense of joy ... in entering on such a possession, conscious of the power to set it even partially in order'.[17] Her mother described her at that time as busy as a bee − 'very like a bee in her happy murmurings whilst at work, and her evident pleasure in it'.[18]

The labour involved however was hard and detailed. Sometimes she thought that 'really it would be a small cost in value to pay any sum, however tremendous, to get rid of this annoying small perpetual care, if the work could be done as well; but then it couldn't; it is only when the detail is managed on as great principles as the whole plan that a work becomes really good. And so, I suppose, being really the school of training tenants most effectually, I must still keep it, and hope that it will not finally make one either small or mean or bitter'.[19]

The success of this housing experiment in the centre of London quite soon became widely known. Visitors, including the Queen's daughter, Princess Alice, who came incognito, began to arrive, somewhat to Octavia's dismay, for she hated the invasion of the tenants' privacy. 'There is nothing to see, only much to do' she complained. George Eliot offered money. George MacDonald came with his family to produce theatricals.

Whilst she was running the housing project, Octavia had to continue to earn her living and copy drawings for Ruskin. The strain was too great. She suffered the first of several breakdowns and had to take a long rest on the Continent, whilst her sisters and friends, in particular Janey Senior, the wife of Nassau Senior and sister of Tom Hughes, carried on the school and the housing work.

After her return, and as the work extended, she became better able to delegate responsibility. Money was now no problem. Offers came in from all sides from people who liked to engage in philanthropy at 5%. New properties were acquired. Expansion was limited by the supply of workers, the training of whom became Octavia's main task.

All the managers and rent collectors were women. As Octavia explained, 'Ladies must do it for it is detailed work. Ladies must do it for it is household work: it needs, too, persistent patience, gentleness, hope'.[20] At first these were ladies who gave a little of their time. But it soon became necessary to train volunteers who could give whole days to the work, each taking complete responsibility for a court. They had first to learn how to deal with people, to understand the conditions in which they lived and the ways in which these could be improved. They then had to collect rents, keep accounts, superintend cleaning and advise on repairs. They needed some knowledge of sanitary science and to be familiar with the laws relating to landlord and tenant and with the various agencies for helping the people, which often asked the workers to act for them.[21]

Octavia was very conscious of the danger of keeping too much control in her own hands, or that she might 'spoil all by growing despotic or narrow minded, or overbearing or selfish: such power as I have is a quite terrible responsibility; and so few people tell me where I am wrong'. But she was a vigilant supervisor. 'It is of no use to have the right spirit', she told her volunteers, 'if the technical matters, all the sanitary and financial arrangements, are in a mess. Beware of well meant failures!'.[22]

Apart from her work in housing, Octavia took a leading part in the founding of the Charity Organization Society. The severe winter of 1867–8 caused great distress, and large funds for relief were collected by the Lord Mayor of London. The way in which these were spent appeared to many social workers to be so lavish and haphazard as to increase pauperisation. In 1868 The London Association for the Prevention of Pauperisation and Crime (later to become The Charity Organisation Society) was set up. Ruskin paid two thirds of its expenses.

Initially the task of the C.O.S. was to coordinate the work of organisations which gave relief and to prevent duplication and overlapping. Under the influence of Octavia Hill, Rev. Samuel Barnett, and its dynamic secretary, C.S. Loch, however, it came to assert principles of relief, in particular the application of sci-entific method to each individual case, so that a correct forecast could be made of the effect of the assistance given. This led to a distinction between the deserving and the undeserving poor, and appeared to many to be a negation of Christian charity. The leading members of the C.O.S. not only placed restric-tions on voluntary aid but resisted state or municipal action in the provision of housing, medical care or old age pensions. Canon Barnett and his wife, living in Whitechapel, eventually changed their views and came to believe that the inquisitions of the C.O.S. did more harm than good, and advocated old age pensions. Octavia never changed her view.[23]

In 1868 shortly after the C.O.S. was founded, Octavia Hill read a paper to the Society on 'The Importance of Aiding the Poor without Alms Giving'. In this she restated the principle that was fundamental to all her work, the importance of the worth and value of the individual. She urged that the poor should be regarded 'primarily as husbands, wives, sons and daughters, members of households, as we are ourselves, instead of as a separate class', and that 'relief funds should be used to make them independent, not dependent'.[24]

The Rector of Marylebone, Rev. W. Fremantle, now invited her to apply her principles in the Walmer Street district, one of the poorest in his parish. In doing so, she abolished the wholesale handouts of coal tickets, free meals and money, insisting that every case of distress, and the whole resources of each family, must be examined carefully before any dole could be given, that work should be offered to the able bodied workers, and relief withheld if it were not done. She and the Charity Organisation Society aroused bitter resentment not only among the poor but many of the clergy, to whom the giving of alms was a traditional Christian duty and to whom the C.O.S. appeared to be 'all Organisation and no Charity'. The principles gradually came to be accepted by the Bishops, and Octavia through her membership of the Central Committee of the C.O.S. came to know and be trusted by Lord Shaftesbury, James Stansfeld and others as one of the leading philanthropic and social workers of her day.

She became widely known when the Government in 1875 introduced the Artisan Dwellings Act, largely based on her recommendations, as was recognised in debates in the House of Commons. Her mother observed that Dr Southwood Smith's mantle had fallen on his granddaughter. Octavia however wrote 'I wish someone would explode me. It is so difficult to unhumbug oneself'.[25]

Octavia's need to earn a living by teaching and copying whilst carrying on her housing work had probably been a factor in her first breakdown. A number of wealthy friends then, without her knowledge, organised a fund whose income she reluctantly accepted in order to make her free to devote all her time to social work. She was never affluent however. Personal poverty, she wrote, was a help to her. 'It keeps me simple and energetic, and somehow low and humble and hardy in the midst of a somewhat intoxicating power'.[26]

Octavia believed that urban dwellers needed four kinds of open spaces: places to sit in, to play in, to stroll in, and to spend a day in.

At first she was preoccupied with making small open spaces available to her tenants — what she called open air sitting rooms for the poor. She tried to persuade churches and chapels to open disused burial grounds to the public, and was accused of irreverence. She asked School Boards to keep the school playgrounds open in the evenings and on Sundays. She approached Corporations, City companies and the Metropolitan Board of Works with requests that they should buy open spaces or provide for them in new building schemes. This proved one of the hardest of her struggles. With her sister Miranda she formed the Kyrle Society whose purpose was 'the diffusion of beauty'. It planted small gardens, organised a choir which sang at services in poor parishes and ran singing classes. Always a disciple of Ruskin, she put up inscriptions in multicoloured tiles donated by her friends. One which ran along the faces of the houses said 'Every house is builded by some man, but He that built all things is God'. It was perhaps fortunate however that she failed in an effort to blazon Kingsley's words 'Do noble deeds!' on the side of Waterloo Station.

Her interests gradually became broader, and she worked to preserve from the developers the remaining green spaces of London. She took a leading part in the unsuccessful attempt to save Swiss Cottage Fields and in the successful campaigns to preserve Parliament Hill and Vauxhall Park. She was the originator of the term 'The Green Belt' and inevitably was drawn on from seeking to preserve spaces in towns to fighting for the preservation of the countryside when Canon Rawnsley drew attention to the threat of urban development in the Lake District. It soon became apparent that there was no legal means of making gifts of land and houses to the public; in 1894 with Canon Rawnsley and Sir Robert Hunter she therefore took the lead in the establishment of the National Trust.

At weekends Octavia would tramp along disused country paths to preserve the rights of way. A companion on these walks was Edward Bond, a barrister who helped her to organise a men's club at Barrett's Court, one of her most difficult properties. Bond had achieved a Double First Class degree and was a Fellow of Queen's College, Oxford. His private means enabled him to lead a life of voluntary public service and he was later to become a Member of Parliament. Beatrice Webb described him as 'a fine figure of a man, with handsome features, and large soulful grey eyes, who alternated cultured comments with thrilling silences'.[27]

In 1877, when she was 38 and he was 33, they became engaged. Bond's mother however, with whom he lived, vehemently opposed the marriage of her only son. He became hesitant, and urged delay. The short engagement was ended and they never met again.[28]

This emotional crisis coincided with a break between Octavia and Ruskin, who wrote to demand an explanation of a criticism which he had been told she had made of certain of his projects. Reluctantly she replied that, much as she admired his ideas, she felt that he lacked the capacity for management of great practical work and had a tendency to trust the wrong people. Ruskin published the correspondence in *Fors Clavigera*, including his bitter complaint to Octavia that 'Of all the injuries you could have done – not me – but the cause I have in hand, the giving the slightest countenance to the vulgar mob's cry of "unpractical" was the fatalest.'[29]

On top of the broken engagement and the unwilling quarrel with her old mentor, whom she did not know to be mentally ill, came the death of her closest male collaborator, Sydney Cockerell. She now suffered a serious breakdown which kept her out of the field for two years, most of which time she spent travelling on the Continent with her friend Harriot Yorke.

After she resumed work, the Ecclesiastical Commissioners asked her in 1884 to take charge of their courts in Southwark and Deptford. Her position was now very strong and she insisted to the Commissioners that in their rebuilding schemes open spaces should be provided for the tenants. As the Bishop of London, Temple, said 'When she had talked to us for half an hour we were quite refuted. I never had such a beating in all my life! Consequently I felt a great respect for her. So fully did she convince us, that we not only did what she asked us on that estate, but proceeded to carry out similar plans on other estates'.[30]

The high property value of London sites made it expedient in Southwark to replace cottages by blocks of flats. Octavia generally deplored this, believing that the cottages, however shabby, 'with the separate yard for chair for invalid, swing for child, place for creepers and bulbs, space for man to make a little workshop, the separation from other families, make them incomparably better than anything however spick and span we can build now'.[31] She prevailed on the Commissioners to save as many cottages as possible and even to build some new ones. The work spread to Leeds, Liverpool and Manchester, then abroad to Germany, Holland and America. In Berlin an Octavia Hill Verein was formed. She had created a new profession, and eventually salaried workers came to be employed to work alongside the volunteers.

Although she never gave up her direct contact with tenants, Octavia came to spend more of her time on public bodies. In her evidence to the Royal Commission on the Housing of the Working Classes in 1884 she suggested that it was now necessary to discriminate between two types of tenant. The reasonably prosperous artisan could be housed by the Building Societies at an economic rent. But poorer tenants, living on the edge of poverty, still needed the kind of help that she and her Managers could give. They required simple, cheap accommodation, which they could not damage. She strongly opposed the provision of subsidised housing by State or Municipal Authorities which she considered would bring down the level of wages.[32]

In 1905 she served as a member of the Royal Commission on the Poor Laws. She took her duties very seriously, delegating most of her normal work to colleagues, and visiting many work houses and other institutions throughout the country. The Commission was charged to examine not only the working of the Poor Laws, but also relief measures outside them, which included relief of unemployment. Octavia signed the majority report on Poor Law Reform but wrote a memorandum of dissent from the proposals regarding unemployment, because she objected to the creation of 'artificial work'.

Shortly before her death, when she was over 70, it was fitting that her last campaign should have been on behalf of one of Ruskin's causes, to rescue the River Wandle, which he had described in *The Crown of Wild Olives* as 'trembling and pure like a body of light', from the rubbish tips of London authorities.[33] It was successful, and the banks of the stream below Mitcham Bridge came to be vested in the National Trust as a memorial to her.

In her last years she shared a house in the Marylebone Road with her sister Miranda and Harriot Yorke, spending week-ends in the latter's cottage in Kent where they worked vigorously, digging up flints from the garden and tramping along paths to assert the traditional rights of way.

In the spring of 1912, when she felt herself to be failing, she handed over her nine banking accounts to the successors she had trained. She could be content with her housing work. 'I might have given it a few more touches', she said, 'but I think it is all planned now, very well'. She died in August 1912. Her family refused the offer of a tomb in Westminster Abbey and she was buried beside Miranda in her village home of Crockham.

Octavia Hill was one of the least theoretical of reformers. Her various work started from individual problems. As one of her biographers has pointed out – 'Her housing work had its origin in an effort to find a house for one family. The seed of the National Trust and all her work for open spaces was planted in a tiny playground in Marylebone, and the spirit which inspired all her efforts for the C.O.S. and the reform of the Poor Law first expressed itself in an effort to help improvident little toy-makers to save their own money to pay for their 2d dinner'.[34]

Despite her public work she always remained more interested in individuals than in problems of general welfare. From F. D. Maurice she had learnt that nothing was more important than spiritual development, or in lay terms, growth of character. The material help which she gave she always saw as a means to a spiritual end.

Her objection to undiscriminating charity was not only that it demoralised the recipient but often the donor, who by paying a cheque might feel himself relieved of all responsibility for those social conditions from which he might derive part of his income.[35]

Although she started life as a Christian Socialist, she regarded the function of the State not as to provide directly for the needs of its citizens, but so to organise society as to enable everyone to keep themselves and their families in independence. On this point came her fundamental divergence on the Poor Law Commission from the Fabian, Beatrice Webb. Her success was due to combining vision with a great attention to detail, whether in dealing with the problems of the poor or of the environment. She was pertinacious and undaunted. 'I am always ready for failure in preparing the hearts of people for any new thing', she said, 'Someone must pay the cost in disappointment, and I am quite ready to do so'.[36] She was a typical mid-Victorian woman in her deference to males, particularly if they were in Holy Orders, and she opposed women's suffrage. Sydney Cockerell described her as 'an unobtrusive plainly dressed little lady, everlastingly knitting an extraordinarily fine piece of work ... of great force and energy, with a wide open but well stored brain, but withal as gentle and womanly a woman as can be'.[37]

Some of the women who knew her however left a somewhat different picture. Dame Henrietta Barnett had been one of her housing managers before she married Samuel Barnett, the Vicar of Whitechapel. She greatly admired Octavia and the influence which she had exerted in first interesting Canon Barnett in social questions. She described her as 'strong willed, but the strong will was never used for self. She was impatient in little things but persistent with long suffering in big ones, often dictatorial but humble to self effacement before those she loved and admired ... She evoked more admiration than love, but she loved love ... She was nicest when she was made passionate by her earnestness'.[38]

Beatrice Webb also served for a time as one of Octavia's volunteer housing workers. She started by regarding her as 'a sort of ideal of the attraction of woman's power', but thought that this power was 'sometimes shown in a despotic temper'. After the breakdown which followed her broken engagement, Mrs Webb considered that Octavia had 'sought retirement in the detail of endless practical work in the subordination of other and inferior workers. As a great leader of woman's work she assuredly takes the first place. But she might have been more if she had lived with her peers and accepted her great sorrow'.[39] It is doubtful if Beatrice Webb either knew or understood Octavia Hill's character well, for from the latter's own letters it can be seen how she understood the danger of being corrupted by power; it was partly as a safeguard against its temptations that until the end of her life she occupied herself with humble details and still transplanted daisies round Paradise Court with her own hands.

Although Octavia Hill sometimes wrote about religion in her letters, she did not often talk about it. Too much, she considered, was said to the poor about God. She had no sympathy with those who tried to force their religion on others. She despised the attempts of the clergy to lure the poor to their churches with free meals and coal tickets and believed that religious teaching had suffered incomparably more than it had gained by the confusion of temporal gifts with spiritual teaching. 'For God's sake let His truth stand on its own merits' she wrote. 'Preach it by word, by deed, by patient abiding, but do not use bribes or even what look like bribes to make men take it in'.[40]

She was happy in the Church of England, in its sense of order and in the beauty of its liturgy. There continually opened out to her new visions of ways in which the Church would expand and become more comprehensive, would adapt itself to new needs and give more responsibility to laymen. She advised her friend Janey Senior however that if she felt alienation and antagonism, rather than support and fellowship, within the Church of England, she should leave it. If she did this, she said those who loved her would never feel her further from them.[41] Indeed she cared little about denominations. When a friend tried to persuade her to become a Quaker, she replied that she already felt herself to be one.

When Ruskin spoke to her wistfully of the glories of life in convents, she replied robustly, 'Convents helped to educate learned men and taught great illuminations. But I don't think that people who thought to escape evil in them found rest. Evil must be fought with and conquered, not run away from'.[42] Reflecting on the story of Martha and Mary, when she was only 18, she felt that Martha's would have been the better part, if she had only learnt to worship as she worked. But 'the resolution to make pauses for quiet thought is a most difficult duty. I believe the difficulty is connected with pride and want of faith. Attention to details is blessed if it springs from simple obedience, but restlessness and anxiety arise from a lingering doubt whether God can really arrange His world without our help'.[43]

The privilege of work she viewed almost with awe. 'What are we', she asked, 'that we should ask more than that God should let us work for Him among the tangible things which He created to be fair and the human spirits which He redeemed to be pure?'.[44] She had a strong sense of providence, that God required each person to cultivate his own garden, and that He had prepared her for her own work, But this was not to be solitary work. From Maurice came the vision of the Christian Community; from Maurice too a theology which accepted that God could bring good out of evil and that human suffering was sanctified by the suffering of Christ.

The early accounts of Octavia Hill were quite uncritical; later her reputation suffered from the able attacks of Beatrice Webb, and the ethos of the Welfare State, whose coming she opposed. More recently sympathy has revived, in an era of privatisation, for her distaste for bureaucracy. How and why she developed from being an enthusiastic Christian Socialist into an almost Calvinistic belief in free enterprise is something of a puzzle when it is recollected that her banker father had been broken by that system through no fault of his own. What, we may wonder, was the fate of her undeserving tenants and of their innocent families who were evicted because they failed to pay the rent?

Yet in practice Octavia's economic and social principles were tempered by her Christianity. Evictions in fact seem to have been very few, and even when families were evicted she continued to try to help them. As Canon Barnett observed, 'She brought the force of religion into the cause of wisdom, and gave emotion to justice'.[45] Her passionate and sensitive care for individuals kept bursting out. 'I would wish most lovingly to grasp the whole purpose of each life', she resolved when she was 20.[46] She noticed how a slum child 'comparatively without affection, utterly indifferent to home, is hardly touched by kindness, but at the sight of flowers her face lights up, her eyebrows raise, her whole being seems expanded'.[47]

She had the great gift of joy. It was joy in nature when, in her long walk home from her work with Ruskin, watching the sunset or rooks' nests against the sky, she would repeat the Magnificat; joy in people, in the parties which she organised for her tenants, with the games and the flags and processions and the organ grinder; and perhaps most of all joy in the work which she felt that God had given her, and for which He had prepared her. In the last year of her life she wrote to her fellow workers, 'As I write to record what has been done, a sense of thankfulness seems to be singing in my heart as I think of the many and great mercies which have been with us, of the joy which has been sent to us and of how, day by day, strength has been given to follow the way and light to see it, not far ahead but sufficiently for daily guidance'.[48]

She had too the gift of love. All work done as routine without love, she said, is quite despicable and *all* done with love most honourable.[49] It saddened her that, as Henrietta Barnett observed, she was sometimes unable to convey this sense of love. 'I wish I were gentler and better able to let people see what I feel', she wrote. 'In one way I can conceal nothing − everyone knows what I think, right or wrong − but few know how I care for them'.[50]

She wanted 'to get *near* people and get their spirits into harmony with God's will and purpose, and make them feel that one only wants *that* done'.[51] Yet it was absurd to try to teach grown up people anything until 'you have warmed the heart and unfrozen the tongue'.[52] Although she never married, she was very much a family person, living happily with her mother and her sisters, and constantly expressing her gratitude for their support, without which her achievements would not have been possible.

Much of her success was due to that patient study and masterly grasp of detail which impressed her contemporaries. As has been seen, at times she feared that the fight for mere existence, references, notices, rents and repairs, might make her mean or small or bitter: yet she believed that 'It is by the small graciousnesses, by the thoroughness of the out of sight detail that God will judge our spirit and our life'.[53]

Her religion caused her, except during her illnesses, to be an optimist and an activist. She was particularly fond of St Christopher 'because he learnt that the good thing was the strong thing'. 'There is a rest and certainty of our Father's loving rule and loving care', she said, 'which we carry about with us always and which never leaves us'. 'Whatever fact we meet in life', she wrote to Sydney Cockerell, 'that is God's own permitted fact or truth, possibly not eternal, but meant for us to accept or resist, but always to deal with, for which effort He gives us great strength'.[54] Yet in her activism and optimism she remained Maurice's pupil in her attitude to the problem of suffering. At the age of 70, on the death of Miranda, who had been her dearest sister and closest colleague, she wrote 'Our modern way of looking upon suffering as a thing which by good arrangement we can get rid of often misses that solemn sense of its holiness which those who live in constant memory of Our Lord's suffering enter into'.[55]

When, late in life, her portrait was presented to her by her friends, she said in returning thanks, 'When I am gone, I hope my friends will not try to carry on any special system or to follow blindly in the track which I have trodden. New circumstances require various efforts, and it is the spirit, not the dead form, that should be perpetuated'.[56] As she thus foresaw, some of her ideas fell out of date. One recent writer finds her social attitudes almost incomprehensible.[57] Yet her attitudes to housing were profoundly religious and if 100 years later the way in which she reached them is sometimes hard to understand, her own wise words may be remembered:

'I think one often has to hold two truths apparently utterly inconsistent in one's mind, knowing that, both being proved true, there must be some possibility of reconciling them by some unknown third truth which time may reveal'.[58]

Further Reading

Octavia Hill, *Life As Told In Her Letters*, ed. C.E. Maurice, London 1913, and *Octavia Hill, Early Ideals*, her earlier letters edited by Emily S. Maurice, London 1928, are valuable sources.

Octavia Hill, *Letters to Fellow Workers*, London 1933, and Octavia Hill, *Homes for the London Poor*, London 1970, are reprints of her articles and circular letters.

Of the biographies, Gillian Darley, *Octavia Hill, A Life*, London 1990, draws on much unpublished material but E. Moberly Bell, *Octavia Hill*, London 1942, remains useful. W.T. Hill, *Octavia Hill*, is mainly concerned with her work for the National Trust.

Beatrice Webb, *My Apprenticeship*, Cambridge 1979, and Henrietta Barnett, *Life of Canon Barnett*, London 1918, contain interesting critical references to Octavia Hill.

There is a perceptive essay on her, particularly as regards her religious ideas, in Nancy Boyd, *Josephine Butler, Octavia Hill, Florence Nightingale*, London 1982.

Notes

1. W.T. Hill, *Octavia Hill*, ('Hill') London 1956, p. 24.
2. C.L. Lewes, *Dr Southwood Smith*, London 1898, p. 156.
3. E. Moberly Bell, *Octavia Hill*, London 1942, p. 13.
4. *Octavia Hill, her Life as told in her Letters*, ed. C.E. Maurice, London 1913 ('Life'), p. 4.
5. Bell, pp. 21–2.
6. *Life*, p. 23.
7. E.S. Maurice, *Octavia Hill, Early Ideals*, London 1928, p.40.
8. *Early Ideals*, op. cit., pp. 131, 146, 156.
9. Gillian Darley, *Octavia Hill*, London 1989, p. 63.
10. Hill, *op. cit.*, p. 56.
11. O. Hill, *Homes of the London Poor*, London 1883, reprinted London 1970, p. 20.
12. *Ibid.*, p. 18.
13. *Ibid.*, p. 27.
14. O. Hill, *Homes*, p. 42.
15. O. Hill, *Homes*, p. 19.
16. Ibid., p. 24.
17. O. Hill, *Homes*, p. 26.
18. Bell, op. cit., p. 117.
19. Ibid., p. 85.
20. O. Hill, *Letters to Fellow Workers*, London 1933, p. 23.

21. Bell, p. 121.
22. Bell, pp. 122–3.
23. Beatrice Webb in *My Apprenticeship*, London 1926, p. 194 ff. makes an able attack on the C.O.S. and its leaders.
24. Bell, op. cit., p. 108.
25. Bell, op. cit., p. 116.
26. *Life*, p. 270.
27. B. Webb, *My Apprenticeship*, London 1926, pp. 263–4.
28. Bell, pp. 156–8; Hill, p. 110.
29. J. Ruskin, *Collected Works*, ed. E.T. Cook, London, Vol. 29, 1878, p. 354.
30. Bell, p. 185.
31. Bell, p. 188.
32. Bell, p. 257.
33. Hill, p. 164.
34. Hill, p. 17.
35. Bell, p. 280.
36. Bell, p. 282.
37. *Life*, p. 269.
38. H. Barnett, *Life of Canon Barnett*, Vol. 1, pp. 30–31.
39. Beatrice Webb, *Diaries*, Vol. 1, p. 170.
40. Bell, p. 112.
41. *Life*, p. 280.
42. *Ideals*, p. 124.
43. *Ideals*, p. 92.
44. *Homes*, op. cit., p. 53.
45. *Life*, p. vii.
46. *Life*, p. 112.
47. *Life*, p. 86.
48. O. Hill, *Letters on Housing*, London 1933, p. 64.
49. *Life*, p. 161.
50. *Life*, p. 288.
51. *Life*, p. 405.
52. *Life*, p. 335.
53. *Life*, pp. 229, 335.
54. Hill, p. 114; *Life*, p. 509.
55. *Life*, p. 572.
56. *Life*, p. 582.
57. D. Owen, *English Philanthropy 1660–1960*, Cambridge, U.S.A., 1964, p. 387.
58. *Life*, p. 282.

2

Pandita Mary Ramabai and the Widows (1858 – 1922)

'The first Christian to be enrolled in the Calendar of Indian Saints'

Sarojini Naidu, 1924

Pandita Ramabai was pre-eminent among Indian women of her time as a social and educational reformer, Sanskrit scholar and translator of the Bible. She was devout in her faith and saved thousands of women and girls from lives of misery. Yet the Anglo-Catholic sisters of the Community of St Mary the Virgin, who were responsible for her conversion, watched her remarkable career unfold with as much dismay as gratification: for on becoming a member of the Church of England she continued to regard herself culturally as a Hindu, and she welcomed Ministers of all Christian denominations to conduct worship in the great church which she built for her widows and orphans. She refused to accept correction of her ecumenical attitude and practice. As her baptismal sponsor, Sister Geraldine, sadly observed, 'Christian liberty and Christian hierarchical government, with its ramifications and discipline, her mind was unable to harmonize ... She wished to fly with the swallows or soar with the lark and would have none of the corporate life of the rooks or starlings who were marshalled under the command of a leader.'[1]

Her early life was an extraordinary and tragic adventure. Her father, Anant Shastri, was a Sanskrit scholar of the caste of the Chittapana Brahmins, many of whom occupied positions of distinction in Western India; he was a follower of the Bhakti faith, which focused on personal union with God. His main eccentricity was to believe in the education of women; at the age of forty, when his first wife died, he married a girl of 9 and taught her Sanskrit. The religious leaders of the

45

neighbourhood protested that this was against tradition, so he moved into the forest on the top of a peak in the Western Ghats where he established an ashram. Here six children were born to him, of whom three survived; the youngest of these was named Ramabai, after the sister of Ram who was Goddess of Light. The cost of entertaining pilgrims and visitors gradually caused him to sell off the rice fields and coconut plantations upon whose rents he depended. The family were obliged to leave their home and live as pilgrims; the little Ramabai was carried down the mountain on a man's back in a cane box.

From the age of 8 until she was 16 she was instructed in Sanskrit literature by her mother. The family earned their living as Purunikas, or religious pilgrims, moving from village to village and reading or reciting the Sanskrit Puranas. For the audience it was an act of merit to reward them with food, clothes or money, and in normal times they were never in want. When the father became blind the mother and children did the reading. In 1876–77 however the family were overtaken by the great famine which swept through Southern India, in which high caste families, unaccustomed to hard labour and poverty, suffered worse than the lower castes. As Ramabai bitterly remembered, 'We had all the sacred learning necessary to lead an honest and religious life, but the pride of caste and superior learning and vanity of life prevented us from stooping down to acquire some industry whereby we might have saved the precious lives of our parents.' The family's remaining money was spent in giving alms to Temple Brahmins in order to propitiate the gods, but 'nothing came of all this futile effort to please the gods – the stone images remained as hard as ever and never answered our prayer'.[2] Ramabai's father, mother and sister died of starvation within months of one another, leaving only herself and her brother. Her father's last words to Ramabai were 'Remember, my child, you are my youngest, my most beloved child; I have given you into the hands of our God; you are His, and to Him alone you must belong, and serve Him all your life'.[3]

The faith of Ramabai and her brother in their religion however had now grown cold and they were not so strict about obtaining secular education or the means of earning their living. Eventually in 1878 they arrived at Calcutta, then the capital city of India. Here for the first time they came in contact with Christians and attended religious services, where, when the congregation knelt, Ramabai thought that they were worshipping their chairs. They also met learned pundits who asked Ramabai to lecture to women on their duties according to the Shastras. In studying books of Hindu law whilst preparing her lectures, Ramabai was struck by the fact that although the sacred books were inconsistent on many things, they were unanimous in holding that women as a class were bad, worse indeed than demons. Their only hope of liberation from millions of rebirths and suffering was through worship of a husband, with no other pleasure in life than the most degraded slavery to him. Women had no right to study the Vedas, and without knowing them no one could know the Brahma; without knowing Brahma no one could obtain liberation. Therefore no one could obtain liberation whilst incarnate as a woman.

Similar rules applied to the Sudra class. If a Sudra dared to hear or recite the Veda, according to the law he was to be punished by having his ears filled with liquified lead or having intensely hot liquor poured down his throat. As for the lowest castes, their only hope of promotion in a future life was through service to Brahmans. They must live on the outskirts of villages and towns and were barred from the temples.[4]

Ramabai became disgusted with these doctrines and she and her brother came to associate with the Brahmo Samaj, the reformist group which drew much from Christianity as one of the various paths to the True God. Its leader, Keshab Chandra Sen, encouraged her to read the Vedas, despite the tradition that women might not do so. The Brahmo theistic concept of life, with its sense of justice and its tolerance of all teachings of truth and religious attitudes, had a considerable appeal for Ramabai, though it failed to satisfy her deeper religious longings.[5] It was nothing, she said later, but what a man makes for himself, having no other foundation than man's own natural light.[6]

Her lectures on the rise and fall of the Aryan race and on female emancipation, and above all her knowledge of the sacred books, caused something of a sensation. Calcutta University, on the advice of a Committee composed of one Indian and two British scholars, conferred on her the title 'Saraswati,' after the Goddess of Learning. Later a gathering of scholars also awarded her the title of Pandita, the first Indian woman to be so honoured. Her modesty did not allow her to mention these honours in any of the articles which she wrote about her early life.

Suddenly, when a sufficient income was being earned by their teaching, and when they were developing a satisfying intellectual and social life, Ramabai's brother Shrinivas died. Until then, under his protection, she had never contemplated marriage, but at the age of 22 she now married a friend of her brother's, Bipin Behari Medhavi, a Bengali school teacher and lawyer, who was 7 years older than herself and not a Brahmin but a member of the Sudra caste. It was a civil marriage with no religious ceremony, and she also broke with tradition in calling him by his first name. In the following year a daughter, Monorama — or Heart's Delight — was born. It seems to have been a happy marriage, although Ramabai annoyed her Brahmo husband by receiving visits from a Baptist missionary and declaring her intention of becoming a Christian. After less than two years of marriage however her husband died of cholera. She had no wish to remain in Bengal as a widow and be perpetually accused by her husband's family of responsibility for his death. She returned therefore with her daughter to Maharashtra, the home of her ancestors, and settled in Poona, then the intellectual centre of Western India. Here the eminent reformer M.G. Ranada and his wife welcomed her. Now, and for the rest of her life, she wore the short hair and white sari of the widow and no ornaments.

She earned her living by lecturing, mostly on social questions and on the position of women; she also started women's committees which discussed female emancipation. In 1882 she gave evidence to the Hunter Commission on Education when it visited Poona. In this she advocated the appointment by the Government of women school inspectors, maintaining that 99% of educated men in India were opposed to female education. She also urged the Government to make provision for the study of medicine by women, pointing out that many Indian women would rather die than discuss their ailments with a man.[7]

She now decided to go to England, firstly to improve her English and then to study medicine. Many of those who had heard her lectures contributed money for her passage; this was supplemented by royalties on a book by her in Marathi on 'Morals for Women.' Its message was that women's salvation lay in their own hands, and that their first duty was to educate themselves. In preparation for the journey she and her daughter took English lessons from Miss Hurford, Principal of the Government Female Training School; Miss Hurford agreed to this on condition that she should also be allowed to impart the Gospel Story. Through her Ramabai met Sisters from the Community of St Mary the Virgin (C.S.M.V.) whose headquarters were at Wantage in England. She also met, and seems to have been considerably influenced by, Father Nehemiah Goreh, a Maratha, who at this time was a member of the Society of St John the Evangelist (S.S.J.E.), or Cowley Fathers, who shared the same Anglo Catholic beliefs as the Wantage Sisters. The Sisters offered to receive Ramabai and Mono at Wantage where Ramabai could teach Marathi to them and learn English until further plans were made. Ramabai before departing from India was reported in the press as saying that she would never be induced to become a Christian. In 1883 together with her daughter and her friend Anandibai Bhagat, who had received a scholarship to study abroad, she set sail for England; they obtained a six berth cabin to themselves as 'no European passengers cared to share with natives.'

Within five months of their arrival in Wantage, Ramabai was baptized and confirmed into the Church of England. The reasons for her precipitate decision are far from clear. She was in the care of Sister Geraldine who had served the Community in India and been invalided home. Sister Geraldine, who was to be a very critical friend to Ramabai for the rest of her life, attributed the conversion to Ramabai's admiration of the work of the Community and in particular of the loving care which they extended to sick prostitutes in London.[8] Ramabai on the other hand says that it was Father Goreh who was responsible, through a very long letter written to her from India to dispel her doubts and to point out how close the Brahmo faith which she held was to the Christian position.[9] Eventually Ramabai would probably have become a Christian in any case, but not, given time for reflection and comparison, an Anglo Catholic.

The impulse may well have been a reaction to the shock of the suicide of Anandibai who was also staying with the Sisters at Wantage. According to Max Mueller, with whom Ramabai stayed in a highly nervous state in Oxford after her conversion, Anandibai had been frightened by the idea that she and Ramabai would be made Christians by force and tried to strangle her to save her from this fate; failing in this she took poison.[10]

After all arrangements had been made for Ramabai to attend medical lectures in Oxford, it was found that her hearing had become so affected by her early privations that she had to give up the idea of a medical career. The Sisters therefore arranged for her to attend Cheltenham Ladies College to study English, Mathematics, Natural Sciences and Greek, and to teach Sanskrit in return. Dorothea Beale, founder and Principal of this first Girls' Public School to be established in England, took direct care of her and arranged through the Prime Minister, W.E. Gladstone, for a grant from the Queen's Bounty to cover her expenses. This somewhat embarrassed the Sisters, who thus could not constitute themselves her 'guardians' in the crisis which now occurred, because Ramabai was of full age and was not financially dependent on them.

Ramabai had now come to have considerable doubts about the Anglo Catholic position and felt confused by its rites and ritual. In letters to Sister Geraldine she explained that she could not accept the doctrine of the Holy Trinity, nor the Athanasian Creed, particularly its declaration that all who do not hold the Catholic faith shall perish everlastingly: she refused to believe that her dear and pious parents were eternally damned because they had not been Christians. She had reservations about the Virgin Birth and the Resurrection of the earthly body of Christ. The 39 Articles were difficult for her to swallow whole. The exclusivity of the Church of England was not only puzzling, but the idea of membership of a national Church was repugnant to someone who lived under an imposed British rule; it also seemed to her incongruous for the Church of England to regard Nonconformists as being outside the Holy Catholic Church, when in turn, as she learnt from reading Roman Catholic literature, the Church of England itself was not regarded by Rome as being part of the Catholic Church.[11]

As Ramabai's long letters reached Wantage from Cheltenham, Sister Geraldine was at first soothing. Understanding of these mysteries would come gradually, she urged, if Ramabai would recognize that she was still only a child in the faith; she must take much on trust from the Church. Then and later, when Ramabai based her contentions on her reading of the Bible, Sister Geraldine maintained that the Church was older than the Bible. Unable to persuade, she became sharp and quoted St Paul – 'Let a woman learn in quietness and all subjection'.[12] She now brought up bigger guns. Canon Butler, the Community's spiritual adviser, expressed his displeasure that Ramabai did not go to Confession. He also told her bluntly that she must accept the Church's teaching because it had been doctrine for 1900 years. When she persisted that she should have a voice of her own in proving or choosing a new religion in place of her old one, he contemptuously told her 'Go and work or stay with the Brahmos, or do what you like'.[13] After this unfortunate exchange, he wrote to Sister Geraldine that Ramabai had been spoilt by the attention she received. 'The Indian native', he asserted, 'is prone to vanity'.[14]

Charles Gore, the outstanding theologian who was Principal of Pusey House, Oxford, was brought in to discuss Ramabai's difficulties with her on the basis of a long string of Biblical texts, but he, too, failed to satisfy her about the Trinity.

Whilst Ramabai was in Cheltenham during term time, the Sisters cared for Mono. Returning to Wantage in a vacation, Ramabai heard Mono's prayers and was indignant to find that she had been taught to invoke Father, Son and Holy Ghost. Somewhat unreasonably, she demanded that the Sisters omit the Trinity from Mono's teaching. The trouble was, they suspected, that Ramabai was falling into the hands of 'Protestants.' Certainly she appeared at this time to find the company of Nonconformists more congenial, but, as Gore advised, the Community would be unwise to try to control her movements.

For the Anglo-Catholic community to assert Church discipline in beliefs was understandable but it was exasperating to Ramabai when they tried to censor her conduct. At Cheltenham she had the opportunity to teach Sanskrit to pupils in the boys College who hoped to enter the Indian Civil Service; she could thus earn money which she badly needed. She was forbidden by the Sisters however to do this; the unfortunate Anglican bishops of Bombay and Lahore were disturbed from their furloughs to write letters to the effect that Ramabai's reputation and influence in India would be ruined if she were known to have taught members of the opposite sex. Ramabai took it as an insult that the views of foreigners should thus be evoked to overrule the experience and opinion of herself, a widow aged 27, who had read the Sanskrit Scriptures to male audiences with her father's approval, and had written a book about the morals of Indian women.[15]

And then there was nagging about her diet; Sister Geraldine wrote to rebuke her for refusing to eat cakes at Wantage, presumably because they contained animal fat.

Miss Beale, a committed Anglican, who however had her own experience of crises of faith, was more understanding and more sensible. Allowance must be made, she told Sister Geraldine, for Ramabai's imperfect hearing and knowledge of English; and it should be borne in mind that she was under heavy attack from her former friends in India because of her conversion. She found Ramabai 'very learned and thoughtful.' 'We must not be anxious,' she continued, 'but really trust God with that wonderful mind and character that He has fashioned for her. She will never perhaps think exactly as we do but if she did she would not so well be a teacher for India.'[16]

The more she was rebuked, the more obstinate Ramabai became, saying 'I am not bound to accept every word that falls down from the lips of priests and bishops; I have just freed myself from the yoke of the Indian priestly tribe ... I must be allowed to think for myself. God has given me an independent conscience. .... You are all too learned and too spiritual, too wise, too faithful to your faith which you profess from your childhood, to understand my difficulties in accepting wholly the religion taught by you. You have never had the experience of choosing another religion which was foreign to you as I have.'[17] And, again to Sister Geraldine, she wrote 'I am not free of all my caste prejudices, as you are pleased to call them, I like to be called a Hindu for I am one ... My parents were Hindus. I have thoroughly imbibed within me all the good Hindu lessons of morality they taught me.'[18]

Eventually Ramabai was refused permission to take Communion with the Sisters; at this she wrote defiantly to Miss Beale 'What matters it to me if they will not let me communicate with them . . . The door of the Universal Church is not shut against me and I believe the Holy Catholic Church is not confined within the walls of the Anglican Church. I will take Jesus for my guru and study the Bible.'[19]

The Wantage Sisters had caught a Tartar, and it must have been a relief to all concerned when at this point Ramabai received an invitation from Dr Rachel Bodley, Dean of the Women's Medical College at Philadelphia, to visit the University for the graduation ceremony at which her cousin, Anandabai Joshi, was to become the first Indian woman to receive a medical degree. All expenses were paid, and in 1886 she sailed with Mono, now aged four and a half. Dr Bodley took them into her house. Although originally Ramabai had only intended to stay a few months she once more tried to be accepted like Anandabai as a medical student. When her hearing defect prevented this, she decided to prepare herself to be a teacher and perhaps to start a new educational institution in India where training of the hand as well as the head would be taught. She took a kindergarten teaching course and studied the various school systems of America. Gradually she came to realize that what she most wanted to do was start a school for child widows. To obtain financial support for this in India would be hard, but in America nothing seemed impossible.

She now wrote her best known book *The High Caste Hindu Woman*, the first book by an Indian woman to be published in the English language. In this she began by describing the hateful sentiments about women in the Laws of Manu — how in childhood a woman must be subject to her father, in youth to her husband, and then to her sons after he was dead. She explained how 'though destitute of virtue, or seeking pleasure elsewhere or devoid of good qualities, a husband must be constantly worshipped as a god by a faithful wife.' She drew attention to the recent case of Rakhmabai, a well educated lady who had refused to live with a man of bad character to whom she had been married as a child without her consent; she had been committed to jail by a British magistrate for her recalcitrance.

Against this background Ramabai described the situation of the most miserable group of all, young Hindu widows. These had often been married to men much older than themselves. If their husbands died they were treated as outcastes. Their heads were shaved; their bangles were broken and they were stripped of all clothing except for a coarse sari. They were allowed only one meal a day and must not eat with others. Their widowhood was regarded as a punishment for crimes in their past life and, unless they had children, they were tolerated only as slaves. Many were driven to prostitution or suicide.

Ramabai estimated that there were 670,000 widows under the age of 20 in India. She pointed out the need for institutions in which widows could be educated as teachers, governesses, nurses, housekeepers and in handicrafts. It was hopeless, she said, to expect to find money for this cause in India where the great majority of men were opposed to the education of women. She therefore appealed to the American public to help her to set up an institution which would be managed by a committee of Hindu ladies and gentlemen, and which American teachers would help to staff.[20]

Dr Rachel Bodley, in an eloquent introduction to her book, described Ramabai's remarkable life and warmly supported her appeal; she proposed that interdenominational committees be set up to raise $15,000 to inaugurate the work and then $5,000 annually to support it for the next ten years. She ended by quoting Ramabai's remark to her that the women of America should be reminded that it was 'out of Nazareth that the Redeemer came; that great reforms have again and again been wrought by instrumentalities that the world despised. Tell them to help me to educate the child widows; for I solemnly believe that this hated and despised class of women, educated and enlightened, are, by God's grace, to redeem India.'[21]

Short, clear and colourful, the book had an immediate success. A 'Ramabai Association' was formed in Boston. Its officers were Episcopalian, Unitarian, Baptist and Methodist. The Board of Trustees consisted of eminent business and professional men; the Executive Committee was composed entirely of women. The Association pledged itself to support for ten years a school for widows in which no religious instruction, either Hindu or Christian, would be given. The Bible and the Vedas were to stand side by side in the library for reference. Caste rules were to be observed, but there were to be no public religious observances. Sixty circles of the Association were formed throughout the United States, often by Ramabai herself who had developed into a powerful speaker in English. She spent much of her time writing, or translating from English, school text books in Marathi, with lithograph illustrations.

Mono had been sent back to the Wantage Sisters. It is creditable both to Sister Geraldine and Ramabai that the harsh letters exchanged after the latter's conversion never destroyed their friendship. Right up to Sister Geraldine's death Ramabai continued to write to her as 'My dear old Ajeebai' (Granny) and sign herself 'Mary Rama.'[22]

The American experience did much for Ramabai. Although at Cheltenham she had declared her intention to devote her life to study, in America she found herself through action. She was to introduce many American educational methods in India. More important, her self confidence was strengthened by working with the able, inspired and indomitable women who were emerging in various reform movements of the late 19th century. One of those who influenced her most was Frances Willard, leader of the Prohibition Movement, who described Ramabai's public speaking as 'full of archness and repartee' and her disposition as 'incarnate gentleness, combined with celerity of apprehension, swiftness of mental pace and adroitness of logic'. She was 'captivated' by Ramabai and corresponded with her for the rest of her life.[23]

Ramabai was strengthened also in her love of liberty. Boston and Philadelphia, which were her bases, had been in the forefront of both the American War of Independence and the movement for Abolition of Slavery; on the cover of the magazine of her school was to be depicted the Liberty Bell of Philadelphia. Whilst her Anglican friends in England had been strong supporters of British rule in India, in America she caught at least a whiff of anti-Imperialism.

Where she worshipped in America does not seem to be recorded. This may have varied, according to the practice of her different hosts on her travels. Her experience of working closely with people of various Christian denominations was to confirm her belief in the concept of 'a Universal Christian Church' which she was to put into practice in the non-denominational character of her work in India.

This progress was not welcomed by Anglo Catholics. Rev. C.E. Garner in his Life of Father Goreh was to observe that in America Ramabai 'was exposed to temptations which she was not prepared to resist. . . . She found herself in the midst of those who called themselves Christians, each holding various elements of the Christian Creed. . . . It was not surprising that she lost her spiritual footing.'[24] Indeed Ramabai herself was to admit that she was dazed by the religious diversities in America.

At the end of 1888 Ramabai returned to India from California by the Pacific route, bringing with her the Marathi textbooks which she had prepared – a primer and five graduated readers, a geography, a natural history textbook, and 600 plates for illustrations. On the way she lectured in Japan under the auspices of the Women's Christian Temperance Union.

On her arrival in Bombay she stayed in the house of the Wantage Sisters, where she was reunited with her daughter. Sister Eleanor wrote back from Bombay to Sister Geraldine in Wantage – 'That she has lost her infidel tendencies is a matter of great thankfulness but she is evidently in a fog of dissent. However it may be for us with gentleness to draw her with Catholicity.'[25]

Ramabai was relieved to be able to revert to Indian customs: 'O my feet have been imprisoned for five years,' she wrote, as she resumed her sandals. Sister Eleanor noted glumly that after all the care which the Sisters had taken over Mono's education she was now encouraged to eat her meals with her fingers, sitting on the floor.[26]

Within two months of her return to India Ramabai had opened a school for high caste widows and orphans, both as boarders and day scholars. Its Board of Management included R.G. Ranade, Sir Ramakrishna Bhandarkar and other western

Indian philanthropists. At the inauguration Ramabai boldly told the mainly male audience 'Just as we do not have an Indian citizen as our representative in the British Parliament, which naturally is ignorant about the real state and situation in India, likewise we women folk have not been given an opportunity to place our representative in the Parliament of India.'[27]

The school was named 'Sharada Sadan' – The House of Wisdom. By the end of the first three months there were 22 pupils. Some of them had found their own way to the House, such as Saraswati, a widow whose husband's relatives had arranged to sell her as a prostitute, and Yamuna whose husband had been transported for the murder of a prostitute. In November 1890 the House was moved from Bombay to Poona, which was healthier and cheaper; it was also the centre of Hindu orthodoxy in Western India. Here Ramabai was joined by an outstandingly capable Indian colleague, Soonderabai Power, an Episcopal Methodist who had made several visits to England in protests against the opium trade. Through her influence Ramabai's work came to receive a strong impression of Methodism. Soonderabai was also responsible for introducing daily Bible reading. Eventually she left to start her own Zenana Home in Poona. Although Ramabai honoured the undertaking that her school would be neutral in religion, she and Monorama and Soonderabai started each day with Bible reading and prayers in her room. Ramabai's custom was always to leave her door open, so that girls could come to see her informally at any time. Gradually a number of them, without any particular invitation, came in to listen to the Bible readings. By the spring of 1893 about half the widows attended. Those who were orphaned and without guardians, and who had thus been adopted by Ramabai, were encouraged to do so. A crisis now arose over a school picnic outing: more than half the girls, instead of going on it, stayed behind with Ramabai for a day of prayer and study of the Scriptures, at the end of which 20 asked to become Christians. The teachers who led the picnic excursion, offended, informed members of the local Advisory Board. There was a storm of criticism in the Indian Press. The Trustees in America were considerably disturbed. Twenty-five of the pupils who had guardians were

withdrawn. Several members of the Advisory Committee submitted their resignations direct to Boston on the grounds that
the school had become a proselytising institution.

Ramabai offered her resignation if the Advisory Committee
in Poona were to be given powers of management. Mrs Judith
Andrew, a lady of 68 who was sent out from Boston to report on
the situation, however found there was no effort to proselytise,
but that the mere force of Christian example was the occasion
of these converts accepting the new faith. Ramabai was exon-
erated, and out of the controversy something positive emerged.
The Orthodox Hindus, with her encouragement, started their
own Widows' Home in Poona.

The vacancies at Sharada Sadan were soon filled. Whilst
some widows found their own way to the House, others were
brought in by Ramabai from Northern India, where she visited
the temples disguised as a pilgrim. Here she found girl widows
who had become temple prostitutes and would be abandoned
when they lost their attractions. She rescued a number of them
and almost lost her life in the process. The school settled down
to develop in line with Ramabai's progressive ideas. After the
miserable lives they had led Ramabai wished them 'to see the
contrast in everything where love rules, to become acquainted
with as many good people as possible, to learn what the outside
world is like from pictures and books, and to enjoy the wonderful works of God as they ramble in the garden, study with
the microscope, or view the heavens from the little verandah
on the roof.'[28] She bought a fruit farm and sought to make the
school self-supporting, growing oranges, limes and mangoes.

The Home was not a place where all the best rooms were
reserved for the staff. The girls were free to come and go in
the drawing room; they followed Ramabai about and 'clustered
around her like bees'.[29] Her methods were unorthodox both in
teaching and discipline. She wrote little songs about birds and
flowers for the younger girls to sing. If older girls quarrelled
they were set to work together at two grind stones.

Ramabai was rapidly being recognised as a public figure. In
1889 she became the first Indian woman to address the Annual
Conference of the Indian National Congress, to which she recommended that Hindi should be used as the common language
of India. She also made a forceful speech at the Indian National

Social Conference in the same year, proposing that it should be made an offence to shave the heads of widows. In 1889 her book in Marathi, 'The Peoples of the United States' was published, which described the social progress which America had made as a consequence of democracy and the education of women.

In 1891 Ramabai passed through a spiritual crisis which she described in her *Testimony*. Although she had been intellectually convinced of the truth of Christianity when she was baptised at Wantage, for some years she felt that something was missing in her faith, and read many books on Christian doctrine without being satisfied. She reverted to reading the Bible itself but still 'I was desperate; I realised that I was not prepared to meet God, that sin had dominion over me, and I was not altogether led by the Spirit of God ...' She needed Christ, she said, and not merely his religion.

She now came under the influence of Dr Pentecost, an American Evangelist, who helped her 'to surrender myself unconditionally to the Saviour, and ask Him to be merciful to me and to become my righteousness and redemption and to take away all my sin ... The Holy Spirit made it clear to me from the Word of God that the salvation which God gives through Christ is present and not something future. I believed it, I received it and was filled with joy.' 'I can scarcely contain the joy and keep it to myself,' she wrote. 'I am bound to tell as many men and women as possible that Christ Jesus came to save sinners like me.'[30]

In 1896–7 a great famine occurred in Central India whose consequences were considerably to expand and change Ramabai's work. With her memories of the manner of her parents' deaths, she could not avoid involvement. Travelling around the Central Provinces she rescued hundreds of women and girls from starvation or prostitution and brought them back to Poona where they were lodged in tents on rocky ground adjacent to the farm at Khedgaon. Her vivid accounts of the famine were published in the Bombay Guardian which set up a relief fund to support her efforts. The new arrivals were not high caste girls, but often wild, untamed, jungly creatures, and the girls from the school joyfully came forward to help them. Some of them had become prostitutes; for these a special home

was established when an American lady with experience in reha-
bilitation arrived to take charge.

A further famine in 1899 came right up to the doors of the settlement, and again Ramabai felt she could not refuse to take in
widows and orphans, 1350 in all, of whom half were under the
age of 14. They were settled at Khedgaon on what now became
known as Mukti (House of Salvation). They were all illiterate;
the first need was to organize a school and enlarge the existing
industries, so everyone should learn some useful work. Fifty of
the brightest survivors of the earlier famine were formed into a
school for training teachers. The new girls spent half their day
at their books and half in the industrial department. Apart
from work in the garden and fields, there was an oil press and
dairy, a laundry and bakery. There was spinning and weaving
of cotton and wool, making up garments, blankets and rugs,
and a printing press.

In 1898, at the end of the ten year period for which the
Boston Committee had guaranteed to support the work,
Ramabai visited the United States to discuss the future. The
plan for the first ten years had been fulfilled at Sharada
Sadan. 350 widows had been rehabilitated and trained as
teachers, nurses, matrons and housekeepers, and a number
had remarried. Influx from the famines however had upset
plans to become self-supporting; American aid continued to be
needed, but, in light of the religious controversies which had
occurred and of Ramabai's own growing evangelical enthusiasm which followed her second 'conversion', she sought to
be released from her undertaking of religious neutrality. She
was received generously. The Ramabai Association was recon-
stituted, without the Unitarians, and henceforth her work was
openly acknowledged to be that of a Christian missionary as
well as that of an educator and social reformer.

Now that there was no obstacle to evangelising, a Church
was built at Mukti which could hold four to five thousand
people. Its services were usually conducted by American Methodist Ministers from Poona. The uneducated famine widows
and orphans responded enthusiastically. On one occasion a
procession of seventeen bullock carts carried them, singing
hymns, as they went down to the river to be baptised. In the
two months of December 1901 and January 1902 there were

1,200 baptisms. Nor did the campaign stop there; volunteers went out into the surrounding villages to preach the Gospel.

In 1905 occurred the phenomenon of the Revival at Mukti, which has been treated by Ramabai's several biographers with admiration, puzzlement or reserve. One evening, when Ramabai was reading from the eighth chapter of St John's Gospel, all the inmates, old and young, began to weep and confess their sins. Many felt a sensation of burning which they called a 'Baptism of Fire'. Evangelical work was intensified. Three meetings a day were held in Poona which were attended by non-Christians and by British soldiers. Then the school was closed for ten days, whilst the women and girls 'waited on the Lord' in their huge Church. There was a constant clamour of confessions, of speaking with tongues, and simultaneous prayer. As one visitor observed, 'Waves of prayer go over the meetings like rolling thunder. Sometimes after ten or twenty minutes it dies away and only few voices are heard; then it will rise again and increase in intensity: on occasions it goes on for hours. During these sessions there are usually some confessing their sins, often with bitter weeping which is painful to hear. The conflict seems so great they are almost beside themselves'.[31]

Letters were sent by Ramabai to missionaries all over India asking for names of people to be prayed for; in a short time 29,000 people were being prayed for by name.

It was noticed that although Ramabai welcomed the Revival, she did not herself participate in the loud clamour of confession and simultaneous prayer: indeed she dampened down the manifestations when they began to border on mass hysteria. Yet the Revival brought her a personal message through the Holy Spirit, that she had a duty to translate the Bible into a version which would enable her Bible women to understand it as though they could read it in the original languages. Translations existed, but the earlier ones by Europeans were in faulty 'Padre Marathi'; a later one, made with the help of Hindu Pandits, was in 'Sanskrit Marathi', in a style incomprehensible when it was read out to peasants and shepherds. Ramabai set herself the formidable task of translating the whole Bible into a simple and correct Marathi speech, not from an English version but from the original, with explanatory notes on each page. First therefore she had to learn Hebrew and improve her Greek. For the remaining fifteen years of her life all the time which was not taken in running her institution was devoted to translation. She gave up public speaking, travelling and most personal correspondence. As the chapters were finished, they were printed by the girls on the Mukti press, which also ran off Ramabai's many pamphlets and tracts.

By now Ramabai had ten European or American helpers, but everything continued to be conducted in Indian style. At Communion wheat chappatis and non-fermented grape juice were used. Her staff were chosen with care and were given as much scope as possible for individual development. Monorama wrote a vivid account of a typical day in Ramabai's life in her later days. She would move her 'office' to whatever department appeared to need her most. Often this would be the printing room, sometimes the weaving room; or it might be outside so that she could supervise the masons and carpenters, or on the verandah watching the food being served. When she moved several girls would carry behind her 'Pandita's Ark', a vast, specially made tray with compartments for books and papers.

Early in the morning she would meet the head carpenter, the head mason, the head matron, the chief typesetter and other chiefs of departments to give them their orders for the day. One of the girls stood beside her, ready to look up records and run errands. Next she did the proof-reading; everything put out by the press passed through her hands. Later the weavers might come to her; the pieces of cloth which they had made were weighed and the price decided. Then a merchant might appear with samples of his grains; a price must be established by bargaining and the contents of his sacks weighed. Or it might be someone with spices and groceries for sale. Girls trained as accountants would enter the transactions in their books. Once a week there was a market day where vegetables would be brought for sale and Mukti's products sold. Whenever there was a lull, Ramabai would return to her translations and there were intervals for meals and prayer. She always found time to visit the hospital and pray beside each bed. She had a special place in her heart for the mentally deficient, who she called her friends, and would chat with them as they were employed in cleaning the buildings and weeding the grounds.

She was devoted to animals. Twenty Persian cats answered their dinner bell; there was usually one of them sitting on her writing table, helping with the translations. She kept a little zoo, and once a year her animals and birds were invited to a special tea party. There were tubs of grain for the buffaloes and bullocks and oil cake for goats, sheep, dogs, cats and squirrels. Perhaps her favourites were the bullocks, for we would never get on without them, she said, to draw our water, bring us building materials and carry out our refuse and take our workers to the villages.[32]

Monorama was now Ramabai's right hand. She had, as Sister Geraldine wrote to complain, undergone a frequently interrupted education. At three different times she had stayed with the Wantage Sisters. She had studied at two schools in England and one in Poona. She was about to take her B.A. degree in America in 1900 when she was called back by Ramabai to help her. She graduated however at Bombay University and thus qualified to serve as Principal of the High School at Sharada Sadan. There now occurred a strange incident, as it is recorded by Sister Geraldine. The Committee in Boston proposed the separation of Sharada Sadan, of which Monorama as Head would become directly responsible to Boston, from Mukti, which would continue under Ramabai. Thereupon Ramabai sent Monorama at a few days' notice to Australia and New Zealand to raise support. Shortly afterwards the Sharada Sadan was moved to Mukti. [33] Monorama was only 19 at this time and Ramabai may well have felt her to be too young to carry complete responsibility. Later, in 1912, Monorama opened a Christian school in the State of Hyderabad which did not survive long.

Ramabai was a great institution builder. In addition to the girls departments, an orphanage for boys was set up. Eventually it provided husbands for many of the girls, and Christian families became established in houses around the settlement. Then there was the Priti Sadan, or House of Love, whose 500 little girls were lovingly known as rabbits. There was a Home of Peace for the elderly and a Sunset Home for the aged sick. At the time of the Revival Ramabai experimented with faith healing and Christian Science, closing the clinics and sending away the doctors. Later this policy was reversed and a 60 bed hospital established with two resident women doctors.

During an outbreak of the plague in Western India Ramabai made a public statement attacking the Government for the brutal way in which Indians, including some of her own girls, were treated in the quarantine measures. Shortly afterwards two European officers who were engaged in anti-plague work were murdered and Ramabai was severely criticised in Government circles, and by the ever vigilant Sister Geraldine in England, as having some moral responsibility for this crime. In time the incident was forgotten; one day Mukti was visited unexpectedly by the Governor of Bombay. Her one great thought, Ramabai said after he departed, leaving a very pleasant impression, was that Our Lord Jesus Christ is coming some day just in this unexpected manner.[34] For she had a strong conviction of the imminence of the Second Coming and constantly admonished her staff and girls to be prepared for it. In 1919 the Government conferred on her the Kalser-i-Hind medal, a high decoration given for outstanding social work.

In 1921 Ramabai suffered a sad blow on the death of her daughter who had been so well prepared to succeed her. Ramabai survived her by only a few months. Her great translation accomplished, she now spent much of her days and nights in praise of the Lord. In April 1922 she died quietly in her sleep. The funeral was in the great church which she had built; her girls took it in turns to carry her body to the grave. Shortly before her death she had designated her secretary of many years, Lissa Hastie, as her successor.

The work went on, gradually appearing more orthodox, as many of its lessons came to be applied by the Government and by voluntary agencies all over India. At the hundredth anniversary of Ramabai's birth in 1958 800 women and children were being cared for at Mukti. A report in 1982 showed how orphans and unwanted and deserted babies were still coming in. The teachers training and the printing press continued. So too did the evangelization work in the villages, despite, the report said, the efforts of Satan to frustrate it by thefts, beatings and dog bites.[35]

Ramabai's achievements had been of many kinds.

As an educationist she was a pioneer in India of methods which combined brainwork and handwork. Her demonstration of the capability of girls for both was far ahead of her time. Not only did the girls operate her printing press and maintain and clean its engine, but as masons and carpenters they constructed many of the Mukti buildings. In her schools she introduced fresh approaches, teaching her girls to organize themselves into societies, such as those for Christian Endeavour and Temperance Work, which elected their own officers and used Parliamentary procedures. Because she considered that Hindus tended to despise their bodies, she made her girls study physiology, as well as botany, to enhance their understanding of nature. She introduced kindergarten methods into India and the use of braille for teaching the blind. In spite of frequently living in financial uncertainty, the girls were encouraged to remember the problems of others. They would sometimes volunteer to go without meals so that money could be sent to sufferers in Armenia and in China and even to orphans in America.

As a social reformer, Ramabai's work aroused an increasing sentiment against child marriage and in favour of Hindu remarriage and female education. Her example inspired the establishment of widows' homes elsewhere in India, often with her help. In persuading her high caste girls to sweep floors, and in emphasizing the dignity of labour she set an example similar to that of Mahatma Gandhi.

Recognized as a scholar and writer, in addition to her great Bible translation a number of her books became part of the curriculum of Bombay University. Several of her hymns also were included in Marathi hymn books; these were in the Evangelical tradition: 'I have found a Friend in Jesus' and 'Have You been to Jesus for the Cleansing Blood.' She was a brilliant lecturer, earnest but witty. In modern India she was the first woman to emerge as a leader in public life. She was probably unique in her time as an Indian who headed an international staff coming from Britain, America, Canada, Australia, New Zealand, Denmark and Sweden.

What was she like as a person? Max Mueller, meeting her in her twenties, described her as 'truly heroic, in appearance small, delicate and timid, but in reality bold as a tigress.'[36]

At that time she foresaw her life as that of a scholar, but in later life she no longer read widely, finding a Bible and Concordance sufficient for most of her needs. With responsibility the timidity disappeared. A visitor to Mukti found her 'very charming and humble, and at the same time imperious'.[37] Many people noticed how her faith kept her 'unworried and unharried' and remembered her cheerful face and ringing laughter even when no one knew how to pay for the next week's meals for the staff and pupils and the hundreds of unforeseen lodgers who had been rescued from famine. 'Send a wire to your Heavenly Father who can supply' she would say to her despairing staff and, when they had reduced meals to one a day, a cheque always seemed to come in.[38]

Above all, witnesses recalled, that although – perhaps in the circumstances inevitably – autocratic, she invariably attributed the successes of the project to God and, as the Canadian Mrs Nalder put it, 'She radiates the Lord Jesus'.[39] Rev. Nicol MacNicol, who was her contemporary and first biographer, wrote that 'None of the great Saints acknowledged more fully than she that dependence on divine creative power with which alone the holy life is begun, continued and consummated'.[40] This genuine characteristic of attributing all achievements to God was acknowledged even by Sister Geraldine. MacNicol also observed how in her Christian life there was a continuation of all that was best in her Hindu life.

Her manner of living, like that of Gandhi, was one of extreme simplicity; she owned nothing but her clothes and books. Her progress, also like his, was an experiment with truth which sometimes led her into mistakes which she recognized, such as too great a reliance on faith healing. 'I wanted to find out the truth about everything, including religion, by experiment,' she wrote.

Sister Geraldine, shortly before her own death in 1917, read through her 30 year long correspondence with Ramabai and pondered its lessons. She felt 'thankfulness that through her instrumentality the Kingdom of Darkness is being weakened in India' but 'heart sorrow that she has failed to rise up to the highest spiritual gifts, chiefly through the unhappy divisions among Christians';[41] for the experience of Church missionaries, she generalized, was 'that it is almost impossible to impress Indian people with such a sense of loyalty to the Church that they will refrain from joining in undenominational worship.'[42]

Ramabai wrote to the Wantage Sisters, 'The debt of loving kindness that I owe you I can never repay,' though she did in fact manage to repay them financially. Yet she was unfortunate in the narrow denominational attitude of her godmother. Eventually her kind of Christianity rather than that of Sister Geraldine was to be accepted by Indian Anglicans when they joined with the main Nonconformist denominations to form a single Church. To the spirit of that Church, which set an example of ecumenical brotherhood to Anglicans everywhere, Ramabai's life made a vital contribution.

Further Reading

Pandita Ramabai Saraswati, *The Hindu High Caste Woman*, Philadelphia, 1887.

P. Sen Gupta, *Pandita Ramabai Saraswati*, London, 1970, is the most useful biography.

S.M. Adhav, *Pandita Ramabai*, Madras, 1979, contains extracts from her memoirs and writings as well as a bibliography of books by and about her.

Letters and Correspondence of Pandita Ramabai (ed. A.B. Shah), Bombay, 1977, contains her lifelong correspondence with Sister Geraldine.

Helen S. Dyer, *Pandita Ramabai*, London, 1923, is a memoir by a close colleague. Nicol MacNicol, *Pandita Ramabai*, is another account by someone who knew her. There is a chapter on her in Stephen Neill, *Builders of the Indian Church*, London, 1934.

Notes

1. *Letters and Correspondence of Pandita Ramabai*, ed. A.B. Shah, Bombay, 1977, p. 404.
2. P. Sengupta, *Pandita Ramabai*, London, 1970, p. 53; Muriel Clark, *Pandita Ramabai*, London, 1920, p. 11.
3. Jennie Chappell, *Pandita Ramabai*, London, 1923.
4. P. Sengupta, *op. cit.*, p. 16.
5. Ramabai's Testimony in H.S. Dyer, *Pandita Ramabai*, London, 1923, p. 27.

6. Ibid., p. 32.
7. Sen Gupta, *op. cit.*, pp. 96–98.
8. *Letters and Correspondence of Pandita Ramabai*, ed. A.B. Shah, Bombay, 1977, p. 396/7.
9. Sen Gupta, *op. cit.*, p. 138.
10. F. Max Mueller, *Auld Lang Syne*, Series 2, London, 1899, p. 127.
11. *Letters, op. cit.*, pp. 108, 150, 167.
12. *Ibid.*, pp. 339, 99.
13. *Ibid.*, pp. 131–133.
14. *Ibid.*, p. 76.
15. *Ibid.*, p. 63.
16. *Letters*, p. 78.
17. *Letters, op. cit.*, pp. 130–134.
18. *Ibid.*, pp. 108, 189.
19. *Letters*, p. 405.
20. Pandita Ramabai Sarasvati, *The High Caste Hindu Woman*, Philadelphia, 1887.
21. *Ibid.*, p. xxiv.
22. Jennie Chappell, *Pandita Ramabai*, London, 1938, pp. 36, 38.
23. Sen Gupta, *op. cit.*, p. 164; Ruth Bordin, *Frances Willard*, Univ. of California, 1986, p. 191.
24. Sen Gupta, *op. cit.*, p. 165.
25. *Letters, op. cit.*, p. 231.
26. *Ibid.*, p. 240.
27. Sen Gupta, *op. cit.*, p. 183.
28. Chappell, *op. cit.*, p. 43.
29. Helen S. Dyer, *Pandita Ramabai*, London 1923, p. 13.
30. Dyer, *op. cit.*, pp. 37, 42.
31. Dyer, *op. cit.*, p. 102.
32. Dyer, *op. cit.*, p. 147.
33. *Letters, op. cit.*, p. 364 ff.
34. Dyer, *op. cit.*, p. 51.
35. Mukti Annual Report in *Prayer Bell*, Poona 1982.
36. Max Mueller, *Auld Lang Syne*, Second Series, London 1899, p. 122.
37. R.K. Dongre and J.F. Patterson, *Pandita Ramabai*, Madras, 1969, p. 123.
38. Ibid., p. 42.
39. Chappell, *op. cit.*, p. 75; Dyer, *op. cit.*, p. 42.
40. Nicol MacNicol, *Pandita Ramabai*, Calcutta, 1926, p. 1.
41. *Letters*, p. 423.
42. *Ibid.*, p. 405.

3

Eglantyne Jebb and the
World's Children (1876–1928)

'As Christians we are under an obligation to every single person we meet'
Eglantyne Jebb, 1926

'Elle était plus flamme que femme'
Count Carton de Wiart, in the League of Nations
Assembly, 1929

In 1930 Sir Philip Gibbs, perhaps the best known war correspondent of his time, reflected how at the end of World War I:

'There was a litter of ruin, not only the ruins which covered the old battlefields but in the hearts of men and women, and smouldering fires were waiting to light the torch of war again. Many nations of the world were filled with starving people. It was a ghastly time.

There are very few of us who realized how thin was the ice which covered the dark winters of anarchy and despair and disease. It was at that time that a company of men and women made an appeal to the British nation which I honestly believe helped to save the soul of the world which otherwise would have been damned and doomed. They raised the cry of "Save the Children," a whisper at first, it was heard by those who hated each other and appealed to human instincts stronger than even those of race and nationality; and there was a great surging up of charity in the heart of a stricken world.'[1]

Eglantyne Jebb who, with her sister Dorothy, founded the Save the Children movement in 1919 and was to become its mainspring, was not well known at the time. Indeed, at the age of 42, she regarded her life up to then as a succession

69

of failures in her attempts to find an adequate outlet for her dynamic Christian desire to serve her neighbours. In retrospect however it can be seen how each of the apparent failures equipped her with experience which she was to need for the great work of the last nine years of her life.

Eglantyne Jebb was born in 1876 in Ellesmere in Shropshire. Her father, Arthur Jebb, had practised as a barrister and had been a schools inspector before settling down as a country landowner. He had a strong social conscience and founded the Ellesmere Literary and Debating Society at which he and his children and his servants and tenants would debate social questions together. Eglantyne's mother was distressed by the dreariness and lack of incentive in the lives of rural labourers and their children; she started Arts and Industries classes for them in her home at which wood carving, basket and cane work, carpentry, mosaics and painting were taught. Eventually the Home Arts movement which she started spread throughout Britain. Eglantyne grew up in the midst of this cause in a house pervaded by her mother's undogmatic religious spirit. Whilst her brothers went to boarding schools, the girls were educated at home by governesses; one of these came from Alsace and not only successfully taught them French and German, but left an impression on them of how it felt to be a member of a minority under a conqueror's rule. Eglantyne was editor of the family paper, the *Briarland Recorder*, to which she herself contributed numerous poems, stories and sketches.

As well as her parents, an important influence was her father's unmarried sister, Louisa (Aunt Bun), who lived with the family, and was a Victorian New Woman and Suffragette. When the question of university education for the girls arose, Arthur Jebb demurred, writing to his wife 'If a girl were marked with smallpox and had good abilities, if she were so shortsighted as to make spectacles a perpetual necessity and had great common sense, if she were obliged hereafter to gain her livelihood as a teacher at some sad seminary, there might be something to be said for Cambridge'[2] ... and besides, it would be too expensive. Aunt Bun prevailed and put up some of the money. Eglantyne's elder sister Lill went to Cambridge, and Eglantyne herself to Lady Margaret Hall, Oxford in 1894, the year of her father's death.

For Eglantyne Oxford was her 'Jerusalem' and 'blissful paradise.' Her brother Dick was up at New College; the greatly outnumbered women undergraduates, particularly those as handsome as Eglantyne, were in constant demand. She punted and played hockey but above all she loved to dance. She was coached by A.L. Smith in Political Science with such brilliance that she felt like dancing all the way back to her college after his tutorials. She went to lectures by Charles Gore on Christianity and Property, by Scott-Holland on Tolstoi, and by William Morris on Socialism. She read Browning to Miss Wordsworth, her Principal, and went on reading parties in the vacations. Her contemporary, Ruth Wordsworth, remembered her as the 'very ideal of a Burne-Jones beauty, a mixture of extreme shyness and dignified poise.'[3]

Mrs Arnold Toynbee was Treasurer of Lady Margaret Hall, and her friendship was important when Eglantyne came to consider what to do with her life. She arranged for her to visit Toynbee Hall, the settlement in the East End of London founded in memory of her husband, and persuaded her that there was an important need for university educated women to bring a new spirit into elementary education. Perhaps Eglantyne would not have taken this road had she obtained a first class degree. She had literary ambitions but wrote somewhat gloomily, 'I do not believe that my literary capacities justify me in leading a wholly literary life. I am very far from saying that I think teaching would be altogether congenial and delightful ... I think it suitable'.[4]

So, as her Oxford friend Dorothy Kempe, described her, off she went to Stockwell Teachers Training College with 'a weak voice, eyesight already overtaxed, little ear for music or power of discipline, little taste for handicrafts such as needlework, but an absolute determination to win through'.[5] The other trainees, who were not university graduates, as she described them to her sister, 'wore aprons, had accents, and sisters who served in shops', but they were very friendly. Eglantyne had to learn to teach 20 subjects to classes of 60 children. Her teaching was ruthlessly criticized, and she was 'truly grateful to have an uncompromising person to tell me the truth, and I must just pull myself together'.[6]

When she completed the course, she chose to teach in St Peter's Elementary School at Marlborough; her uncle, who taught at the boys Public School there, had recently become a widower, and the family felt that he and Eglantyne could cheer each other. She lived alone however and went for long solitary walks and bicycle rides on the Downs. She became depressed, fearing that her mind would go blank before her class, wondering whether her teaching even harmed the children, and apprehending a lifetime spent in an occupation which was infinitely worse to her than breaking stones.

It was at this point that she experienced what she came to regard as a moment of revelation which was to shape her life. In her class room hung a cheap print of the head of Christ, crowned with thorns.

'I saw an expression of unspeakable suffering', she wrote to her sister, 'but suffering which was conquered by resignation. He looked upward to Heaven, but the pain was of the earth. Then in the moment of my sorrow I found a happiness which, please God, shall light my life and make my lips speak praise until death ... To worship Him in nature, to admire the dim reflection of His love in those we meet, this crowds life with joy ... for He has given us Christ, who in our difficulties will help, in sorrow comfort, in loneliness befriend. To experience this we need only trust and obey — obey by following His example of service to men ... He has chosen us, and not we Him'.[7]

The question of liking her work and of its utility, she wrote, had now sunk into insignificance. Her letters became more cheerful —

'I almost think I am getting fond of my children', she wrote. 'They often wait about for me outside the door of my lodgings and when I come out, fall upon me with shrieks and howls and inarticulate sounds, resembling those of little pigs when they see the food coming. They beam up at me all the way to school, just as though they did not know I was going to bully them all day'.[8]

She visited the children in their homes and was horrified by the conditions in which many of them lived, and by the lack of opportunities for bright girls who were doomed to become washer-women.

Her health suffered and her doctor advised her to give up the work. Her widowed mother, perhaps subconsciously because she wanted her company, insisted that she resign. She did so sadly. 'I have not only been beaten in the battle', she wrote, 'I have been found sleeping at my post'.[9]

Between 1900 and 1914 Eglantyne was mostly based in Cambridge where her mother had moved. Here her uncle Sir Richard Jebb, Professor of Greek and Member of Parliament for the University, and his American wife Carrie brought her into the centre of the social circle of the University. It was at first a welcome change from the life of an elementary school teacher. She had never, she said, been so happy – 'You know the feeling when you have been cold and someone rubs you warm'. She rode with Lowes Dickinson. She organized 'reformed dinner parties with three courses and Truth Aims: a healthier social intercourse and social propaganda ... Think of Cambridge people attempting simplicity and sincerity! If I am not too frightened I shall laugh'.[10]

From her photographs it can be seen that she was very beautiful at this time; she received several proposals of marriage but was so unselfconscious that they came as a surprise. She herself fell in love with a man who however married another woman. In her distress she felt a need to lead a more useful life. She had wanted to follow part of the university course in Theology but found that 'Christianity is not much studied: they count up words and make minute researches in Greek and Hebrew'.[11] She read broadly, and hung in her room portraits of a somewhat surprising trio of her 'spiritual ancestors': Marcus Aurelius, Warren Hastings and William III. She collected money for the Queen Victoria Fund, and she tutored her young cousins by correspondence. She went to lectures on Political Economy, a subject which she described as 'dry as last week's bread'. When Mrs Alfred Marshall asked her why she did no philanthropic work she replied that she had always failed in what she attempted.[12] Nevertheless Mrs Marshall and Mrs J.N. Keynes drew her into the Charity Organization Society and she became Honorary Secretary of its Cambridge branch. She mournfully described its committee meetings – 'Case after case noted, stories of drunkenness, debt and disease: one goes on to the next tea party'.[13]

The work with the Charity Organization Society led her to write a book, *Cambridge — a Brief Study in Social Questions*. The experience in gathering and assessing material for this was to prove invaluable when she moved onto a wider stage.

Published in 1906, when she was thirty, the study is an unusual combination of factual analysis and expression of broad principles. It commences with statistics on rents, occupations, trades and unemployment, as well as on housing and water supply. It then becomes a tract in which the segregation of rich and poor is attacked — 'We think we love our neighbours, but are glad that all our neighbours happen to be as well off as ourselves'. In religion, the citizens are described as wishing to be secure, not holy: 'They exercise as much influence over the preacher as he does over them, so that the religion he gives them is divorced from ethics, and may form as great a barrier to social progress as admitted irreligion'.

The writer appeals to all citizens to undertake some form of social service: 'Everyone is born to work for others ... Anyone with head or hands can work with them for others. What is preeminently wanted is love'. Above all, 'Almost anything can be done with the young. Workers are needed in youth clubs — 'to catch the brave young wage earner of fourteen; to help him bye and bye to turn into a man, instead of degenerating into a criminal, a drunkard, a loafer'. Secular clubs can do much good but it is widely recognized by workers of experience that religion is their only safeguard when they are brought to face the worst difficulties and dangers.

Her book follows the official C.O.S. line in arguing that indiscriminate charity does more harm than good, and that private charity should aim at prevention and cure of distress, leaving the State to offer relief to those who cannot care for themselves. 'The more we cultivate love for our fellow man, the more it will compel us not to allow our momentary impulses to create disorder in their lives, but to bring to their service the same forthright zeal and self restraint which are necessary to the successful pursuit of our own interests'.

Some of her strongest criticism is directed at voluntary societies — 'The results they have to publish are often in exact inverse proportion to the good which has really been done ... The whole tone of social work is lowered by the necessity which philanthropic societies are often under of shouting the loudest before they can get a hearing. Bare faced and impudent begging, which would be resisted by imprisonment in the case of a tramp, is supposed to be justified by a good cause'.

The book is uneven, showing traces of various hands which have contributed to its drafting. Eglantyne's distinctive note however emerges. She adopts Aristotle's definition of a city as a place where the citizens live a common life for a noble end. Everyone has a contribution to make in helping his neighbour and the community, but needs to be shown how to do it; social welfare should become a science.[14] Later she was to express the same principles for the international community.

In 1908 Eglantyne resigned as Secretary of the C.O.S. on grounds of health. In her diary she wrote, 'Seclusion is to me a heaven on earth: the seclusion in which I can pray and meditate and delight myself in all the beauty of nature, literature and art. Yet He seems to command me to leave all this: to go forth and grapple with evil, even at such close quarters that beneath its shadow I lose consciousness of the light . . . In the rough and tumble of the struggle all my baser passions come out, and I am entrapped in the meshes of the wrong against which I fain would struggle'.[15] At times she almost wished for death, writing, 'Life, which is what I call a separation from God, seems intolerable'.[16]

She canvassed for her sister Dorothy's husband, Charles Roden Buxton, in Parliamentary elections. She wrote a novel for which she could not find a publisher. For long periods she accompanied her mother to health resorts in Switzerland, Italy and Austria. From one of them she wrote 'A hotel like this is for the rich rather what the workhouse is for the poor — the gathering point for the aimless and shiftless'. She liked to escape to go rock climbing. The apparently pointless travelling gave her a fluency in foreign languages which was shortly to be needed.

In February 1913 Eglantyne was sent to Macedonia by the Macedonian Relief Committee. Charles Roden Buxton and his brother Noel were ardent Gladstonians, inspired by the rights of small nations and by horror at the barbarity with which the Turks treated their Slav subjects. In 1903 they had formed the Macedonian Relief Fund. In the Balkan War of 1912 Serbia,

Greece, Bulgaria and Montenegro at last liberated Macedonia from Turkish rule. Eglantyne was asked to go out and allocate relief funds both among the victorious Serbs and the defeated enemy, particularly the Albanians, who had fought on the side of the Turks and had become refugees when they fled from the burning villages into Monastir. When Eglantyne passed through Belgrade, the British Ambassador entrusted her with a bale of goods for Turks. The British Consul in Skoplje also asked her to find out what truth there was in rumours of atrocities – such as that four or five thousand Catholic Albanians had been massacred in Prizren and 30 mayors tied together and shot.

It was a challenging assignment for someone who was a newcomer both to international relief work and to the Balkans, with their fierce and complicated history of racial, linguistic and religious conflict. The Serbian Army attached an officer to her who, however helpful, had to be shaken off before the Albanians would talk freely to her. The anti-Serbian prejudices of the British Consul had to be understood in light of the fact that the Serbs had won the war – 'The Englishman is ever and always on the side of the bottom dog', she wrote, 'in fact as soon as the dog gets to the bottom he forgets that it is after all the same old dog which he knew and disliked in the days of its prosperity'.[17]

She discharged her mission successfully, mostly in French. She reported that though there had been massacres of civilians, the numbers had been greatly exaggerated, and that although deplorable, they could be understood in light of the Serbs' fear of brigands.

Whilst the experience of aid diplomacy was to be important for her later, perhaps even more so was the personal contact with refugees. They had come into town with their possessions loaded on their small wooden carts, even the children having to walk for 50 miles. They had sheltered in the mosque and in outhouses of rich men. The oxen which had drawn their carts were commandeered by the military. One by one their cooking utensils, extra clothes and bedding were sold for food and they were reduced to begging. Many died from starvation, pneumonia or influenza. The British Consul implored her to obtain funds from England to keep the survivors alive until they could return to their villages. As she went back to England with memories of shacks so crowded that the refugees took it in turn to sleep, and of shivering children waiting for the bread and soup doled out through the Macedonian Relief Fund, she could not refuse, in spite of her hatred of public speaking, to address meetings up and down England and Scotland, quoting the Consul's words, '2d a day would keep a man alive and less a woman or child'.

When the need to raise money for Macedonia diminished, Eglantyne was employed by the Agricultural Organization Society, of which her sister Lill was secretary. As Editor of its journal, *The Plough*, Eglantyne brought to the work a concern, derived from her Cambridge survey, with the plight of smallholders and labourers who had to abandon the land. She fell in love with the Agricultural Cooperative Movement, which she saw as a gateway to human regeneration, and wrote much on the success of cooperatives which she had observed in Denmark and the Balkans. A colleague remembered her at this time as 'a personage, who in company dominated those present not by talk but by some spiritual force ... She was selfless without a grain of conceit but her work was beautifully done.'[18] Her frequent illness and depression were now diagnosed as due to thyroid deficiency and goitre. She was sent to recuperate in a small village in the Highlands of Scotland, where she acquired a great admiration for the women in the cottages round her. They would be capable of going anywhere and doing anything, she considered, if it were not for the loss of their teeth, because they could not afford dental treatment – a fact which Eglantyne regarded as a disgrace to the community. She underwent a successful operation and returned to *The Plough*. Shortly afterwards she joined her sister Dorothy Buxton in an enterprise which was to lead to the most important work of her life.

Dorothy and her husband joined the Independent Labour Party and the Society of Friends in 1917. Dorothy was particularly concerned at the effect of the British wartime propaganda machine, which depicted all Germans as united in a ruthless and savage desire for world conquest and as Huns, with no redeeming features, who had brought back the Dark Ages. She deplored the manufacture of atrocity stories. She persuaded the Prime Minister, Lloyd George, to arrange for a licence to be given to her to import from Scandinavia newspapers of neutral and enemy countries. Extracts from these were translated and published in the *Cambridge Magazine*. Military news was excluded, but items were included on the aims and causes of the war, peace discussions, reprisals, treatment of prisoners, atrocities and neutrality questions, as well as the idea of a League of Nations and the impact of the war on social conditions. Eglantyne took over responsibility for supervising translations from the French, Swiss and German newspapers. The extracts were read regularly by Smuts, who was a member of the Cabinet, by the former Foreign Secretary, Lord Lansdowne, and many other influential people. They showed that there was a movement in Germany in favour of a negotiated peace and even of the creation of a League of Nations.

But the *Cambridge Magazine*'s eight weekly pages had room for only a small part of the available information. Dorothy Buxton and Eglantyne were aware from their wider reading of the brutal details of the starvation and high mortality in Germany and Austria as a result of the Allied blockade. After the Armistice put an end to hostilities in November 1918, the blockade and the censorship continued. Dorothy and Eglantyne were shocked that peace had brought no relief, and with their friends formed a Fight the Famine Council under the chairmanship of Lord Parmoor; among its members were 13 Bishops, leading academics, economists and writers. Its objectives were to raise the blockade and to arrange for an international loan to be organized to restore Europe's war torn economy. Pamphlets were issued and speeches made up and down the country, but as Maynard Keynes noted, the fundamental problem of a Europe starving and disintegrating before their eyes was the one great question in which it was impossible to rouse the interest of the Big Four statesmen, Woodrow Wilson, Lloyd George, Clemenceau and Orlando, who were meeting in Versailles to settle the future of the world.

For the sisters exhortation was not enough: the Fight the Famine Council set up a Save the Children Fund of which Dorothy was the first Honorary Secretary; shortly afterwards Dorothy handed over the office to Eglantyne, when she herself reverted to the political work of the Council.

Eglantyne's debut was spectacular. In May 1919 she was prosecuted at the Mansion House for distributing a pamphlet with pictures of starving Austrian babies without previously submitting it to the Press Bureau for censorship. She was fined £5 but obtained a contribution to the campaign from the prosecutor. The publicity helped the success of a meeting which filled the Albert Hall a few days later, and at which Robert Smillie, President of the Miners Union, pledged £10,000 on its behalf to the Fund.

Early in 1919 Eglantyne appeared in the consulting room of a young London doctor, Hector Munro, who was trying to resume his practice after the war. Though it was highly inconvenient, 'When she spoke', he recalled, 'everything else seemed to lose its importance', and he found himself on his way to Vienna. His report on this mission described children dying in the streets, and women with spontaneous fractures of the hips whose bones had lost all solidity. Babies were thrown into the Danube or left in hospitals where they were ranged on shelves to die.

Deeply religious herself, Eglantyne on the basis of this report approached the Archbishop of Canterbury who declined however to make an appeal to the Church of England to help. So, snatching Dr Munro from his practice again, she went with him to see the Pope with whom she had a remarkable success. In 1919 Benedict XV was a sad figure, who had been bitterly reviled from all sides for his position during the war. Eglantyne sensed his intense loneliness 'and felt as if I wanted to make him comfortable'.[19] He kept her and Dr Munro for over two hours in a discussion in French. Seizing this opportunity for a constructive initiative, he declared that he would arrange for collections to be made in all Roman Catholic Churches. He followed this up with an Encyclical, which mentioned the Save the Children Fund by name, and insisted that help must go to all needy children and not to Roman Catholics alone. The Archbishop of Canterbury could now hardly do less, and on Holy Innocents Day in December 1919 collections were made throughout the Roman Catholic and Anglican world, as well as in the Orthodox and Free Churches.

At first the Save the Children Campaign was criticized by

those who argued that it was 'saving children who would grow up to fight against us', and recollected that the Prime Minister, Lloyd George, had after all declared that 'We must squeeze Germany till the pips squeak'. However, as the newspapers started to carry reports of the occupying British troops sharing their rations with German children, feeling changed. At the end of June 1919, a few days after the Peace Treaty with Germany was signed, not only was the blockade lifted but the Government declared that it would provide one pound for every pound raised and spent by charitable organizations for the relief of distress in Europe.

Initially the aid was concentrated in Vienna and in Germany. Eglantyne was quite pragmatic in deciding whether the Fund should operate directly or through existing agencies. In Vienna the greater part of the aid was channelled through the Friends (Quaker) War Victims Relief Committee and used for feeding young children and those in institutions. This was done with the help of Austrian doctors and volunteers, some of them schoolgirls. One of her inspirations was to start an 'adoption' scheme, still in practice, by which donors could support individual children. She was also far-sighted in using the aid to build up Austrian welfare institutions, which could take over its administration. In Germany, similarly, food was provided through the Friends and the Salvation Army in a programme which was described by the Minister of the Interior as not only 'bringing material help to thousands of children, but also helping to overcome the spiritual wounds of the war'.[20]

The Pope's initiative had internationalized the Save the Children movement. Societies were formed in European countries and collections held throughout the Empire. With great skill and diplomacy Eglantyne brought the national Societies together in January 1920 in a Conference under the patronage of the International Committee of the Red Cross. Out of this emerged the Save the Children International Union; Eglantyne was to spend as much time at its office in Geneva as in England. She seemed to travel incessantly. After the Fund's aid in an earthquake, the King of Bulgaria personally drove her round the affected area in a railway engine. A village in Albania was named Xheba after her.

Much of the success of the Save the Children Fund in London

was due to Eglantyne's skill and persuasiveness in finding the right collaborators. Lord Weardale, the Chairman, had been a member of the House of Commons and then of the Lords almost continuously for 35 years; and on the international scene he was well known as a former Chairman of the Inter Parliamentary Union. Supporting him were two men imbued with the high minded spirit of the Balliol College, Oxford, of Jowett's time. One of them, the Vice Chairman, Sir Percy Alden, had been Warden of Mansfield House University Settlement in London, and Editor of the Liberal evening paper, the Echo. The other, the Treasurer, Harold Watson, was a retired Indian Civil Servant. The salaried General Secretary, L.B. Golden, had been a business man and newspaper correspondent in Russia, had served in the Foreign Office, and then with a relief mission to the Baltic States.

Just as the situation in Austria and Germany began to improve, the SCF received a cable from Nansen, the League of Nations' High Commissioner for Refugees, asking it to send out its own workers to organize and supervise feeding schemes in Russia. After the Russian famine came the desperate plight of more than a million Greek refugees turned out of Asia Minor following the Greek defeat by the Turks at Smyrna. Then there was the settlement of the Armenian refugees in Syria where the SCF pioneered the building of model villages for them. There were commitments too which had somehow become on-going, such as aid to the work-schools in Budapest and to the only children's hospital in Yugoslavia.

Eglantyne had a flair for publicity. Despite the apprehensions of her colleagues, she paid £1000 for full page advertisements in the Daily Mail and Daily Mirror which turned out to bring in ten times their cost. Galsworthy was persuaded to contribute a poem beginning 'The statesmen debate. The children die.' George Bernard Shaw, to counter criticisms that the Fund was aiding the enemy, made a statement that 'I have no enemies under seven.' The Fund's appeals were not only to emotions but to self interest. 'Disease knows no frontiers' proved a powerful argument in light of the influenza epidemic of the winter of 1918 which killed thousands of those who had survived the war. Three hundred local committees were formed in Britain. The Fund sent a cameraman to Russia who came back with a film of the death carts and mass burials which moved audiences to tears in Churches, Trade Unions, Chambers of Commerce, and schools.

Eglantyne Jebb's guiding rule was to save as many children as possible, irrespective of all considerations of country or creed. And so, despite the irony of critics and fury of partisans, the Fund fed both the children of 'White' Russian refugees in France and of 'Red' Russians in the Volga Valley. It cared for Armenian orphans and the children of Turks who had taken part in the Armenian massacre. She was far ahead of her time in proclaiming that 'the world is now one village'.

The SCF responded to the criticism that it was interested in saving all the world's children except Britain's own; it campaigned for and supported the establishment of 'open air schools' where sick elementary children from industrial areas could recuperate. It set up a model school at Broadstairs to which Eglantyne urged that each member of the London office should come with the gift of a piece of equipment. In the long miners' strike of 1926 Eglantyne's belief in mutual aid was confirmed when the City Council of Vienna voted to make a substantial donation to provide food and clothing for the children of the British miners who had helped Vienna through the SCF in 1919.

When Eglantyne and Dorothy Buxton had launched the SCF they had seen it as an emergency operation, but even after the series of relief operations slackened, it became clear to Eglantyne that serious questions of a very long term character remained to be faced. First she came to recognize that 95% of the suffering and problems of children which the organization encountered were unnecessary. What was needed was universal agreement on the basic rights of children, accompanied by training, resulting from scientific research, in child welfare. Secondly, the work should be extended to what we now call the Third World where the condition of perhaps the majority of children was permanently as bad as that of those in Europe who had been the subject of emergency relief.

She was remarkably well placed to take the initiative in putting the work on a long term basis through her three capacities as Honorary Secretary of the SCF in Britain, as Vice President of the SCF International Union in Geneva, and as an assessor to the League of Nations Advisory Committee for the Protection of Children, for whose creation she had been largely responsible.

Her systematic mind saw the need for a document which would assert the principle that every child is born with the inalienable right to have the opportunity of full physical, mental and spiritual development. With other social workers in Britain and abroad she elaborated a 'Children's Charter' in 44 clauses. Such a lengthy document was unlikely to capture popular imagination, and one day in 1923 she climbed to the top of Mont Salève, which remains in the sun even when fog covers Geneva below. There she sat down and reduced the Charter to a statement of 5 clauses, each of one sentence. This became the Declaration of Geneva. By her charm and diplomacy, and aided by Charles Buxton who was a member of the British delegation sent to the League Assembly in 1924 by the Labour Government, she obtained its unanimous adoption by the Assembly on the proposal of its President.

The text, given below, was, for an international resolution, remarkably short and clear. Its balance reflected Eglantyne's philosophy that not only did the community have the duty to protect and ensure the development of the child, but that the child in return must be brought up to be aware of, and discharge, its duty to the community.

The Declaration of Geneva

By the present Declaration of the Rights of the Child, commonly known as the 'Declaration of Geneva', men and women of all nations, recognizing that mankind owes to the child the best that it has to give, declare and accept it as their duty, that beyond and above all considerations of race, nationality or creed:

I.   THE CHILD must be given the means requisite for its normal development, both materially and spiritually.
II. THE CHILD that is hungry must be fed; the child that is sick must be nursed; the child that is backward must be helped; the delinquent child must be reclaimed; and the orphan and the waif must be sheltered and succoured.

III. THE CHILD must be the first to receive relief in times of distress.
IV. THE CHILD must be put in a position to earn a livelihood, and must be protected against every form of exploitation.
V. THE CHILD must be brought up in the consciousness that its talents must be devoted to the service of its fellow men.[21]

The passing of the Declaration perhaps marked the high point of Eglantyne's career. She was invited to preach from Calvin's former pulpit in the Cathedral of Geneva. In her sermon she urged, 'In spite of all our sins and follies and bitter, bitter failures, across the wreckage of our broken world, still sounds the divine voice "Be ye perfect, as your Father in Heaven is perfect". May He then put it into our hearts to strive and strive and never cease from striving till we have clean swept away this appalling blot which disgraces our civilization, this iniquitous child suffering'.

She also organized an ecumenical thanksgiving service at St Martin in the Fields in London in honour of the Declaration as well as Summer Schools in Geneva to discuss its implications.

After the Declaration was adopted, it was ratified in many ceremonies, including its signature by each of the Prime Ministers of the British Empire during an Imperial Conference in London. Eglantyne now turned her attention from Europe to Asia and Africa. She was haunted by knowledge that children of 8 in Rhodesia, under an Act of 1926, were 'contracted' to work for the settlers; by the torture of those who collected rubber in the Congo; by the marriage of immature girls in India; by the misery of children of 6 or 7 who were forced by hunger to work 10 or 11 hours by day or night in China – 'worked with as little regard as if they were a spade or a saw, which is used until it is broken and then thrown aside'.[22] Her imagination soared as she saw the magnitude of the task and she would quote the saying of the Dean and Chapter of Seville, 'Let us build a church so great that those who come after us may think us mad to have attempted it'.[23]

She began to learn Chinese and started to ride again. Perhaps to set an example against luxuries which sometimes depended on exploitation, she took to wearing regularly a plain brown dress and a large wooden cross.

Eglantyne approached the problems of society from two standpoints, the religious and the economic-scientific.[1] From the first she liked to quote how Pestalozzi, turning his wild child beggars into a family, exclaimed, 'When I survey the real extent of my task, I see that no man on earth could have been more unequal to it than I. It is love that did it: love has a divine power which is real and does not fear the cross'.[24]

Yet the campaign, she said, must be scientific. It must have the same clear conception of its objects, and seek to encompass them with the same care and the same intelligence, as is to be found in the best commercial and industrial enterprises.[25] As her old Cambridge mentor, Mrs J.N. Keynes, noted, 'Enthusiasm with her was no cover for hasty or ill informed action'.[26] She repeatedly insisted that the systematic collection of data was the only possible basis for a scientific policy of child saving. She emphasized the need for adaptation of child welfare and educational policies to meet local conditions in Asia and Africa, and planned to establish demonstration centres there.

Herself a former teacher, she had progressive ideas on education, praising Austrian schools in which competition between children had no place and cooperation was fostered and encouraged. She deplored a bookish education which inspired no love of books and which turned out excessive numbers of boys and girls who wished to be clerks but were ill qualified for clerical life. Most severely of all, she attacked the custom by which upper class English girls when they left school were discouraged from having any serious interests for fear of diverting them from the entertainments in the course of which they were expected to meet prospective husbands.[27] In Africa she criticized school curricula which dwelt on Hengist and Horsa rather than helping the African to learn to understand and utilize his surroundings and to work in accordance with the genius of his own race.

Her colleagues noticed how amidst the challenges Eglantyne shed her former diffidence and hesitations and developed into an outstanding diplomat, sensing the line of least resistance, circumventing difficulties, shedding harmony around her and drawing together discordant elements, and all the while switching back and forth between three languages.[28] 'She lived,' said her cousin and disciple, another Eglantyne Jebb, 'transcendentally, but was saved for over intensity ... by her keen sense of the ridiculous and her readiness to laugh at herself.'[29] She was an idealist with a very large share of common sense. She believed that as Christians we are under an obligation to every single person we meet. This belief was reflected in the impression which she conveyed to each of her friends that their importance was unique. Sometimes she was proved too sanguine when the first impulsive reaction of people to her vitalizing influence petered out, but her sense of humour protected her in the disappointments.[30]

She counted on prayer as the most important of all her activities. Her Oxford contemporary Dorothy Kempe noticed how 'the old passion for physical freedom, the supersensitivity, had been transcended by a gracious power of loving, a spiritual freedom, a calm that were reflected in her face. There was a neatness and a love of order. There were no secrets. The reserved woman who had once been distracted between her longing for solitude and for service had reached a harmony by keeping her eyes on Him who shared with others everything that they were able to receive.'[31]

When she was at Cambridge she had written of the difficulty she found in life to hit on a modus vivendi with her ideals. Now she seemed to have achieved it. And since her disappointment at Cambridge there seems no indication that she ever considered marriage. 'How unfortunate, how very unfortunate,' she reflected, 'geniuses seem to be in matrimony.'[32]

For all her outward calm and cheerfulness, however, she was often depressed by the task of raising money to feed her children. She felt obliged to travel about frequently, and in the cheapest possible style, to collect money, 'as an example to friends who seemed to me to shirk this disagreeable part of the work ... But I am not a good speaker, and I dislike speaking and friends told me that I appealed for money so badly that it positively pained them. There were long journeys, painful for someone in poor health. And these efforts were useless. I did not collect any money to speak of, and no one, so far as I know, was in the least influenced by my example.'[33] She could never forget the messages she had received from Pope Benedict XV, 'Do not turn back. Work harder.' Her thyroid problem accentuated depression. In the early days of the SCF the miseries of the world's children so weighed upon her that when she crossed a bridge or the high landing of a staircase she heard a voice saying 'Throw yourself down.' Later the fear of not having enough money was with her day and night. When she was told that she would die, her first feeling was 'one of great thankfulness that I should not have to catch a train'; only then she recalled that raising money had become an obsession and that God could do without her.[34]

Her friends believed that anxiety for the financial future of the SCF caused her final collapse. As she lay dying in a clinic in Geneva, she murmured a verse from the 84th Psalm, 'Blessed is the man who going through the vale of misery uses it for a well: and the pools are filled with water.' Even the miserable sense of sin and weariness, she said to her sister, could be replaced by a joyful realization of the opposite qualities as revealed by God. Until then she had been tormented by her own shortcomings. Now she felt 'an assurance with joy and triumph that God has given me leave to speak the truth — a sense of a wonderful new power as if someone had made me the present of a Rolls Royce and chauffeur.'[35] In this new mood of confidence she told Dorothy, 'I can trust God with the future of the SCF. How very odd, how ridiculous it would be if I could not.'[36] The last few months when she knew she was dying appeared to be the happiest in her life.

Looking out from her bed towards Mont Salève where she had written the Children's Charter, she asked to be buried there. She was given a temporary grave while money was collected for a tomb on the mountain; but then came another crisis for the SCF and it was spent on relief in Ethiopia. This, is no doubt what she would have wished.

How widely Eglantyne Jebb was recognized to be a saint could be seen from tributes paid at the time of her death. There was a delightful irony in the fact that it was Viscount Cecil, who had been Minister of Blockade when Eglantyne had been prosecuted at the Mansion House, who contributed the foreword to her posthumous book, *Save the Child*, in which he wrote,

'Eglantyne Jebb belonged to that small company of men and women who may rightly be called saints'.[37] Former colleagues and friends saw various aspects. To Kathleen Freeman she was a saint whose dedicated spirit took possession of all her gifts and talents, turning them with joy and courage to the carrying out of God's purpose.[38] Others compared her with St Catherine of Siena, with St Teresa and with Elizabeth Fry. L.H. Green saw in her character an integration which has distinguished many women saints.[39] Alice Salomon pointed out how creative women who have brought about great reforms have seldom been sentimental but have had a will of iron; Eglantyne Jebb, she considered, had an almost fanatical faith which had cast a spell over her collaborators.[40]

Eglantyne would never have seen herself as a saint, though she did see herself as an instrument of God's purpose; for she was aware, almost too aware perhaps, of her shortcomings. If she would have been embarrassed to have been called a saint, perhaps of all the tributes paid she would have appreciated none more than that of W.A. Mackenzie, the Roman Catholic whom she had charmed the Pope into plucking out of a religious publishing house to become Treasurer of the SCF. 'With all her dominant seriousness, there was no solemnity, not a shred, but always a constant frankness, a gay simplicity, a happy timidity'.[41]

Throughout the years when she worked for the SCF, Eglantyne wrote poems, because, according to her sister Dorothy, she could not help doing so: 'Her inner experiences left her no peace until they had found peace in rhythmic words'. Dorothy had some qualms at rescuing many of them from the wastepaper basket, recognizing that 'She had not, I imagine, quite all the qualifications of a poet in the full sense of the word'. One volume, *The Real Enemy*, was published in the last year of Eglantyne's life. It is infused with indignation and bitterness at the sufferings imposed on children by industrialism and war. It is full of disgust at the standards of society's parasites who profit from, or wilfully ignore, that suffering, and it contains her often quoted poem 'The Amoeba', a savage attack on the values of 'a Christian gentleman'.[42]

Dorothy decided to publish the second volume, *Post Tenebras Lux*, posthumously because she thought that the poems might help others. She explained how Eglantyne had passed through a time when horror of death, not for herself but for others, became almost an obsession. After a period of intense suffering individual confidence was rebuilt. 'Long before death came to break the last fragile bond, one felt ... that her spirit had already found a very large measure of release'.[43]

And indeed in her poem 'The Strength of God' in this second volume, there is a note of resignation quite absent from the first:

'What if my strength ebbs lower day by day,
Yet Thou art strong. I will commit to Thee
The answer of my heart to suffering's call.
All that I could not do and could not be,
The prayers I strove to pray and could not pray,
The help I fain had brought, my vain essay,
Failure and fear and doubt − Thou knowest all.'[44]

In her long final illness she left 'A last message':

'If I be dead, yet still I am not there,
    For what you love is not my mortal frame;
I would not be confused with a corpse,
    O! Let not, then, a corpse assume my name!

Call it not me, for I am fire and life,
    And deeds and words, not what your touch discerns,
Call it not me, for it was never me
    And is not me when it to dust returns.

If you must think me dead, yet dare not think
    That you can place me 'neath the heavy sod,
Yet rather turn from thoughts of death, commend
    My living spirit to the living God.'[45]

Eglantyne was only 52 when she died. Had her life enjoyed a normal span she would have seen almost all that she had worked for internationally destroyed. The critics were shown to be right. The German and Austrian children she saved did grow up to fight against Britain and bomb its cities. Her optimistic belief that her campaigns would bring about an international solidarity was proved futile by Hitler and

Mussolini. And yet, if she had survived the Second World War she would then have seen, in the work of UNRRA and UNICEF and the recognition of the international community's responsibility towards the Third World, a renewal of the expression of her ideals on a grander scale than even she could ever have anticipated.

Further Reading

Books by Eglantyne Jebb: *Cambridge – A Social Study*, Cambridge 1906; *The Real Enemy* (poems), London, 1928; *Post Tenebras Lux* (poems), London, 1929; *Save the Child, a Posthumous Essay*, London, 1929.

The only substantial biography is *Rebel Daughter of a Country House* by Francesca Wilson, London, 1967. This says little about the period of Eglantyne Jebb's work for the SCF. On the latter the most useful books are *The White Flame – the Story of the Save the Children Fund* by Dorothy Buxton and Edward Fuller, London, 1931; *The Right of the Child* by Edward Fuller, London, 1951; and *If Any Man Build* – the History of the Save the Children Fund, London, 1965. A typescript of Eglantyne Jebb's letters to Dorothy Kempe, and the latter's interspersed comments on them, are in the SCF Library in London. There are various other accounts and impressions of her in the papers which are kept in her childhood home in Ellesmere.

Notes

1. *S.C.F. Pictorial News*, Spring 1930.
2. Francesca M. Wilson, *Rebel Daughter of a Country House*, London, 1967, p. 54.
3. 'Recollections of Eglantyne Jebb' by Ruth Wordsworth, p. 12, Eglantyne Jebb Papers, Ellesmere, Box 3/7.
4. Wilson, *op. cit.*, p. 80.
5. Eglantyne Jebb M.S. Letters, S.C.F. Library, London, p. 71.
6. Wilson, *op. cit.*, p. 84.
7. Wilson, *op. cit.*, pp. 88–9.
8. Letters, *op. cit.*, p. 44.
9. Wilson, *op. cit.*, p. 91.
10. *Ibid.*, p. 101.
11. Letters, p. 145.
12. *Ibid.*, p. 240.
13. *Ibid.*, p. 233.

14. Eglantyne Jebb, *Cambridge, a Social Study,* Cambridge, 1906.
15. Wilson, *op. cit.*, p. 110.
16. *Ibid.*, p. 111.
17. Wilson, *op. cit.*, p. 132.
18. Wilson, *op. cit.*, p. 150.
19. *World's Children*, April 1929, p. 108.
20. Dorothy F. Buxton and Edward Fuller, *The White Flame*, London, 1931, p. 42.
21. *White Flame, op. cit.*, p. XI.
22. Eglantyne Jebb, *The Real Enemy*, 1928, p. 20.
23. Edward Fuller, *The Right of the Child*, London, 1951, p. 35.
24. Eglantyne Jebb, *Save the Child*, London, 1929, p. 2.
25. Fuller, *Right of the Child, op. cit.*, p. 11.
26. *White Flame, op. cit.*, p. 15.
27. E. Jebb, *Save the Child, op. cit.*, pp. 48, 58.
28. Mrs C. de Bunsen, *World's Children*, Feb. 1929, p. 75.
29. Kathleen Freeman, *If Any Man Build*, London, 1965, p. 22.
30. Eglantyne Jebb Papers, Ellesmere, Box 3/1.
31. *Letters*, p. 8.
32. *Letters, op. cit.*, p. 45.
33. *White Flame, op. cit.*, p. 15.
34. E. Jebb Papers, Box 3/1.
35. Dorothy Buxton in *World's Children*, Feb. 1929, p. 75.
36. Wilson, *op. cit.*, p. 214.
37. E. Jebb, *Save the Child*, London, 1929, p. V.
38. Freeman, *op. cit.*, p. 146.
39. Edward Fuller, *The Right of the Child*, London, 1951, p. 11.
40. Alice Salomon, *Eglantyne Jebb*, Geneva, 1936.
41. Wilson, *op. cit.*, p. 217.
42. Eglantyne Jebb, *The Real Enemy*, London, 1928.
43. Eglantyne Jebb, *Post Tenebras Lux*, London, 1929, p. 8.
44. *Ibid.*, p. 16.
45. Eglantyne Jebb, *Post Tenebras Lux, op. cit.*, p. 16.

4

Caroline Chisholm, the
Immigrants' Friend (1808 – 77)

*'The fifth part of the world, Australia, has up to now
but one saint, one legend ... The richest and most
powerful government in the world ... failed in colonization ... where a simple woman succeeded by her
force of character and her vigour of soul'*
Jules Michelet, *La Femme*, 1862 (Translation)

In the Alternative Service Book of 1980 five Roman Catholic
saints who lived since the Reformation are commemorated.
All are Continental Europeans who were professed religious
and only one of them, St Teresa of Avila, is a woman. There
may be room therefore for one more Roman Catholic who was
a British wife and mother and whose unique work, inspired by
her religion, was undertaken in happy cooperation with, and
for the benefit of, people of all denominations in a place and
time of considerable religious intolerance.

In Australia Caroline Chisholm, though neglected for years
after her death, is now firmly established as a national heroine;
her portrait has appeared on a bank note and on a postage
stamp, and a Parliamentary constituency bears her name. In
Britain, where she spent as much of her life and where for
a few years in the 1840s and 50s she was perhaps the most
famous woman in the country except for the Queen, she is
seldom remembered; for when she returned to Australia in
1854, the Crimean War produced a new British heroine,
Florence Nightingale, who followed her example, exploited
her tactics and gained a more lasting reputation. At the end
of that war, Mrs Chisholm was far away, back in Australia;
Australian emigration was no longer topical. Perhaps more
significantly, a Roman Catholic heroine could be an embarrassment at a time when the activities of the Roman Catholic

92

Church in England were a subject of mistrust among the ruling class and were fiercely attacked in the press.

Caroline Jones was born in 1808 in Wootton, near Northampton, the youngest of a large family, and was baptized in the Church of England. Her father was a prosperous yeoman farmer who died when she was six; she was brought up by a pious evangelical mother to interest herself in the elderiy poor and visit them with baskets of food. She recollected that when she was a child she listened to an old soldier talking about his travels, and was thus inspired to make her dolls play at colonization, travelling out over a basin in boats made of bean bags, and sending back wheat in the returning ships. She was educated, together with her sisters and cousins, by a governess. Bored by the callow youths whom she met at country balls, she was attracted by a more serious and older man, Archibald Chisholm. He was an officer in the East India Company's army who came from a Roman Catholic clan in the Scottish Highlands, many of whose members were being ruthlessly evicted by landlords in their determination to replace the crofters by more profitable sheep pastures. When he asked her to marry him he was thirty four and she was twenty one. She accepted him on the condition that he would leave her free to undertake philanthropic work. He was to honour this condition nobly. In return Caroline took her husband's religion.

They married in 1830 and went out to Madras in the following year. They had no children for six years and Caroline was thus free to devote much of her time to setting up and running what she called an Industrial School for British soldiers' young daughters who were leading a demoralized life in the barracks. It was run on quite original lines. The girls indeed learnt reading, writing and arithmetic and received religious instruction; but they were also however taught to keep accounts and were formed into committees, one of which took charge of the stores, whilst another looked after small children who were brought in for care; a third studied the symptoms and treatment of those who were sick. The girls who were thus trained were much in demand as wives and servants.

In 1836 the Chisholms' first child, a son, was born; he was followed a year later by another son. In 1838, instead of taking leave in Britain, the family decided to spend it in the milder climate of New South Wales, and handed over the school to the Madras Government. At the time when they arrived in Sydney transportation of convicts from Britain was about to end, and most of those already in Australia were emancipated or on ticket of leave. Immigration of free colonists was now being financed from the sale of lands. Bounties were paid by the Government to agents who brought immigrants on to the ships. Once the immigrants arrived in Sydney they were turned loose with no shelter or help in obtaining employment.

It was Archibald Chisholm who first became aware of the distress of the newly arrived immigrants. He met a group of fellow Highlanders who only spoke Gaelic and could find no work. He lent them money to buy tools and set them up as wood choppers. After talking with them he shared with Caroline his impression that the situation of single women was far worse even than that of the men whom he had helped. Under the convict system about ten times as many males as females had been brought to New South Wales. To redress the balance large numbers of young women were being shipped out. They were often abused by the ships' officers. On arrival impostors would board the ships, pretending to employ 'servants,' but in fact taking the women to brothels. Ironically, although through the efforts of Elizabeth Fry a reception barrack had been provided for female convicts, this no longer existed. The free women immigrants thus had nowhere to sleep and many became prostitutes.

The needs of these women and girls provided Caroline's first cause in Australia. She would meet them coming off the boat, would shelter as many as nine in her house, and find posts for them with ladies in Sydney. She frankly told their prospective mistresses however that the previous system by which convicts were assigned to them as domestic helpers had spoilt them a little, and that they must get used to losing a little power and learn to bear and forbear with these free servants.[1]

She wrote several letters to the Governor, Sir George Gipps, to suggest that a home be provided for the girls who came off the ships; when at last through his wife she obtained an interview, he recorded his surprise. He 'expected', he said, 'to have seen an old lady in white cap and spectacles, who would have talked to me about my soul. I was amazed when

an aide introduced a handsome, stately young woman who proceeded to reason the question as if she thought her reason and
experience, too, worth as much as mine'.[2]

She failed however to persuade him to do anything, and
struggled with her conscience as to whether it was her duty
and within her capacity to take action herself. It would be a
hard and unpleasant task, and both as a woman and a stranger
to the colony she felt diffident. The work would take her from
her family and involve expenses which she could barely afford.
She would have to reclaim prostitutes and argue with pimps
and procuresses, and when she sought help there would be a
prejudice against her in influential circles because she was a
Roman Catholic.

Yet when she tried to persuade herself that this was not her
responsibility, 'the delay pressed on my mind like a sin. I was
impressed with the idea that God had in a peculiar manner
fitted me for this work. During the season of Lent I suffered
much ... but on Easter Sunday I was enabled at the altar of
Our Lord to make an offering of my talents to the God who
gave them. I promised to know neither country nor creed, but
to serve all justly and impartially. I only asked to be enabled
to keep these poor girls from being tempted by their need to
mortal sin, and resolved that to accomplish this, I would in
every way sacrifice my feelings. I felt my offering was accepted
and that God's blessing was on my work. But it was His will to
permit many serious difficulties to be thrown in my way and
conduct me through a rugged path of deep humiliation'.[3]

If any doubts remained after this religious experience, they
were dispelled when, walking by the sea, she encountered a
beautiful Highland girl called Flora, seeking to drown herself. Caroline argued with her, found her lodgings and heard
her promise not to kill herself. 'My spirits returned; I felt
God's blessing was on my work. From this time, I never
thought of human help ... From the hour I was on the beach
with Flora, fear left me'.[4]

She now obtained the help of the press in exposing the
wretched condition of the female immigrants. Through Lady
Gipps the Governor was reluctantly persuaded to make the
abandoned convicts' barracks available as a temporary home,
provided that the Government incurred no expense. Mrs

Chisholm slept there herself, feeding the rats who ran all over her bed on bread smeared with arsenic. She began to gather in girls not only as they arrived but also from the streets.

At night she would pass through the dormitories and if she found a girl sleepless and in tears would take her to her room and share her troubles. She set up a free Registry Office in the building, where she drew up contracts in triplicate between employers and the women which stated and registered the latters' rights. She persuaded the leading ladies of the colony to form a Committee of Management and to raise funds. The barracks were too unhealthy for her to keep her three children there, and they were boarded with friends.

Though some jobs for the women were found in Sydney, the greatest demand for unskilled labour was in the country. Caroline sent out circulars to clergymen, police magistrates and other responsible people to obtain information on local employment needs and wages. The Governor agreed to frank her letters.

The Anglican Bishop was at first highly suspicious having, he said, 'an instinctive dread of every undertaking in which the influence and policy of Rome can find scope to act', but he found her 'a ladylike person and very prepossessing and interesting from the earnestness with which she has taken up a good cause'. He authorized his clergy to collaborate with her.[5] It was a disappointment on the other hand that influential members of her own Church refused their support because her project aimed to help women of all denominations.

When the needs of the various districts had been ascertained, arrangements were made to transport the women free of charge in the drays which were returning empty to the farms after they had unloaded their produce in the city. But the women, terrified of bushrangers, blacks and bunyips, refused to travel without her. So she went along with them from farm to farm, placing them in employment with, an observer noted, 'an earnest admonition to the heads of every family to be careful of those whom she said she regarded as her children, and with an earnest injunction to the young immigrants to let her know how they got on, and if they had any complaint to communicate it to her.'[6]

After her first journey she set up depots in several country towns in the charge of clergymen and respectable citizens who would receive the women and interview prospective employers. Warmly supported by the press, she received gifts of food and shelter for her caravan along the way, as well as loans of carriages to carry the sick. Now those journeys took place, often lasting several weeks at a time, for which she became famous. Caroline would ride at the head of her company on her white horse, Captain, sometimes breaking away in a gallop when they neared a farm which might provide accommodation, and would jolly along her bewildered urban girls when occasionally they had to camp in the bush. Occasionally a desperate bushman would leap onto the road and seize her horse's bridle, imploring her to find him a wife. Unperturbed, she would refuse to act as a matrimonial agent, though she would carefully place her girls in family farms where there were bachelors nearby.

On one occasion indeed she admitted to doing rather more. She received a letter from an emancipated convict, well established with 50 acres, 10 head of cattle and several hundred sheep. His wife had died and he asked for a servant who would look after his child. 'I wouldn't mean, on any account in the world', he declared, 'to be bound to marry, but I don't wish it altogether to be left out'. Mrs Chisholm made enquiries and found that when he had gained his freedom he had sent money to his parents in England and that he had nursed his wife devotedly in her last illness. She was touched. 'Who', she asks, 'would not get up early to serve such a man! I did, for I knew that early in the morning is the best time to find a wife. I went first to the governess room – all asleep; I unlocked the Home door. Some dressed, some half dressed, some, too, very cross: I have often remarked that early in the day is the best time to judge a woman's temper. I went through the Home and tents and found a girl at the wash tub at work with spirit, very neat and tidy'.[7] She asked the matron to keep an eye on the girl, was satisfied with her report, and sent her up to the widower in the care of a married couple related to her who had also been engaged by him. A successful marriage came about.

Pretty girls, whatever their qualifications or characters, were difficult to dispose of, for farmers' wives seeking servants were nervous of the roving eyes of their husbands and sons. 'O, it is a comfort to have something a little repulsive' exclaimed one lady as she gratefully accepted the plainest of Mrs Chisholm's charges.[8]

In the Home and on the journeys many of the girls told Caroline how brutally they had been treated on the voyage. Convinced that such treatment could only be stopped by bringing a prosecution, she collected facts with her usual thoroughness and told the Governor, who was alarmed at her temerity: 'I am ready to prosecute: I have the necessary evidence and if it be a risk whether I or these men go to prison, I am ready to go to prison'.[9] A case was brought against the Captain and surgeon of an immigrant ship who had behaved with outstanding savagery; both were convicted, fined and jailed. The sentences and the publicity which they received in Britain and Australia did much to stop the abuse of women immigrants at sea.

At the end of her first year's work Mrs Chisholm published a pamphlet written 'with the hope of attracting attention to some of the evils attending the present system of allowing female immigrants to make engagements on board' and 'of inducing H.E. the Govenor to promise that young women sent to the colony shall be received and protected until suitable situations are offered to them'. She attacked the bounty system and the dishonesty of its agents and revealed the disgraceful conditions on the immigrant ships. But she also gave a vivid, and often amusing, account of her own experiences in pursuing seducers, rescuing recent immigrants, and finding them employment. The publication was tactfully dedicated to 'the clergy of Australia'. It also appealed to the hard headed. 'The expense of tending 10 bad women (who every year get worse)', she argued, would more than pay for the protection of 400.[10]

Although Caroline Chisholm's first task in Australia was undertaken on behalf of single women, she saw this within the broader context of the founding of families, for throughout her life the welfare of the family as a unit was her main concern. Many employers were reluctant to engage men with children because they would need more rations than would bachelors. Mrs Chisholm again set off on expeditions inland, this time with unemployed men and their families, visiting farmers and persuading them that in the long run employing sober family men was a sensible investment. Once more she rode at the head of a caravan, fording rivers with a child on each side of her saddle. She was remarkably successful, but this was not enough. She knew that what most immigrant families eventually wanted was their own homes and land. She proposed a plan to the Government by which groups of families would be settled up country. An area of uncultivated land would first be cleared communally. Then it would be divided between families. In addition to cultivating their own land, some men would provide specialized skills to their neighbours, for which they would be repaid in labour. A schoolmaster would receive land rent free and would be paid by each family, either in labour or in produce, for the education of their children. The cost and ownership of expensive machinery, bullocks and carts would be shared. When the Legislative Council refused to finance such a scheme, Mrs Chisholm obtained a gift of land from a supporter and supervised the settlement of 23 families along these lines as a pilot project, doing the surveying herself.

As she talked with her people on the road, Caroline came to hear much about the untruthful descriptions of New South Wales given by the bounty agents who had recruited them in England, and how little they had known of the conditions into which they were coming. On the other hand, the English press was full of alarming statements at this time about the effect of a temporary depression in New South Wales, and these discouraged the kind of prospective immigrants who were most wanted. She asked the Government therefore for £300 to pay for her to conduct a survey which would collect and record the experiences of some 3,000 recent settlers and which could be published in England. When the Legislative Council failed by one vote to appropriate funds for this, she undertook the survey herself. Her husband, who had returned to his regiment in 1840, had now come back to Australia after retiring on pension. Together they prepared a questionnaire and travelled to farms and stations, taking down statements in homes, by the roadside or sometimes in a field, using the plough as a table. Mrs Chisholm was so well known to the settlers and they were so anxious to send news through her to their friends at home that they invariably related their circumstances with the greatest readiness and cheerfulness. Although without government backing it was not possible to reach as many settlers as she had hoped, the brief biographies of some 600–700 families, before and after reaching the colony, were recorded in their own words.

It was Caroline's intention to use the information which she gathered in support of proposals for a new immigration policy which she would publish and put before the Home Government. In 1846 she sailed for England with her husband and three children. Another child was born on the voyage.

Her achievements during her seven years in New South Wales had been remarkable. Her name, it was said, had become a talisman.[11] With no official authority she had settled 11,000 people and reunited 600 families. She had greatly raised the status of immigrant women and brought about hundreds of happy marriages. She had caused higher standards to be expected among doctors and captains of immigrant ships, though she was to effect further improvements when she reached England. She had come to be regarded as an institution in Sydney and had been the only woman to be invited to give evidence before Government Committees on Immigration and on Unemployment. Her influence with the colony's leaders and the press, carefully and sparsely used, was usually highly effective in exposing scandals and in raising money for causes. Thus she had, for example, shamed the citizens of Sydney into subscribing for the purchase of a hearse so that the dead no longer travelled to their resting place in a cart shared with the carcases of dogs. In all this she had been able to overcome prejudice against the intervention of women in public affairs and, by her evident fairness and lack of sectarian bias, to make a nonsense of allegations that she discriminated in favour of Roman Catholics and Irish and was a tool of the Papacy. It had been, she reflected, a 'God-like occupation' to find employment for the immigrants and help them to found families. When she left, Robert Lowe told the New South Wales Legislature that she was 'the only person in the colony who had done anything effective to mitigate a crying evil and national sin and to fix families on our lands in place of bachelors'.[12] Even the Governor apologized publicly for having at first poured cold water on her schemes and, when he returned to England, gave her valuable support.

On her return to England Caroline had several aims.

Firstly she hoped to arrange for publication of what she called her 'Voluntary Information', obtained from her interviews with settlers, which would provide the factual ammunition for the skirmishes with the British government which she foresaw.

Secondly she wished to arrange for the wives and children of emancipated convicts and immigrants to join them in Australia, and she brought with her hundreds of letters and notes to enable them to be traced.

Thirdly she wanted to form a connecting link between employers in Australia and prospective immigrants in Britain.

Her fourth and most ambitious objective was to bring about an overall plan for the colonization of Australia.

Caroline's organization of her campaign, with only her husband's pension to finance it, was masterly. The Chisholms first rented a house in a humble area near the London docks where working class people for whom they had messages from relatives in Australia, as well as those who sought information, were not embarrassed to visit them. Here, whilst still needed at home by the new baby, she both gave out and gathered information. Then the Chisholms moved closer to Whitehall; Mrs Chisholm's mother came to stay with them and look after the children. Caroline now made continuous visits to the Colonial Office, Home Office, and Land and Emigration Commissioners, armed with the statistics and other information which she had collected in England and Australia. A contemporary observed, 'It is one of the characteristics of Caroline Chisholm that she never makes a claim or charge – whether it be against a government department or a commercial system, which she is not prepared to establish with the strongest judicial proof. Met by Emigrant Commissioners in the case of deserted children first with delay and then with evasion, for a whole winter, while snow lay ankle deep in the streets, she passed with her neatly tied evidence between her lodgings in King Street, Covent Garden, and Downing Street, Park Street and Whitehall. They began, as is the custom with officials, by denying the facts; but as each doubt was hinted, a bundle of papers was produced, untied, and such particulars as the following were detailed – John Brown and Mary, his wife, sailed from Liverpool May the – 1836. Ship name – , Emigrant Agent – . The third time was enough. "That will do", said the bland Commissioner, and the order was given that transferred two shiploads of children from workhouses to their parents.'[13]

By her persistence, patience and charm she eventually persuaded ministers and officials to make reluctant breaches in the principles of laissez-faire. Funds were made available for wives and children to be reunited with husbands and fathers who had been sent out as convicts. Assisted emigration, which had been suspended because the sales of land which financed it had diminished owing to the high price set, was resumed on a restricted scale; unmarried women went out in the first batch. Regulations which excluded both men over 40 and large families came to be tacitly ignored.

Then she proceeded to broaden the campaign and in open letters to Cabinet Ministers raised the question of a national colonization policy. In a letter to Earl Grey, the Colonial Secretary, written at the height of the Irish famine, she asked, 'Is it not a lamentable thought that deaths should daily result from starvation among British subjects, while in this valuable colony good wheat is rotting on the ground for want of hands to gather it in? That tens of thousands of fine sheep, ... thousand upon thousand of fat cattle were slaughtered and boiled down as tallow whilst the vast refuse was cast into the fields to be devoured by pigs and dogs, and yet no effort is made by England to provide for her struggling people by a humane system of colonization?'[14]

She dwelt on the commercial advantages for Britain of emigration to Australia, pointing out that whilst of 100 settlers sent to Canada, 65 moved on to the U.S.A., of those who went to Australia 99% remained in the Empire; also that whereas each emigrant to Canada spent between £1 and £5 on British manufactures, in Australia the figure was between £7 and £10.

With a lack of squeamishness unusual in contemporary public debate, particularly on the part of a woman, she described how the sex imbalance in Australia was resulting in prostitution, homosexuality and the extinction of the aborigines whose women were stolen. She argued that priority should therefore be given to systematic arrangements for the reception and employment of single women, for in the long run, she declared, wives and children were 'God's police'.

She bluntly stated that the Commissioners in London were the agents of the squatters who owned the great sheep runs and were therefore opposed to the immigration of smallholders and their families; and she attacked the system of high land prices which worked in favour of the large landlords.

As an appendix to her letter to Earl Grey, she included eighteen of the voluntary statements of successful settlers; she never was able to afford to publish them in full. These sample personal histories, which were also reprinted separately for a wider public, all carried the conviction that Australia was, as one woman put it, 'a good country to live in, with meat, bread, milk, eggs, butter and cheese in plenty, with not too much toil'. George B., who had a farm, a dray and a team of bullocks, in his statement asked Mrs Chisholm to urge his brothers to come and join him. Ellen W. similarly wanted her sisters to come out, 'O what a difference there is between this country and home for poor folks' she declared. 'Old England is a fine place for the rich but Lord help the poor'. A ticket of leave man asked for his wife to be brought out. A mother interviewed had been obliged to leave one child at home and had sent money back to bring her to join the family in Australia; but the money had been stolen and there was no news of the child.[15]

As the only woman witness, Mrs Chisholm gave evidence both to a Committee of the House of Lords on the Execution of the Common Law and to another on Colonization from Ireland. To these Committees she outlined a new approach to emigration. Under the existing policy emigrants had been given free passages but were left to sink or swim on arrival. Her philosophy on the other hand was that immigrants should pay for their own passages, thus insuring that provident men and women would be selected, but that they should then be helped to obtain land and employment on arrival. To bring this about she proposed a Land Ticket Scheme; under this, intending immigrants would purchase interest-bearing tickets which could be cashed as payment for their passage and for land on arrival. However her scheme was blocked by the interests of wealthy landowners who were opposed to closer settlement.[16]

She repeatedly encountered prejudice against Irish immigrants, but when asked by the House of Lords Committee whether she found them turbulent and insubordinate replied, 'Not at all. I found I could manage the Irish best. I found them exceedingly good tempered. It latterly became a point with me first to explain to two or three sensible Irish the line that I intended to take. I endeavoured to give them hope; and having succeeded in that, I used to let them loose amongst the others ... If I had taken the Scotch or English first, I should have had more difficulty'.[17]

Though she was politely received and successful with particular schemes, she failed to persuade the Government to embark upon what she called a national system of immigration; she decided therefore that a private society needed to be set up for the purpose. In 1849 the Family Colonization Loan Society was formed. The eminent philanthropist Lord Shaftesbury (then Lord Ashley) was Chairman. Among its members were Sidney Herbert, who as a Cabinet Minister was later to launch Florence Nightingale on her career, and several other Members of Parliament. Branch committees were formed in Britain and Australia. Funds were raised by voluntary subscription to enable people wishing to emigrate to form themselves into groups of not less than three, and not more than twenty, families. These were expected to raise half the cost of the voyage, the remainder being advanced by the Society. On arrival the immigrants would be found employment by the Society's agents and would repay the loans. The money recovered would be used to finance further groups.

Through her influence with Angela (later Baroness) Burdett Coutts, Caroline arranged that small sums could be remitted from Australia to England through Coutts Bank; Australian banks at that time were charging £15 to remit £50. The immigrants as they made good could thus arrange for relatives to join them.

Every week the Chisholms held a group meeting for people who had enquired about emigration. They included mechanics, governesses, servant girls, dock labourers and unsuccessful doctors and lawyers. A letter to the *Morning Chronicle* described one of these meetings –

'At seven p.m. a number of respectable men in their Sunday best, with their wives and children, assembled in two small rooms on the ground floor. On the table were laid original letters from emigrants to their relatives at home, as well as colonial newspapers, for the perusal of all parties; and several heads of families, who were present, pulled out of their pockets, with gratification and honest pride that was delightful to observe, letters from their children in the colonies and which were read by a gentleman present, all speaking of their well doing. The females were first assembled in the back room where Mrs Chisholm and an Australian lady, a resident of 24 years, gave them information and explained to them the sort of outfit etc.'

A list of the names and addresses of those present was circulated so that they could become further acquainted. 'On one occasion', the writer continued, 'I observed a respectable father consign to another family his daughter ... saying to the mother, "I place her with confidence under your care upon Mrs Chisholm's recommendation". Most of the families had been for the last twenty months economizing their means so as to entitle them to a loan; and they expect to leave in the same ship'.[18]

The room was furnished with a model of the sleeping berths on the Society's ships, with the utensils recommended, such as spoons, pint pots, strong cheap mugs, a filter and a medicine chest.

Caroline Chisholm's enthusiasm for the forming of groups was partly due to her belief that the system raised moral standards, so that the group would exercise pressure on its members to repay loans but, more important, she considered it degrading for girls to be dumped as a body in Australia to marry the first men they met. As members of a family group they could exercise a choice, and marry with dignity.

The letter in the *Morning Chronicle* was no doubt part of Mrs Chisholm's publicity campaign, which was as successful in England as it had been in Australia. Robert Lowe, previously her friend in Sydney, was now a powerful supporter as a leader writer for the London *Times*. But above all it was Charles Dickens who made Mrs Chisholm and the Society famous. Dickens had become interested in emigration whilst travelling in America and writing *Martin Chuzzlewit*. He was now writing *David Copperfield*, at the end of which not only the steady Peggottys but the improvident Mr Micawber were to emigrate to Australia, where the latter surprisingly made good and became a magistrate. Dickens visited Mrs Chisholm at the suggestion of Mrs Sidney Herbert. He came away with a bundle of immigrants' letters and brief histories. Many of these he published in his paper *Household Words* which had a huge readership and influence among the middle and working classes. They were accompanied by articles warmly praising Mrs Chisholm and the Society because they relieved starvation and diminished crime through combining charity with the industrious and frugal efforts of the working classes themselves.

Mrs Chisholm made effective use of the members of her Committee in obtaining an Act of Parliament which obliged immigrant ships to provide adequate space and sanitary facilities for all passengers and to allow them access to the deck. This proved one of her most dramatic achievements, for the results could immediately be seen in the reduced mortality rates. The Society contracted for ships to be built to carry their immigrants which were considerably more spacious than was required under the new law, having only one class and with cabins for all passengers. The public were invited to inspect them and the finest was named *Caroline Chisholm*. Mrs Chisholm was strongly attacked by owners of the existing insanitary immigrant ships who accused her of corruption and jobbery.

It now became important for the Society to have an energetic and effective agent in Australia to organize committees for the reception of the immigrants and subsequent recovery of loans. So in 1851 Archibald Chisholm, unremunerated, characteristically volunteered to go out and undertake the laborious task of establishing branches in Melbourne, Adelaide, and Sydney. In that year gold was discovered in Australia. Men in all walks of life dropped what they were doing and rushed to the gold fields. There was a clamour for labour of every sort to replace them. Wealthy London merchants and capitalists now became interested in Australia, but all their enterprises needed manpower. They eagerly subscribed £10,000 to the Society; a number of them also joined its Committee, which could now afford a paid secretary in London and agents in Australia to replace Archibald Chisholm. Indeed within a few years economic development in Australia had advanced so rapidly that loans were no longer necessary to encourage immigration, and the Society could be dissolved.

Just before the effects of the gold rush were felt, Mrs Chisholm can be seen at the height of her fame in Britain. The venerable Walter Savage Landor addressed an ode to her asking:

> 'Chisholm, of all the ages that have rolled
> Around this rolling globe, what age hath seen
> Such arduous, such heaven guided enterprises
> As thine? Crime flies before thee and the shores
> Of Austral Asia, lustrated by thee
> Collect no longer the putrescent weeds
> Of Europe, cast by senates to infect
> The only unpolluted continent.
> Thither thou hast conducted honest toil
> Fainting of hunger on the wealthy street ...
> Thither the maiden in whose pallid face
> Lust thought he saw his victim ...
> These thou has watched over, nor hast look't
> Beyond, where glory sits awaiting thee ...
> Nor wouldst thou hear with any fresh delight
> What sages in their histories will record,
> That the most potent empire of the earth
> Was planted, some five centuries before
> Under God's guidance, by His Chisholm's hand ...
> Thy grander soul threw open a wide world
> With one command, Be Virtuous and Be Free.'[19]

Even more widely quoted was *A Carol on Caroline Chisholm* in *Punch* in 1853, robustly preferring her work to that of missionaries in Africa —

> 'Beyond the roaring ocean, beneath the soil we tread
> You've English men and women, well housed and clothed and
>   fed
> Who but for help and guidance to leave our crowded shores
> Would now be stealing, begging or lie starving at our doors ...
>
> Who led their expeditions and under whose command
> Through dangers and through hardships sought they the
>   promised land?
> A second Moses, surely, it was who did it all,
> It was a second Moses in bonnet and a shawl.'[20]

Both poems were reprinted as broadsheets, with her portrait.

The boom in emigration to Australia which followed the discovery of gold caused a number of guidebooks and manuals to be published, often including 'Memoirs' of Mrs Chisholm as an indication of their authenticity. A 'Chisholm tent' was marketed; 'Chisholm recipes' were printed on packets of patent flour. Dinner sets were made with her portrait on every piece. The *Westminster Review* wrote that Mrs Chisholm had done more for the moral regeneration of the Australian colonies than all the clergy: 'She did moreover what they could not do – what you felt no one could have done but herself. Like many other moral heroines, she seemed born just for her work.'[21]

In 1853 Caroline visited Rome to fetch back her son William whose health had broken down there whilst he was studying in a seminary. She was received by the Pope who presented her with a gold medal and a marble bust of herself. In London her portrait, seated at her desk with a map of Australia in the background, was painted by Sir George Hayter, and exhibited at the Royal Academy. Before each of the Society's ships sailed a great public meeting was held for the emigrants and their well-wishers. At one of these in 1852 Mrs Chisholm reached her apogee, with more than 2,000 people present and the Chairman, Lord Shaftesbury, ending his eulogy of her talents and self-denial by declaring 'The children shall arise and call her blessed.'

Amidst all this fulsome praise Mrs Chisholm continued with her practical work, daily receiving some 80 visits and writing 40 letters, with no help except a clerk and an old woman to open the door. Once, when asked to define a gentleman, she described him as one who when he writes includes a stamp for a reply. Much of her work was detailed and tedious, answering enquiries, tracing relatives of those she had met on bush journeys and transmitting small sums of money. From Ireland alone 5,000 enquiries were received. Visitors came even on Sundays, the only day when those in domestic service were free. Her advice to immigrants was practical and down to earth. The best shoes for wearing on ships, she told them, have moderately stout soles and no heels. Rather than boxes, immigrants were advised to pack their possessions in barrels, which could be rolled along by children. They need not waste their money on special clothing, for they could keep warm on board by wrapping cloth round knees and ankles.

Each day she put aside time for her children, of whom her seventh and last was born in 1851. They wandered happily around the office and parlour at other times. 'I dream of Mrs Chisholm and her housekeeping', wrote Charles Dickens to his patroness, Miss Coutts. 'The dirty faces of her children are my constant companions'.[22] A more sympathetic writer was saddened that 'a head and heart that might with happiness to the world found and govern a colony toils and moils over the petty economy of household duties in order to save for "my poor emigrants"'.[23]

Mrs Chisholm had planned to return to Australia with her children in the Society's ship which was named after her. But in 1854 the Crimean War broke out. It was perhaps symbolic that the *Caroline Chisholm*, with her well executed bust as its figurehead, was taken over as a troopship. Immigration was now crowded out of the newspapers by despatches from the Crimea.

When she sailed for Australia Caroline could look back on her seven years in Britain with satisfaction. She had despatched the wives and families of emancipated convicts to Australia and had persuaded the Colonial Office to reintroduce the scheme whereby women were given free passages. Travelling around England, Scotland and Ireland, she had sought out many children and parents of free immigrants and enabled them to join the bread winner in Australia. As for her vision of a 'national colonization policy', although she had not persuaded the Government to take it up, much had been achieved through the Family Colonization Loan Society which had sent out over 3,000 immigrants. Her scheme for remittances of money from Australia had been particularly effective. She had brought about greatly improved conditions for passengers on immigrant ships. Perhaps most important of all in the long run she had made Australia known to thousands who previously had not considered going there.

In July 1854 she arrived in Melbourne with her six children and was reunited with her husband. A public reception was held in her honour. A committee collected £2,500 for a testimonial, to which the Victoria legislature added £5,000. With some of this money 'Chisholm and Son' opened a large general store.

Though Caroline was now disposed to retire from public life, she could not rid herself of a feeling of responsibility towards those whom she had encouraged to emigrate. To bring herself up to date with their problems, shortly after her arrival she visited the gold fields at Bendigo and Ballarat in a covered cart, taking one of her sons as escort. Here she found the miners, most of whom had left their wives behind, living in disgusting conditions, 'entering their blankets at night more like dogs than men'. Talking with them, she found that their great grievance was the difficulty in securing land on which they could settle and establish their families. The main obstacle which prevented the families from joining them was the lack of accommodation along the roads. When she returned to Melbourne therefore she set up a society to build and maintain shelters which provided simple accommodation at low prices along the route to the gold fields. The Government made a grant, but she probably spent much of her testimonial money on this project.

Addressing a meeting to raise money for the shelter fund, she spoke about the land problem. She never could and never would, she declared, have recommended any man to come to Australia if she had not believed that lands would be freed to provide homes for the people. She conducted a long correspondence in the Melbourne *Argus* about her land ticket scheme.

In 1855 she suffered a severe illness. She recovered sufficiently to inspect her shelters and lived for a time in the small town of Kyneton, where the family set up a new and seldom profitable store. But her doctors told her that her only hope of survival was to move to the healthier climate of Sydney. Here she and her husband lived in straitened circumstances, borrowing money and pawning the Pope's medal to buy their food. For Archibald the only work available to an elderly retired major was as a draper's assistant, whilst Caroline decorated cakes for confectioners and gave occasional English lessons to Chinese. When two of their sons joined them and found jobs, the situation improved and Caroline set up a boarding school for girls.

From time to time she gave public lectures, for which she was probably paid. No longer being responsible for projects, she could express her views with less restraint. Once more she urged that the land should be opened to the people and attacked the great landlords for preventing this. She advocated adult suffrage, the secret ballot and payment of members of the legislature. She called for shorter hours for shop assistants.

In 1866 Caroline and her husband returned to England in order to complete the education of their two youngest children, both girls, in Europe. Shortly after her arrival she received a pension of £100 a year from the Royal Bounty Fund. For the last five years of her life she was completely bedridden, cared for by a daughter and enjoying her grandchildren. She was sustained not only by her faith but her sublime sense of the ridiculous which once caused her to relate how a priest, not aware that she was conscious, remarked to the doctor – 'As I was a strong minded woman, he would be excused if asking how many hours I might live, as he had a pressing engagement'.[24]

On the Feast of the Annunciation in 1877 she exclaimed several times 'Take me home! Take me home!' and died the same day, a few months before her husband. The *Times* only devoted ten lines to her death and the Australian press hardly mentioned it.

Australian writers have recognized Caroline Chisholm's importance handsomely. Sir Keith Hancock has said that 'It is scarcely an exaggeration to assert that Mrs Chisholm established the dignity of womanhood and of the family in New South Wales'.[25] Sir Douglas Copland has called her 'the greatest of women pioneers in Australia'.[26] Her religion was the dominant force in her life. It was broad and comprehensive and was accompanied, as Samuel Sidney who worked closely with her noticed, by a degree of common sense that amounted almost to genius. It was probably that common sense, allied to her unsectarian outlook, which caused her to become a Roman Catholic on marriage in order to avoid a conflict of denominational loyalties in the family. Her religion gave her a generous awareness of Original Sin; though an idealist, she was patient and understanding of the faults of those whom she sought to help.

Politically she became more radical as she grew older. As time went on she found it less necessary to be restrained in expressing her opposition to the export of the English class system to Australia. 'I am not afraid of a row', she wrote in a letter to Lord Shaftesbury in 1857. 'I do not dread a riot; and I may go further and say that I look upon a little bit of wholesale rebellion as one of the best preservatives of the public peace'.[27] Yet though her sympathies were with ex-convicts and men who wanted to become small independent farmers, she had many personal friends among the landlords.

She was singularly fortunate in her husband. He recognized her inspiration and served loyally in a subordinate position under her leadership. Though studious and book-loving by inclination, he spent much of his leave and retirement in tedious clerical and administrative tasks. A considerable part of his salary and hard-earned Indian pension were swallowed up in his wife's good works so that in his old age he found himself impoverished. Yet he never seems to have complained.

As for her children, friends who were closer to the family circle than Dickens remembered the care with which Caroline taught them and the stories she invented to illustrate faults and vices. When small they had to reserve a portion of their dinner and take it out on a clean plate, with pepper and salt, to the tramps and unfortunates who came to the family's door. From quite an early age they enjoyed helping with their mother's work.[28] Her daughter remembered her many years later as 'an immensely clever woman, extraordinarily versatile, capable of directing building of sheds and repair of bullock carts, able to carry our surveying, and gifted as a water diviner, and yet having all the domestic accomplishments, including fine needlework. Above all she was supremely observant ... she saw everything ... there was no need to tell her you had passed a sleepless night or were in pain or sorrow. Nothing escaped her.'[29] It was for her shrewdness as much as her charity that priests used to seek her help and advice. Though she was a formidable critic, she was generous in encouragement. 'Why do we only praise our dead,' she asked, 'why do we not praise the living. It can do no harm, but it can help many.'[30]

Her dry sense of humour caused her to publish without comment as an appendix to *Female Immigration* a list of gifts which she had received from people whom the Home had helped. They included a four pound jar of honey, the first gathering of beans from a garden, Baxter's *Call to the Unconverted* (a surprising present to a Roman Catholic), a Highlander's club for her little boy and 51 pieces of wedding cake from women whose marriages she had helped to bring about. The last she must have appreciated most of all.[31]

Perhaps the final word on Caroline Chisholm may be left with the eminent French historian Jules Michelet who devoted a chapter to her in his book *La Femme* in 1862 which described her as a saint. He was inaccurate both about the date of her birth and her age at her marriage; he supposed, when he wrote, that she was dead, whilst she still had fifteen years to live; he was sadly wrong in saying that her 'apostolate' had only drawn on the family funds for £16 when in fact it had reduced them to penury. He was provocative in expressing sympathy with her because English prostitutes, among whom she worked, were less amusing than their French sisters. His prediction that her reputation 'would grow greater from age to age' hardly proved correct. Yet all these inaccuracies were less important than his assessment. 'A French or German woman,' he observed, 'could have had as much goodness and generous pity, but I do not know if they would have persisted against so many obstacles. What was needed was an admirable obstinacy in doing good, a sublime stubbornness.'[32]

Further Reading

Among Caroline Chisholm's pamphlets are –
  Female Immigration Considered, in a Brief Account of the Sydney Immigrants Home (Sydney, 1842). This is hard to locate outside Australia.
*Emigration and Transportation Relatively Considered in a Letter to Earl Grey (*London, 1847*).*

Comfort for the Poor! Meat Three Times a Day!!!, Voluntary Infor-
mation from the People of New South Wales (London, 1847).
Family Colonization Loan Society, a Letter to Lord Ashley (London,
1849).
The A.B.C. of Colonization (London, 1850).
    Several memoirs of Mrs Chisholm, some anonymous, were pub-
lished in England in the 1850s. The most useful, much of it quoted
from her letters and writings, is Eneas MacKenzie, *Memoirs of*
Mrs Chisholm (London, 1852). More recent biographies are M.
Kiddle, *Caroline Chisholm* (Melbourne, 1950) and M. Hoban,
Fifty One Pieces of Wedding Cake, A Biography of Caroline
Chisholm (Kilmore, Victoria, Australia, 1973).

Notes

1. Samuel Sidney, *The Three Colonies of Australia*, London,
   1853, p. 138.
2. M. Kiddle, *Caroline Chisholm*, Melbourne, 1950, p. 32.
3. Caroline Chisholm, *Female Immigration Considered*, Sydney
   1842, p. 4.
4. Ibid., p. 5.
5. Kiddle, *op. cit.*, p. 234.
6. Sir Roger Therry, *Reminiscences of 30 years residence in NSW*
   and Victoria, London, 1863, p. 421.
7. *Female Immigration, op. cit.*, p. 46.
8. *Female Immigration, op. cit.*, p. 45.
9. Kiddle, *op. cit.*, p. 53.
10. Ibid., p. 11.
11. Sidney, *op. cit.*, p. 38.
12. Hoban, *op. cit.*, p. 181.
13. Anon, *What has Mrs Chisholm done for New South Wales?*
    Sydney, 1862, p. 4.
14. Kiddle, *op. cit.*, p. 445.
15. Eneas MacKenzie *Memoirs of Mrs Chisholm*, London, 1852,
    p. 243 ff.
16. Hoban, *op. cit.*, p. 212–213.
17. *Ibid.*, p. 213.
18. Hoban, *op. cit.*, p. 246.
19. Hoban, *op. cit.*, p. 323.
20. *Ibid.*, p. 322.
21. Hoban, *op. cit.*, p. 274.
22. Hoban, *op. cit.*, p. 240.
23. *Ibid.*, p. 266 (Samuel Sidney.)

24. '*What has Mrs Chisholm done for New South Wales?*', *op. cit.*, p. 14.
25. W.K. Hancock, *Australia*, London, 1930, p. 49.
26. Kiddle, *op. cit.*, p. 5.
27. Hoban, *op. cit.*, p. 375.
28. *Anon., Emigrant's Guide to Australia with Memoir of Mrs Chisholm*, London, 1853, p. 28.
29. Edith Pearson, *Ideals and Realities*, London, 1914, pp. 71, 91.
30. Pearson, *op. cit.*, p. 90.
31. *Female Immigration, op. cit.*, p. 99.
32. J. Michelet, Oeuvres Completes, Paris, N.D., *La Femme*, p. 657 ff. (translation).

PART II

CONTEMPLATIVES

5

Christina Rossetti (1830–1894)

'My God shall fill my longings to the brim'
Christina Rossetti, 1853

'You were not a pure saint by any means. You pulled legs; you tweaked noses; you were at war with all humbug and pretence. Modest as you were, still you were drastic, sure of your gift, convinced of your vision. In a word, you were an artist'
Virginia Woolf, 1932

It is surprising that no consideration appears to have been given to Christina Rossetti when the list of those to be commemorated by the Church of England in 1980 was prepared; for she was the most authentically Anglican poet since Keble. Indeed several editions of her works are still in print, whilst Keble's 'Christian Year' has long since ceased to be published. As for her life and beliefs, it has perhaps been unfortunate for her reputation that most of what has been written about her since her death has been based on the Memoir and Reminiscences of her agnostic brother William who, though devoted to her, had no sympathy with her religion. Her omission may also partly be due to the fact that by birth and temperament she was a somewhat disconcertingly unEnglish kind of person.

Her father, Gabriele Rossetti, came from Naples where he had been a custodian in the Museum and a poet. He was involved in a revolution against the reactionary Bourbon monarchy and fled to London where he lived precariously by teaching Italian. He married Frances Polidori, a woman much younger than himself, whose father was Italian and mother British. They had four children in rapid succession: Maria (1827), who was to become an Anglican nun; Dante Gabriel (1828), the poet and painter; William Michael (1829), a civil servant and writer; and finally Christina, born in 1830.

The children were baptized into the Church of England. The boys inherited the anticlericalism of their nominally Roman Catholic father; the girls grew up in the devout Anglicanism of their mother who moved from an Evangelical to a High Church faith into which they followed her.

Living in London, the family was poor. There was one servant and no nurse. The education which the children were given by their mother, a former governess, was a very literary one. As there was no nursery, they would listen in the living room to the explosive discussions of the Italian exiles who visited their father: they grew up to be bilingual, speaking English with their mother and Italian with their father.

There was little visiting except to the suburban home of the Polidori grandparents, in whose garden Christina acquired her lifelong love for the creeping and aquatic creatures who were always liable to make their incongruous way into her poems. Grandfather Polidori printed a volume of her verses on his private press when she was 12. The fluency in composition which she attained so early was fostered by the game of Bouts-Rimés played by the Rossetti family, in which sonnets had to be constructed at speed to fit final lines which were announced in advance.

The melancholy note and the preoccupation with death in Christina's poetry owed much to her poor health. At the age of 15 she was believed to have tuberculosis as well as angina pectoris. Later she developed Graves Disease which destroyed her good looks. She was compelled, says William, 'to regard this world as a valley of the shadow of death and to make near acquaintance with promises, and also with threatenings, applicable to a different world.'[1]

When partial blindness disabled the father and Dante Gabriel's fees as an art student needed to be paid, the others had to work, William as a clerk in the Inland Revenue, the mother and daughters as teachers and governesses, an occupation for which Christina felt no vocation or capability. Eventually when old Gabriele died Frances, Maria and Christina moved into William's house.

During the last illness of her father, when she was 13, Christina and her mother started to attend services at Christ Church, Albany Street, whose incumbent, William Dodsworth, was a strong supporter of the Tractarian or Oxford Movement. Under his influence the Rossetti women abandoned their individualistic, evangelical form of religion for one which held the Church of England to be a valid part of the whole Catholic Church. This form of religion came to be the most important aspect of Christina's life. Dodsworth eventually went over to Rome. William considered that Christina too would have been happier as a Roman Catholic, but she inherited both her mother's loyalty to the Church of England and her father's distrust of the Vatican. She asserted sturdily in one of her commentaries on the Saints, 'Great is our privilege as members of the English Church, in that we are not commanded, or invited, or in any way encouraged to assert what contradicts history or override facts by pious beliefs'.[2]

It was in William's house that the Pre-Raphaelite Brotherhood of painters was formed by Gabriel, together with Holman Hunt and John Everett Millais, all then under the age of 21. William became a member, and Gabriel proposed that Christina should also be elected. He was overruled, and Christina would retire from the noisy meetings to write poetry in her room on her washstand, sometimes however being fetched down to help to edit the group's shortlived journal, 'The Germ', to which she also contributed poems.

It was in the P.R.B. that Christina at the age of 17 acquired a fiancé. Among the members of the Brotherhood was James Collinson, the only one to have already exhibited a picture, 'The Charity Boy's Debut', at the Royal Academy and who was now working on a long and rather dull poem on 'The Child Jesus'. James Collinson was described by William as 'small and rather dumpy, with a thick neck; his manner was subdued and somewhat timid and the same was the case with his art'. Like Alice in Wonderland's dormouse, whom he somewhat resembled, he was apt to fall asleep during his own parties. It seems that he was more deeply in love with Christina than she with him. 'As well he might be', William writes tartly, 'for in breeding and tone of mind, not to speak of actual genius or advantages of person, she was markedly his superior'.[3]

According to William, Christina at first rejected Collinson because he was a Roman Catholic, as she was 'firmly opposed to anything that smacked of Mariolatry'. Collinson thereupon rejoined the Church of England and was accepted by her; however, along with many other more prominent Anglo Catholics, he was disgusted by the Gorham Judgement and returned to Rome, whereupon Christina broke off the engagement. William concludes 'He was a well meaning man of timorous conscience. But he had none the less struck a staggering blow at Christina's peace of mind on the very threshold of womanly life, and a blow from which she did not recover for years'.

Christina's only other love, according to William, was Charles Cayley, whom she had known since he had been a pupil of her father and who proposed to her many years later when she was 35. Cayley was a scholar, whose interests were almost wholly in books; he translated Dante into English and the Bible into Iroquois. William describes him as 'inobservant of the ways of the world and indifferent to them', though 'a thoroughly refined gentleman. His manner was absent minded in the extreme ... One awaited his arrival with some apprehension, conscious that some embarrassment would follow ... He was a most unworldly person, which was no doubt in my sister's eyes a merit, not a blemish. His precise religious opinions are not clear to me; he had been brought up in the Church of England. I suppose that like so many men of inquiring mind, he regarded all religions as much the same thing – a mixture of feeling with thought, and also with assumption and legend, not with verification'.[4]

Christina encouraged his dilatory wooing in a lighthearted poem:

> 'My blindest buzzard that I know,
>   My special mole, when will you see?
> O, no, you must not look at me,
>   There's nothing hid for me to show.
> I might show facts as plain as day;
>   But since your eyes are blind, you'd say
> "Where? What?" and turn away'.

Cayley had lost all his capital in a scheme to place advertisements on the walls of railway stations; William generously told

Christina however that if they married they could live under his roof. Finance was a minor consideration for Christina; but when Cayley proposed she probed his religious faith, and, finding this incompatible with her own, refused him. She continued to love him until his death in 1883 and he would frequently visit her.

Before considering Christina's poetry, it is necessary to try to understand her religion, by which it was largely inspired. William described this as 'far more a thing of the heart than of the mind. Her faith was pure and absolute, an entire acceptance of a thing revealed, not a quest for any confirmation in demonstrative proof ...'. There were few things she disliked more than 'evidences of Christianity'. Her attitude was 'I believe because I am told to believe, and I know that the authority which tells me to believe is the only real authority extant, God'.[5]

Whilst she was uninterested in theology, she had a minute knowledge of the Bible, which she supplemented by reading the *Confessions of St Augustine* and the *Imitation of Christ*. She liked to quote *Pilgrim's Progress* and gloried in Dante. She took Holy Communion twice a week, went to Confession, and practised moderate fasting. These practices brought her great comfort; as she once revealed to Gabriel 'I have borne myself until I became unbearable and then I have found confession, absolution and spiritual council and relief inexpressible'.[6]

Although her poems reveal how she went through crises in which her sense of unworthiness made her desperately unhappy, her religious experiences never soured her temper. Cheerfulness she considered to be an essential duty. William described her as 'an Anglo Catholic, and among Anglo Catholics a Puritan', but she was very tolerant of other denominations − 'Let us be provoked to good works', she wrote, 'by those with whom we cannot always agree, yet who in many ways set us a pattern. I at least can learn much from the devotion of Catholic Rome, the immutability of Catholic [sic] Greece, the philanthropic piety of Quakerism, and the zeal of many a Protestant'.[7] In her poems there was no sectarianism.

Her religion made her kind to others; she never used a harsh word about anyone, and would forgive lapses in them which she could not pardon in herself. She could hate the sin but love the sinner. She was more tolerant of immorality than unbelief, and considered it a mistake to try to convert anyone except by prayer and love. Love, she said, was more potent to breed faith than faith to breed love. William regarded religious 'overscrupulosity' as the only defect in her character. Gabriel regretted the 'morbidity' of her work and joked about 'the skeletons in Christina's closets'.

Why the same kind of religion which made her sister Maria supremely happy when she entered an Anglican convent should have so often filled Christina with despair is not easy to understand. Perhaps the spiritual direction which Maria was given equipped her better to overcome any lack of confidence. Perhaps Christina, whatever advice she received from her parish priest, was less able than Maria to tolerate a discipline which, though it might have provided support, would have limited the range of her poetic emotions.

As it was, her poetry reflected, particularly in her earlier years, a constant and unhappy struggle between earthly and divine love, as well as an exhausting tension between what she was and what she thought she ought to be. For years she seemed to live on a treadmill. She loved the world but considered that love to be sinful; she renounced the world and was made unhappy by renunciation; she then condemned her unhappiness.[8] The religion which made her kind to others did not make her kind to herself.

Christina's early poems were submitted in draft to Gabriel from whom she received much encouragement. He in turn sent them to Ruskin, a friend of the family, who replied that no publisher would take them, 'so full they are of quaintness and offence and irregular measure'. But Alexander MacMillan, whose Thursday 'Tobacco Parliaments' were frequented by the P.R.B., accepted several of her poems for *MacMillan's Magazine*, including two which were to become widely popular, 'Does the Road Wind Uphill All the Way', written when she was 27, and 'My Heart is Like a Singing Bird' when she was 26. Encouraged by the reception, MacMillan brought out her first book of poems, *Goblin Market*, in 1862 before either her brother or Swinburne had a volume to their name. The latter indeed hailed her as 'the Jael who led the Pre-Raphaelite hosts to victory'.

Yet was this a Pre-Raphaelite victory? Consider 'A Birthday':

> My heart is like a singing bird
>   Whose nest is in a watered shoot;
> My heart is like an apple tree
>   Whose boughs are bent with thickset fruit;
> My heart is like a rainbow shell
>   That paddles in a halcyon sea;
> My heart is gladder than all these
>   Because my love is come to me.
>
> Raise me a dais of silk and down;
>   Hang it with vair and purple dyes;
> Carve it in doves and pomegranates,
>   And peacocks with a hundred eyes;
> Work it in gold and silver grapes,
>   In leaves and silver fleurs-de-lys;
> Because the birthday of my life
>   Is come, my love is come to me.

The lush second verse, so strikingly contrasted with the simplicity of the first, may appear to be in true Pre-Raphaelite style, but by whom, readers ever since have asked, was the poem inspired? Hardly the dormouse Collinson who had passed out of Christina's life; and her relationship with Cayley was still some years ahead. One biographer has somewhat desperately suggested that she was in love with a married man, William Bell Scott, a conclusion for which subsequent critics have found no evidence.[9] A recent writer on the other hand supposes that 'Probably the poem represents an exceptionally strong mystical awareness of the presence of God – vouchsafed to her perhaps in Holy Communion, perhaps in meditation, perhaps in washing the breakfast dishes'.[10]

Both *Goblin Market* and its successor, *The Prince's Progress*, published in 1866, are divided into sections of secular and devotional poems; but the distinction is fine, for again and again even the secular poems express the disappointment of profane love, and the poet turns to God, as in 'Twice', composed in 1864 –

I took my heart in my hand
   (O my love, O my love),
I said: Let me fall or stand,
   Let me live or die,
But this once hear me speak –
   (O my love, O my love) –
Yet a woman's words are weak;
   You should speak, not I.

You took my heart in your hand
   With a friendly smile,
With a critical eye you scanned,
   Then set it down,
And said: It is still unripe,
   Better wait awhile;
Wait while the skylarks pipe,
   Till the corn grows brown.

As you set it down it broke –
   Broke, but I did not wince;
I smiled at the speech you spoke,
   At your judgment that I heard:
But I have not often smiled
   Since then, nor questioned since,
Nor cared for corn-flowers wild,
   Nor sung with the singing bird.

I take my heart in my hand,
   O my God, O my God,
My broken heart in my hand:
   Thou hast seen, judge Thou.
My hope was written on sand,
   O my God, O my God;
Now let Thy judgment stand –
   Yea, judge me now.

This contemned of a man,
   This marred one heedless day,
This heart take Thou to scan
   Both within and without:
Refine with fire its gold,
   Purge Thou its dross away –
Yea hold it in Thy hold,
   Whence none can pluck it out.

> I take my heart in my hand —
> I shall not die, but live —
> Before Thy face I stand;
> I, for Thou callest such:
> All that I have I bring,
> All that I am I give,
> Smile Thou and I shall sing,
> But shall not question much.

In 'The Heart Knoweth its own Bitterness' (1857), she protests passionately against the inadequacy of her earthly loves, wanting

> 'To give, to give, not to receive.
> I long to pour myself, my soul ...'

but finding

> 'You scratch my surface with your pin,
> You stroke me smooth with hushing breath —
> Nay pierce, nay probe, nay dig within,
> Probe my quick core and sound my depth.
> You call me with a puny call,
> You talk, you smile, you nothing do:
> How should I spend my heart on you —
> My heart that so outweighs you all.'

Then the mood changes

> 'Not in this world of hope deferred —
> This world of perishable stuff;
> Eye hath not seen nor earth hath heard
> Nor heart conceived that full "enough".
> Here moans the separating sea,
> Here harvests fail, here breaks the heart.
> There God shall join and no man part.
> I full of Christ and Christ in me.'

But the search for God, the response to God, the communication with God, all these were hard for her. In 'Bruised Reed Shall He Not Break' (1857), the dialogue is commenced by the Lord —

> 'I will accept thy will to do and be,
>   Thy hatred and intolerance of sin,
> Thy will at least to love, that burns within
>   And thirsteth after Me.
>
> So will I render blessing still,
>   The germs and small beginnings in thy heart
> Because thy will cleaves to the better part'

but the poet's reply is

'Alas, I cannot will.'

Sometimes there is almost a note of despair in the quest, as in 'A Better Resurrection' (1858), with its echo of 'The Birthday' –

> 'I have no wit, no words, no tears;
>   My heart within me like a stone
> Is numbed too much for hopes or fears;
>   Look right, look left, I dwell alone:
> I lift mine eyes, but dimmed with grief,
>   No everlasting hills I see;
> My life is in the falling leaf:
>   O Jesus, quicken me. . . .
>
> My life is like a faded leaf
>   My harvest dwindled to a husk;
> Truly my life is void and brief
>   And tedious in the barren dusk;
> My life is like a frozen thing
>   Nor bud nor greenness can I see
> Yet rise it shall – the sap of Spring –
>   O Jesus rise in me. . . .'

At other times it was the life of devotion which seemed too hard, as in 'Weary in Well Doing' (1864) –

> 'I would have gone; God bade me stay;
>   I would have worked; God bade me rest.
> He broke my will from day to day,
>   He read my yearnings unexpressed
> And said them nay.

Now I would stay; God bids me go;
   Now I would rest; God bids me work.
He breaks my heart, tossed to and fro,
   My soul is wrung with doubts that lurk
And vex it so.

I go Lord, where Thou sendest me;
   Day after day I plod and moil;
But Christ my God, when will it be
   That I may let alone my toil
And rest with Thee?'

Occasionally there was a different, tranquil note, when her perceptive love of natural beauty united with her love of God. At such times she was no more reluctant than Breughel to place a Bible scene in her own countryside. Best of all, this emerges in 'In the Bleak Mid Winter,' published in 1872 but probably written earlier, which has become so widely known as a Christmas carol that it needs no quotation.

It was probably in the late 1860s that Christina wrote the moving sonnet sequence 'Monna Innominata', though it was only published in 1881. In a foreword the author refers to the 'unnamed ladies' addressed by the medieval troubadors, and suggests that these sonnets are what their replies might have been. William Rossetti however maintained that this was a blind to draw off attention from the fact that they were written to a particular person, by inference Cayley.[11] In the poems divine love has a higher claim than human love, yet the two may be reconciled.

'Trust me, I have not earned your dear rebuke,
   I love, as you would have me, God the most;
Would lose not Him, but you, must one be lost,
   Nor with Lot's wife cast back a faithless look
Unready to forego what I forsook.
   This say I, having counted up the cost,
This, tho' I be the feeblest of God's host,
   The sorriest sheep Christ shepherds with his crook.

Yet while I love my God the most, I deem
   That I can never love you overmuch;
I love Him more, so let me love you too;

Yea, as I apprehend it, love is such
I cannot love you if I love not Him,
    I cannot love Him, if I love not you.'

Many of Christina's later poems have had little subsequent appeal. Those in *Sing-Song, a Nursery Rhyme Book*, now seem sugary and sentimental, though occasional charming little verses can be found, such as that commencing 'Hope is like a harebell, trembling from its birth'. There were also many verses written for particular fasts and feasts, few of which are remembered. She had to endure first the collapse of her brother Gabriel, whom she helped to nurse, from laudanum poisoning, and his eventual death, followed by those of Maria and Cayley, and that of her mother, with whom she had lived all her life. There was then the strain of caring for her aged aunts and of her own lingering illnesses. Yet after the renunciation of Cayley the devotional poems become calmer, less desperate. Even when attracted by marriage she had been equally repelled by its consequences as she contemplated a woman who 'grew gross in soulless love, a sluggish wife' or another who 'droned in sweetness like a fattened bee'. In 'The Ransomed of the Lord', now that the possibility of marriage has been put aside, there is a note of hope which had been lacking in earlier years —

'Thy lovely saints do bring Thee love
    Incense and joy and gold,
Fair star with star, fair dove with dove,
    Beloved by Thee of old.
I, Master, neither star nor dove,
    Have brought Thee sins and tears;
Yet I too bring a little love
    Amid my flaws and fears.
A trembling love that faints and fails
    Yet still is love of Thee,
A wondering love that hopes and hails
    Thy boundless love of me;
Love kindling faith and pure desire,
    Love following on to bliss,
A spark, O, Jesu from Thy fire,
    A drop from Thine abyss.'[12]

Now the dialogues between the poet and the Lord end on a reassuring note —

'O Lord, when Thou didst call me, didst Thou know
  My heart disheartened thro' and thro',
  Still hankering after Egypt full in view
Where cucumbers and melons grow?
  — "Yea, I knew." —

But, Lord, when Thou didst choose me, didst Thou know
  How marred I was and withered too,
  Nor rose for sweetness nor for virtue rue,
Timid and rash, hasty and slow?
  — "Yea, I knew." —

My Lord, when Thou didst love me, didst Thou know
  How weak my efforts were, how few,
  Tepid to love and impotent to do,
Envious to reap while slack to sow?
  — "Yea, I knew." —

Good Lord, Who knowest what I cannot know,
  And dare not know, my false, my true,
  My new, my old; Good Lord, arise and do
If loving Thou hast known me so.
  — "Yea, I knew." —

Beneath the Anglo Catholicism of her adult life, the uneasy questioning of the Evangelical religion of her childhood had long smouldered — how could she, who felt herself so unworthy, expect to be of the elect? In her last poems the doubts are dispelled —

  'Lord, what have I that I may offer Thee,
  Look Lord, I pray Thee, and see

  "What is it thou hast got?
  Nay child, what is it thou hast not?
  Thou hast all gifts that I have given to thee:
  Offer them all to Me,
  The great ones and the small,
  I will accept them one and all."

"I have a will, good Lord, but it is marred;
A heart both crushed and hard,
Not such as these the gift
Clean-handed lovely Saints uplift."

"Nay, child, but wilt thou judge for Me?
I crave not thine but thee."

"Ah, Lord who lovest me!
Such as I have I now give Thee".'

In her middle and later years Christina devoted much of her time to writing devotional commentaries, usually for publication by the Society for Promoting Christian Knowledge (SPCK). The most substantial were *Annus Domini, A Prayer for Each Day of the Year* (1874), *Called to be Saints* – *the Minor Festivals devotionally Studied* (1881) and *Face of the Deep* – *A Devotional Commentary on the Apocalypse* (1892).

Apart from some of the religious verses which first appeared in them, these are little read today. In *Called to be Saints* there is a quaint charm in the way in which her observation of nature supports her themes. Each Saint is commemorated by a plant or flower – holly, with its blood red berries and thorns, for the martyr St Stephen; mistletoe for St John, to show that 'Ours is a derived life'; ivy for St Thomas, because like him it needs a prop. Every Saint too is allotted a particular precious stone.

For most of her life Christina earned little from her writing. A brief experience convinced her that her ailments prevented her from working as a governess or teacher, the only professions open to a woman of her background. At various times she contributed to the family finances by undertaking Italian translations and articles for encyclopaedias. In 1876 she described herself as 'exercising my old craft of painting despicable sprigs on notepaper corners for sale at 1d a sheet for the good of the house'.[13]

After she became an Associate of the Sisters of All Saints she took to wearing a plain black dress, with hanging sleeves, and a muslin cap. How far her Puritanism had caused her to diverge from the aestheticism into which the Pre-Raphaelite Movement found its way is seen in the devotional works which she conscientiously turned out for the SPCK. Thus in *Letter and Spirit, notes on the Commandments*, she reflected – 'For the books which we now forbear to read we shall one day be endued with wisdom and knowledge. For the music we will not listen to, we shall join in the song of the redeemed. For the pictures from which we turn, we shall gaze unabashed on the beatific vision ... It cannot be much of a hardship to dress modestly and at small cost rather than richly and fashionably, if with a vivid conviction that we are awaiting the "white robes" of the redeemed'.[14] She became somewhat eccentric. Walking in the streets she would pick up pieces of paper which were blown about, in case portions of the Holy Bible were written on them which could be desecrated by a casual tread.

Such a progress might well have led to the loss of her sense of humour, but she continued to be amused by herself, both as she was and as she had been. 'I was a very melancholy girl, but now I am a very cheerful old woman', she told a visitor in 1885.[15] And as she lost the beautiful girlish figure which he had so often painted, she wrote to Gabriel 'A fat poetess is incongruous, especially when seated by the grave of buried hopes'.[16] To thank Scott for a gift, she sent him a poem beginning

> 'Accept this faint flash of a smouldering fun,
> The fun of a heavy old heart'.[17]

She pasted into her copy of *Poems* (1875) a parody of *A Birthday*, beginning

> 'My heart is like one asked to dine
> Whose evening dress is up the spout ...'

and ending

> 'Work me a suit in crimson apes
> And sky blue beetles on the spree;
> Because the mother of my wife
> Has come − and means to stay with me'.[18]

MacKenzie Bell, her first biographer, who knew her well in her last years, remembered her as being almost incapable of being ruffled by the petty worries of existence, and dwelt on the sweetness, profundity and fascination of her personality.[19]

As she admitted to a visitor in 1885, she lived increasingly in the other world.

For many years Christina worked with the Anglican Sisters among fallen women and factory girls. In the Crimean War she offered to accompany her aunt to work as a nurse under Florence Nightingale, though she was rejected as being too young. Yet social work and loving her neighbours was a duty rather than a vocation.

> 'Yea Lord' – she wrote wryly – 'I will serve them by Thy grace,
>   Love Thee, seek Thee in them, wait and pray;
> Yet I would love Thyself, Lord, face to face
>   Heart to heart, one day'.

She knew and cared little about party politics, but was aware of the moral and social problems of the late Victorian age. 'Alas England', she prophesied in *The Face of the Deep* in 1892, 'full of luxuries and thronged by stinted poor, whose merchants are princes and whose dealings crooked, whose packed storehouses stand amid bare homes, whose gorgeous array has rags for neighbours! From a canker in our gold and silver, from a moth in our garments, from blasted crops, from dwindling substance, from righteous retribution abasing us among the nations, Good Lord deliver us'.[20]

After the death of her mother Christina continued to look after her aged aunts. The effort of doing so left her with little time, and less energy, for writing, for she was herself a semi-invalid. In 1892 she underwent an operation for cancer. She survived her Aunt Eliza by only a few months, and died in December 1894 after a long and painful illness in which much of her time was spent in silent prayer. 'This illness has humbled me', she said, 'I was so proud before'.[21]

Among her papers was found the manuscript of a last poem –

> 'Sleeping at last, the trouble and tumult over.
> Sleeping at last, the struggle and horror past,
> Cold and white, out of sight of friend and lover,
>   Sleeping at last.

No more a tired heart downcast or overcast,
No more pangs that wring or shifting fears that hover,
Sleeping at last in a dreamless sleep locked fast.
Fast asleep. Singing birds in their leafy cover
Cannot wake her, nor shake her the gusty blast,
Under the purple thyme and the purple clover,
   Sleeping at last.'

Christina whose poems were set in the countryside and never in the city, where almost all her life was lived, died and was buried in a thick London fog. William, the agnostic, organized the ceremonies decently. One of her poems 'Lord, Grant Us Grace to Mount Thy Steps of Grace' was sung as an anthem. On her tombstone in the family grave at Highgate was engraved the last verse of her poem 'The Lowest Room' –

   'Give me the lowest place; or if for me
   That lowest place too high, make one more low
   Where I may sit and see
      My God and love Thee so.'

The case for commemorating Christina Rossetti rests mainly on her poems. At the time of her death her reputation was at its height. Edmund Gosse in the *Century Magazine* described her as 'the sister of George Herbert', and her poetry as in the true Anglican tradition – 'a union of fixed religious faith with a hold on beauty'.[22] A.C. Benson in the *National Review* placed her even higher for 'avoiding the elaborate conceit of Herbert, the desperate euphuism of Crashaw and even the pathetic refinement of Henry Vaughan – ahead of the homely domesticity of Keble, the unsure Puritanism of Charles Wesley and the paucity of experience of Newman'. Himself the son of an Archbishop of Canterbury, Benson reflected with some surprise on how the Church of England with its 'decorous moderation, its liberal generosity, its refined ardour' was the passionate Christina's chosen home.[23]

Mr Gladstone recited her poems. An anonymous writer in the *Saturday Review* dwelt on how much good she had done, and how genuinely she was loved by many who had not seen her.[24] This admiration extended into the early 20th century, so that Sir Walter Raleigh, Professor of English Literature at Oxford

University, exclaimed 'The only thing that Christina makes me want to do is cry, not lecture'.[25] Virginia Woolf praised her for being at war with all humbug and pretence, convinced of her vision, an artist, sorrowing but not morbid.[26] Then the Freudians came on the scene; her repressions, dreams and symbolism provided an easy meal for them. Later the feminists discovered and wrote theses on her. Germaine Greer, in an introduction to a new edition of *Goblin Market* in 1975, demolished her with both Freudian and feminist attacks, describing how she 'used the aspirations of piety as a metaphor for her own frustrated sexuality', 'made her life a torture where release from pain was the sweetest pleasure', and 'wilfully set out to waste her life'. But perhaps Ms Greer was not particularly suited to sympathize with her subject, for in a parenthesis she observed — 'To be sure God is a phenomenon of human fabrication'.[27]

One of Christina's most perceptive contemporary critics, Arthur Symons, observed that 'She does not preach, she prays' and that 'We read her as though we were eavesdropping on the dialogue of a soul with God'. It was this aspect, no doubt, which caused Bishop Westcott of Durham, himself a near saint as well as a great scholar, to write to William on her death about the reverent admiration for her which he could not express, and to say that 'Not a week passes, I think, when I do not find some fresh pleasure in your sister's verses'.[28] At the other extreme, the atheistic Algernon Swinburne was a lifelong admirer who, perhaps to her embarrassment, dedicated poems to her. A hundred years after her death, though of her thousand published poems some appear banal and other self-pitying, the best have retained a perennial interest both for Christians and non-Christians for their beauty and as a record of her struggle to find in God a final satisfaction for the abounding love which was the mainspring of her life and action.[29]

Further Reading

The literature on Christina Rossetti is vast. Some 300 books and articles on her appeared between 1900 and 1982. Of those by contemporaries W.M. Rossetti's Memoir in *The Poetical Works of Christina Rossetti* (London 1904) is essential; as is his *Some*

Reminiscences (London 1906) and his edition of *Family Letters of Christina Rossetti* (London 1908). Mackenzie Bell's *Christina Rossetti* (London 1898) is a biography by a contemporary who was a friend in her later years.

Of subsequent biographies Georgina Battiscombe, *Christina Rossetti – A Divided Life* (London 1981) and Margaret Sawtell, *Christina Rossetti, Her Life and Religion* (London 1955) are among the most useful. Kathleen Jones in *Learning not to be First – the Life of Christina Rossetti* (Oxford 1992) makes use of recent research.

E.K. Charles, *Christina Rossetti – Critical Perspectives 1862–1982*, summarizes assessments of Christina Rossetti over this period and contains a comprehensive bibliography.

Virginia Woolf has a stimulating chapter on Christina Rossetti in *The Common Reader,* Second Series, (London 1935) and there is a useful chapter on her in H.N. Fairchild, *Religious Trends in English Poetry*, Vol. IV, Columbia University, 1987.

The best edition of her poems is *The Complete Poems of Christina Rossetti*, edited by R.W. Crump, (Louisiana State Univ. 1979). However, *The Poetical Works of Christina Rossetti* (London 1904), edited by William Rossetti, remains invaluable for his notes on individual poems. In *The Achievement of Christina Rossetti*, edited by David A. Kent (Cornell 1987) a laudable attempt is made 'to exorcise the demon of false autobiography in the study of Rossetti' and to assess her writings on their intrinsic merits.

Notes

1. Christina Rossetti, *Poetical Works*, London 1904, Introductory Memoir, p. 1.
2. Christina Rossetti, *Time Flies*, London 1885, p. 54.
3. W.M. Rossetti, *Some Reminiscences*, London 1904, p. 65.
4. W.M. Rossetti, in *Poetical Works*, *op. cit.*, p. LIII and in *Some Reminiscences*, *op. cit.*, pp. 311–315.
5. *Poetical Works*, *op. cit.*, p. LIV.
6. Christina Rossetti, *Family Letters*, London 1908, p. 103.
7. MacKenzie Bell, *Christina Rossetti*, London 1898, p. 187. It is curious that Greece is described as Catholic.
8. A. Clutton Brock, *More Essays in Religion*, London 1922, p. 11.
9. L.M. Packer, *Christina Rossetti*, Cambridge 1963.
10. H.N. Fairchild, *Religious Trends in English Poetry*, Columbia Univ., Vol. IV, 1987, p. 313.

11. Christina Rossetti, *Poetical Works, op. cit.*, p. 462.
12. The Triad, *Poetical Works, op. cit.*, p. 329.
13. Christina Rossetti, *Family Letters*, London 1908, p.58.
14. MacKenzie Bell, *Christina Rossetti*, London 1898, p. 302.
15. G. Battiscombe, *Christina Rossetti − A Divided Life*, London 1981, p. 192.
16. *Family Letters, op. cit.*, p. 95.
17. W.B. Scott, *Autobiographical Notes*, London 1892, Vol. II, p. 314.
18. *Poetical Works, op. cit.*, p. 481.
19. Bell, *op. cit.*, p. 4.
20. Bell, *op. cit.*, p. 157.
21. *Ibid.*, p. 176.
22. *Century Magazine*, No. 46, June 1893, p. 211.
23. *National Review*, Vol. 24, Feb. 1895, p. 753.
24. E.K. Charles, *Christina Rossetti − Critical Perspectives*, Susquehanna Univ., Canada, 1985, p. 65.
25. *Ibid.*, p. 105.
26. Virgina Woolf, *Second Common Reader*, London 1932, p. 264.
27. Christina Rossetti, *Goblin Market*, New York, 1975. XIX, XIV.
28. Bell, *op. cit.*, p. 174.
29. C.M. Bowra, *The Romantic Imagination*, London 1950, p. 270.

6

Evelyn Underhill (1875–1941)

'The mystic is not a person who has queer experiences, but a person for whom God is the one reality of life; he is a religious realist.'

Evelyn Underhill

Between the publication of *Mysticism* in 1911 and her death in 1941 Evelyn Underhill's reputation stood very high. Many of her 40 books were widely read, *Mysticism* going into twelve editions. She received far more demands for addressing retreats, seminars and conferences and writing articles than she could meet. People from all over the world wrote to her or dropped in on her friendly London house for advice on their spiritual problems.

In the decades after her death however, as Archbishop Ramsey noted in 1975, 'Her name went through a phase of apathy and antipathy', perhaps, he thought, because of a 'cosy' or 'middle class' tinge in her style.[1] In 1958 Valerie Pitt made a severe attack in an article entitled 'Clouds of Unknowing', drawing on a recent biography of Evelyn Underhill by Margaret Cropper which she described as 'a hagiography in the very manner of the retreat world ... a cosy, gossipy world with a private manner of speech, and almost a private cult'. She went on to accuse her of 'discussing the love of God in terms of fairies at the bottom of the garden'. Her visits to the poor are described as motivated by the benefits to her own soul, 'an outrageous insult to personality'. Evelyn Underhill and her associates are depicted as sublimely unaffected by the miseries of mass unemployment and the rise of Hitler. 'In this magic circle nothing, nothing, nothing is seen apart from its possible use in spirituality ... In such an atmosphere ordinary things and real people recede. The world is never seen as it is.'[2] With her prolific output she was later described as the 'Agatha Christie of spirituality.'[3]

Much of this criticism is exaggerated and even untrue. As will be seen, Evelyn Underhill had a social conscience and was not unmoved by the almost apocalyptic events of her time. She considered that her own vocation however was to give help to troubled souls and to keep alive the contemplative tradition, just as earlier mystics had done amidst the dissensions and wars of her favourite 14th century.

Part of the interest of her life lies in the fact that it was a double one. In her comfortable house at 50 Campden Hill Square, London, where almost all her married life was spent, she would, as Mrs Stuart Moore, efficiently instruct her servants on their daily duties. Then she would retreat to her study where, as Evelyn Underhill, she would kneel, half writing half praying, interrupted by the visitors who sought her spiritual advice, and whom, however cranky, she never turned away. Later Mrs Stuart Moore would reappear, lunching with her mother next door, and going to tea parties, entertaining her husband's legal friends or her own literary circle at dinner. It is perhaps unfortunate that both Charles Williams, the admiring editor of the collection of her letters, and Margaret Cropper's biography, which appeared not long after her death, quoted her spontaneous letters so copiously and did not discriminate more carefully between Miss Underhill and Mrs Stuart Moore.[4]

There was little in Evelyn Underhill's early years to indicate that she would become one of the most widely read writers on prayer and spirituality in the first half of the 20th century. She was born in Wolverhampton in 1875 and was an only child. Her father was a barrister who was later to become Sir Arthur Underhill. Shortly after her birth the family moved to London. Although Evelyn was baptized into the Church of England, the family did not attend church. Between the ages of 13 and 16 she went to a small boarding school, Sandgate House, near Folkestone. Her teenage beliefs and aspirations were recorded in her diary on the eve of her seventeenth birthday. The men she then most admired were Mahomet, Giordano Bruno and Jesus Christ; her heroines were Joan of Arc and Catherine Herschel. In politics she was a socialist. In religion she believed in God, and found the Bible one of the best and wisest books the world had ever seen, but not inspired; she had no use for churches. Finally she wrote, 'I hope that my mind will not grow tall to look down on things, but wide to embrace all sorts of things.' She went on to King's College, London where she studied Botany, Philosophy and Social Science.

As an only child she had grown up closely with Jeff and Hubert Stuart Moore, the sons of a neighbour and colleague of Arthur Underhill; their mother died while they were quite young and Mrs Underhill took the boys under her wing. From an early age Evelyn and Hubert were close companions, sharing among other things, a love for bookbinding. Whilst it came to be understood that they would eventually marry, it was to be a long time before they could afford to do so, as Hubert aspired to become a barrister like his father.

After she graduated and was still living at home, Evelyn's first book was published, a humorous collection of verses about the law, *A Bar Lamb's Ballads*.[5] She also wrote short stories, mostly dealing with problems of the supernatural. Between 1904 and 1909 her three novels were published, all concerned with the spiritual and moral problems of characters who lived between two worlds. There was much symbolism, flavoured with theology, and rather little attention to characterisation. Her first novel, *The Grey World*, had a certain success; *Punch*'s reviewer observed 'It fills me with ideas, though I don't know what they are'.[6] She also wrote poems, collected and published as *Immanence* in 1912.

As for religion, 'For eight or nine years', she was to recall, 'I really believed myself to be an atheist. Philosophy brought me round to an intelligent and irresponsible sort of atheism, which I enjoyed thoroughly but which did not last long. Gradually the net closed in on me and I was driven nearer and nearer to Christianity, half of me wishing it were true, and half resisting violently'.[7]

Though holidays were often spent sailing with her parents, every spring Evelyn would accompany her mother on a visit to the continent and it was in Chartres Cathedral and in Italy that she began to become attracted to Roman Catholicism. Back in England, she arranged to spend a few days in a convent but fled after the fourth day, 'otherwise I should have submitted then and there'. The day after this she was 'overcome by an overpowering vision which really had no specific Christian element and yet convinced me that the Catholic religion was true.'[8]

She now came under the influence of Monsignor R.H. Benson, a former Anglican and son of an Archbishop of Canterbury, who was tolerant of her doubts and did not try to hustle her into conversion. Shortly before her marriage she told Hubert of her intention to become a Roman Catholic and was quite unprepared for the 'storm of grief, rage and misery on his part'. Above all, it was the confessional that worried him. He could never again, he said, trust her or have mutual confidence, with a priest between them. She put off entering the Roman Catholic Church for six months and the marriage went ahead. Shortly afterwards a papal encyclical appeared, strongly condemning the modernist theologians by whom Evelyn was mostly influenced. She felt that she could not surrender her intellectual honour; thus she never became a Roman Catholic, although until she was over forty she continued to attend that Church's Masses without taking the Sacrament.

Evelyn was 32 when at last she married Hubert, who was four years her senior. For almost the whole of the rest of her life she lived with him in a house in London, just round the corner from her parents. It was now, after the experiments of the novels, that she wrote the books on mysticism for which she became famous. Her longest and best known work, *Mysticism*, appeared in 1911. At the time when she wrote, the word was suspect: to many it had connotations of fanaticism and hysteria and even of dabbling with the occult. In the first part of the book Evelyn examined the subject from the aspects of theology, psychology and symbolism, and defined mystics as 'the pioneers of the spiritual world'; 'We have no right', she declared, 'to deny validity to their claims merely because we lack the courage necessary to those who would prosecute such explorations for themselves'. In the second part she illustrated the mystic life by record after record of mystical experience. She divided her way into five sections. The first was the Awakening of Self, the second was the Purgation of Self, when all things are stripped from the mystic; this is followed by the Illumination which, however, turns into the Dark Night when the soul is deprived of all sense of the presence of God. Finally the soul enters into the Unitive Life. Here, the writer

insists that the mystic in union with God does not necessarily remain a contented contemplative, but acquires the
creative energy to open the way to the Kingdom of Heaven
to others.

In the final chapter Evelyn linked the experience of the
mystics to the life of contemporary Christians. Far from being
academic or unreal, the history of the mystics, she maintained,
is vital for the deeper understanding of the history of humanity.
Every person who awakes to consciousness of a reality which
transcends the normal world of sense is put upon a road which
follows at low levels the path which the mystic treads at high
levels. 'I do not care whether the consciousness be that of an
artist or musician, striving to catch and fix some aspect of the
heavenly light or music and denying all other aspects of the
world in order to devote themselves to this; or of the humble
servant of science, purging his intellect that he may look upon
her secrets with innocence of eye; whether the higher reality be
perceived in the terms of religion, beauty, suffering; of human
love, of goodness or of truth. However widely these forms of
transcendence may seem to differ, the mystic experience is the
key to them all'. . . . 'We are then', she concludes, 'one and all
the kindred of the mystics . . . Their attainment is the earnest
money of our eternal life. To be a mystic is simply to participate
here and now in the real and eternal life; to the fullest, deepest
sense which is possible to man'.[9]

Mysticism has been described by one of Evelyn's biographers
as 'romantic and engaged rather than dispassionate and
objective, empirical rather than theoretical, actual rather
than historical'.[10] Its success was immediate. At a time when
William James and Bergson were in vogue, its psychological
approach appealed to many, including theologians, who saw
psychology as the key to the understanding of human advance
in intelligence and creativity. It fitted with the effervescent
optimism before 1914 of the cultured class, with its belief in
the 'life force' and in the inexorable progress of the human
race towards a greater fulfilment of its potentialities.[11]

Between 1911 and 1914 the book went through three large
editions. It seemed, commented Dean Inge, that the whole
world was going over to mysticism. Evelyn followed up in
1913 with *The Mystic Way* which has been described as 'a

tour de force, a complete takeover of the New Testament and early church history by mysticism and their thorough reinterpretation almost exclusively as a record of mystical experience'.[12] In 1914 a reviewer in the *Quarterly Review*, confronted by eight mystical works, three of them under Evelyn's name and two more by her under a pseudonym, reflected that the interest in the subject was a reaction to Victorian ideals of material success. Men were becoming introspective and concerned, he said, with the great question of the value of life which is bound up with consciousness and its relation to the universe. This, it seemed, was peculiarly the province of the mystic, and Evelyn Underhill's *Mysticism* had done more than any other single work to popularize the subject.[13]

For Evelyn there were many consequences of the fame which these books brought. She became a Fellow of Queen's College, London. She came to the attention of Rabindranath Tagore, with whom she collaborated in the publication of an English translation of the poems of the Indian mystic Kabir. 'It is almost immaterial', one of her biographers dryly observes, 'that the poems which they gave to the world are almost certainly not by Kabir and gave an impression of his doctrine totally at variance with reality'.[14] Her books brought her the friendship and spiritual counsel of Baron von Hügel. There was a flood of letters from her readers seeking advice on their own spiritual problems. The pattern was thus set by which the rest of her life was to be devoted to religious work, public and private, though frequently punctuated by holidays abroad, usually with her husband. It was ironical that at the time when she first found herself obliged to advise others she herself was tormented by doubts and had found a home neither in the Roman Catholic Church nor in the Church of England.

Eventually, between 1917 and 1920, she became a practising member of the Church of England, but still found herself at times in the depth of misery and despair. In 1920 she persuaded Baron von Hügel to become her spiritual director, which he remained until his death in 1925. It was to him, she said, 'that, under God, I owe my whole spiritual life'.[15]

In agreeing to become her Director, von Hügel pointed out that they were both very busy people but he recognised 'How large is your public. How many souls will be led right or wrong by yourself with your rare charm of style, large knowledge of literature and delicate interestingness of character ... You can and do reach more people than I can ever expect to reach myself.'

Von Hügel was a loyal though critical member of the Roman Catholic Church. His wide international contacts and reputation were such that he avoided censure after the papal encyclical of 1907 which condemned the Modernists, although he had been at the centre of the movement. He had a tolerant attitude to the Church of England and never attempted to persuade its members to cross over to Rome.

Many of the letters between Evelyn and von Hügel survive. In these Evelyn explained how for weeks she knew herself to be unmendably displeasing to God, suffocated by the inescapable sense of sin and utter rottenness. She brooded whether her spiritual experiences might be imagined and subjective. She was, she said, vain about her achievements and reputation. She had doubts which were absolute torture, paralysing her faith at the roots. She questioned the Virgin Birth, the physical resurrection and the miracles in St John's Gospel. She accused herself of egoism in her personal relationships, exercising 'claimfulness and jealousy'.[16]

Von Hügel in reply would gently rebuke her for scrupulosity, for excessive self observation and self reproach. She suffered, he said, from overintellectualisation, and as a remedy he advised her to devote time to visiting the poor. The only mortification which he prescribed was self denying work. He told her that she was mistaken ever to expect absolute certainty about her spiritual revelations. He exhorted her to devote regular times to corporate worship, 'Thus your visible religion will safeguard your invisible religion, and your invisible religion will give freshness and variety to your visible religion.'[17]

When she exclaimed, 'Unless I leave my professional vanity at the Cross, I may as well give up altogether', he told her, 'This is excessive', and that to the end of her life she would have to struggle on after falling into such faults.[18]

Just before he died there was a last exchange of letters in which Evelyn explained that she was still intermittently in constant conflict with hateful feelings of claimfulness, bitterness, jealousy and uncharitableness which swamped her soul in spite of desperate struggles. The Baron in his reply asked her to try to alter the 'vivacious, irritated or confusing attention' which she gave to her soul, 'drop, gently drop by a quiet turning to God and Christ and the poor and you will grow in peace and power'. He also suggested that she cut down on the work which she was doing.[19]

She had felt, she said, 'very safe and happy sitting in his shadow' but she treasured and quoted in turn to those who sought her own advice his remark, 'The best thing we can do for those we love is to help them escape from us'.[20]

Whilst she was thus being helped by von Hügel, and indeed until the end of her life, Evelyn was herself advising an increasing number of people who wrote to her about their spiritual problems after reading her books. Though at first she was dismayed by the 'ever-growing crowd of people who have had visions and want to tell me what they are like,' in time she came to see this counselling as her most important vocation. 'If we educate intellects', she pondered, 'surely we must take account of them in religion, as in everything else ... I feel the ideal thing – and for me the only way – is to get people individually, one by one, when a door is opened to one. The idea of talking generally about anything that really matters makes me squirm'.[21]

Three years after her death Charles Williams brought out an edition of her letters. She never seems to have failed to reply or to invite her correspondents to visit her. Wherever she might be, on her husband's yacht, on their archaeological tours abroad, even in a pause on a country walk, sitting on the ground, she would write modest, firm but loving letters, sometimes to individuals whom she would never meet. At times her letters from her London home are interrupted by the need to organize a party for visiting lawyers or to go down to the garden 'to catch 300 slugs'.

Most often she exercised a calming, decompressing influence. 'Forget the word "progress" for a year'. 'Develop and expand the wholesome natural and intellectual interests of your life – don't allow yourself to concentrate on the religious side only. ... Your spiritual life is still based on too much feeling and not enough on *will* ... Your chief prayer must not be to *see* Him first and always, but to be useful to Him first and always'.[22]

As she grew older she insisted more on the importance of institutional religion; 'A moderate regular sharing in the degree suited to each will in the end enrich, calm and deindividualize our inner life ... No amount of solitary reading makes up for humble immersion in the life and worship of the Church. ... In this one must beware of fastidiousness'. Though she admitted that Protestant hymns of the Church of England were dreary and Roman popular favourites even worse, she explained that 'The Church must provide for all her children at every level of culture, and this is a discipline which it is often hard for the educated to accept. It provides splendid training in character and humility'.[23]

To those who asked her to recommend mortifications she suggested that the austerity of the Saints should be left to the Saints, and that for many of us the most appropriate mortification is that of the tongue, a careful guard on all amusing criticism of others.[24]

Her advice was often expressed in vivid or homely phrases. To one she wrote, 'Knock down the partition between living room and oratory, even if it does mean tobacco smoke and incense getting a bit mixed up'; advising someone not to mope over failures, she declared, 'The one point of real importance is to have enough trust and humbleness not to be discouraged even by really spectacular falls. In the sight of God a few somersaults aren't nearly as bad as going into the garden to eat worms'.[25]

In the First World War Evelyn worked in the Naval Intelligence Office in the preparation and translation of guide books. Here her colleague, Barbara Collingwood, to whom she was known as a respected poet and writer, 'had expected to meet a lady rather exquisitely withdrawn, but no one could have seemed less lofty and remote than Evelyn, meeting everyone and everything with a bit of a grin, and a splutter of laughter and a naughty irreverent joke'.[26] Evelyn even wrote a description of an invented county, complete with flora and fauna, which the proper authorities innocently passed to the printer.

But beneath this amused manner she was coming to grips in her writings with the position of the mystic in wartime.

In her preface to her book *Practical Mysticism* late in 1914 she recognized that 'The deep conviction of the dependence of all human worth upon eternal values, the immanence of the Divine Spirit within the human soul which lies at the root of a mystical concept of life, is hard indeed to reconcile with much of the human history now being poured red-hot from the cauldron of war'. Yet, she maintained, the mystic is not necessarily a quietist. Mystical consciousness indeed gives renewed vitality. She reminds her readers that in the lives of Joan of Arc, Florence Nightingale and General Gordon 'their national value was directly connected with their deep spiritual consciousness; their intensely practical energies were the flowers of a contemplative life.'[27]

During the First World War she published her second book of poems, *Theophanies*. Neither this nor its predecessor *Immanence* (1913) are now much read. As one of her biographers has noted, few things are deader than second-rate metaphysical poetry. She seems indeed to have recognized her limitations, for the last poem of *Theophanies* ends —

> Yet since the humble lover can
>   Ask all things, as the seers have told,
> Within thy mighty metric span
>   My faltering song do thou enfold
> That in the symphony of grace
>   The note of failure finds its place.

Henceforth she wrote no more poetry because she said, 'It was too easy'.[28]

In her three books, *Mysticism*, *The Mystic Way*, and *Practical Mysticism*, Evelyn had explained her view of mysticism, its consequences for those who took the mystic way and her own commitment to it. She had made available a large selection of texts, had reinterpreted the fundamental documents of the Christian religion and written a guide to the practice of contemplation. She had edited and made known to the public the works of medieval mystics such as those of Ruysbroeck, Richard Rolle, Jacopone da Todi, and Julian of Norwich, as well as the anonymous *Cloud of Unknowing*.

From about 1920 her writings were mostly of a different character. Her return to the Church of England

was warmly welcomed. In the disillusion of the post-
war period her writings on mysticism had a refreshing
appeal. She came to be much in demand at first to give
addresses and then to conduct retreats, and it was out of
these that most of her subsequent writings emerged except
for *Worship*.

Her main and frequent publications were now revised
texts of addresses given in the retreats which she conducted. They had a considerable vogue. 5,500 copies of
Abba, for example, were sold within three months of publication.

At first she was almost startled to find herself 'petted and
prosperous' in Church of England circles. 'When treated with
gravity and respect', she wrote to Lucy Menzies in 1923, 'I sort
of shrivel', faced as she described 'with adolescent leaders like
rows and rows of grim bunny rabbits, not understanding one
word'.[29]

Through her membership of COPEC (the Conference on
Politics, Economics & Christianity) in 1924, she came to
work with many of the most influential thinkers in the
Church. A more important contribution was made through
her membership of the Church's Commission for deepening
the spiritual life of clergy and laity.

From 1924 she began to conduct retreats, usually about eight
a year, each lasting for three days, with about 24 participants.
The objects at which she aimed were rest, recreation, renewal
and a recovery of quality and depth. Whilst services were conducted by a chaplain, she herself would lead meditations on
New Testament and other passages. She would prepare in considerable detail, pinning keynote quotations and reproductions
of pictures to the notice board, and would be available for
individual consultation twice a day. She would ask her friends
to pray for each retreat and at the end would reveal their
names. Whilst it was very unusual for a woman in her time
to conduct retreats for the laity, it was unprecedented for one
to be asked to address conventions of priests on their duties
and requirements.

In two addresses to the Worcester Diocesan Convention
in 1936 she spoke of prayer as the unique source of pastoral power, besides which intellectual and organizing ability

counted for little; and of how 'a pastor's first business was to be a friend of God.' 'The vocation of the Christian Minister is a supernatural vocation, and how can he fulfil it unless he leads a supernatural life?' she asked, and pointed out how the achievements of priests such as the Curé d'Ars and Father Wainwright depended on regular periods of absorbed devotion which no call was allowed to interrupt.[30]

She gave addresses to groups of religious teachers, theological students, health workers, wives of the Clergy, and on the BBC. She spoke to Methodists from Wesley's pulpit. Her biographers claim that she was the first woman to appear on the lecture list of Oxford University. Although in many of these activities she was a pioneer of women's roles, in a lecture on the Ideals of the Ministry of Women in 1932 she opposed the entry of women into the priesthood of the Church of England because 'such a break with Catholic traditions cannot be made save by the consent of a united Christendom.' On the other hand she desired the extension of women's ministry, 'gathering little groups around them, creating spiritual families on whom they exercise a transforming power, giving people God in a very unofficial way.'[31]

She often spoke about prayer, teaching that 'all worship must start with adoration, which reveals to us the insignificance of the "luggage" of life over which we make most fuss.' The illustrations in these talks were as homely as those in her letters. As a conductor of retreats, she would explain, 'I am no more the authority over your real journey than the conductor of a bus.'[32] She contrasted the 'Cat Way' and the 'Monkey Way': those who followed the former were as abandoned to God as entirely as a kitten is by its mother who carries it in her mouth. But those who followed the latter must strive to cling to God, just as the baby monkey clutches to its mother with all its little might as they swing through the trees.[33] She taught that the spiritual life and the practical life, the life of sense and the life of spirit, could not be separated. Through prayer the two sides could be reconciled. But the bread of life, she warned, seldom had any butter on it.

Worship (1936), was the most important book of her later years. In the first part principles of Christian worship were examined; in the second this led to discussion of the various traditions of Christian worship. She desired, she said, to show how Roman Catholicism, Protestantism and Orthodox are 'chapels of various types in the cathedral of the spirit' and to dwell on 'the shelter which they can offer to many different kinds of souls, rather than on the shabby hassocks, the crude pictures or the paper flowers'. Her intention was 'to interpret as much as I am able, and to criticize as little as I can'.[34]

As to her churchmanship now, she wrote to a Roman Catholic friend, the Abbot of Downside, in 1931, 'I solidly believe in the Catholic status of the Anglican Church as to Orders and Sacraments ... It seems to be a respectable suburb of the City of God − but all the same part of Greater London. I appreciate the superior food etc. to be had nearer the centre of things. But the whole point is that the Lord has put me here, keeps on giving me more and more jobs to do for souls here, and has never given me orders to move'.[35] The Church of Rome had its attractions, she admitted, but 'if all the Tractarians had imitated Newman's spiritual selfishness, English religion ... would be dead as mutton'.[36] She admired the Tractarians, but was not at home with extreme Anglo Catholics, preferring the tradition of Lancelot Andrewes, Jeremy Taylor and Ken.

Though she dwelt now rather less on mysticism, in her addresses she spoke of 'the passionate longing of the soul for God, the unseen reality, loved, sought and adored for Himself alone ... The mystic is not a person who has queer experiences, but a person for whom God is the one reality of life; he is a religious realist'. Again and again she insisted that great mystics are seldom dreary contemplatives, but people who have been remade in harmony with an overwhelming experience of God and act within a strange originality and power. Not only are Christians of various denominations such as St Francis, St Catherine of Siena, George Fox and Elizabeth Fry given as examples, but those of other creeds, such as Kabir and Plotinus.

Many honours and distinctions now came to her. She was made a Fellow of King's College, London and a Doctor of

Divinity of St Andrew's University. For several years she was religious editor of the *Spectator*.

Bishop Barkway observed that Evelyn's holiness was of the type which hid itself in the apparent ordinariness of her daily life.[37] She was saved from over-intensity by the holidays which she spent with Hubert, in Britain or abroad, bird-watching, observing wild flowers and exploring old churches; these she regarded as part of the pattern of life which God had given her. It was perhaps unfortunate for her posthumous reputation that so many of the letters which she wrote on these expeditions, dashed off lightly in the idiom of her time and class, came to be published. References to 'darling plants and flowers', 'larks shouting Alleluia', the 'heavenly gift of lavender bags' and even to the 'darling Feast of All Saints' have jarred upon the sensibilities of critics of later generations.

To her sorrow, Evelyn was childless. Cats had an important part in her life. They had birthday parties with candles and sardines. They wrote letters to her friends, and one of them even reviewed a book on cats for *Time and Tide*. At Christmas there was a cat's crèche at the tree.

In her later life Evelyn suffered from chronic asthma. In a retreat resolution in 1930 she wrote, 'Since it appears likely that I will have indifferent health for the rest of this life, I must face this quietly and gratefully and determine that it shall be the least possible worry and detriment to others'. Although to those who met her now it almost seemed as though a breath would blow her away, she appeared to give out a feeling of peacefulness, 'like a Chinese sage or a Benedictine monk'. Some were struck by 'the impression of light which came into the room with her'.[38] 'She soothed the tense and over-excited, trying to coax out of themselves the self preoccupied, broadening the horizons of the restricted, urging to desirable objectives the docile and eager'.[39]

Yet even now, as she told Bishop Frere, who had succeeded von Hügel as her spiritual director, she still felt alternations of vivid consolations and deprivations in her prayer, and continued to reproach herself about her failings in love and her privileges.

In the Second World War, unlike the first she maintained a pacifist position, though not aggressively. In its first year she and her husband stayed with friends in the village of Highden where she taught about religion in the primary school and also led a weekly intercession service in the parish church. In mid 1940 the Stuart Moores moved back to London to share a house with friends. During the bombing of London she expressed 'a certain odd satisfaction in being reduced to primitive conditions and having to practise abstinence about something one has always taken for granted, sitting very loose to possessions and much simplification of life.'[40]

She died in London from a thrombosis in 1941. One who was at her bedside recorded: 'She went through a good bit of pain which reached a climax when the distress seemed to be spiritual rather than physical. She was very strange and we thought she was dying. The next morning she became radiantly happy and remained all day in an ecstasy of triumph; from what she said she knew that something had been accomplished and the sufferers would not be disappointed. She was rejoicing in God and Christ in a way which was very different from her normally rather austere devotion. She fell asleep very peacefully. We watched the course of events with the greatest interest and exhilaration.'[41]

How then does Evelyn Underhill's life and work appear some 50 years after her death? There has recently been a major revival of her reputation in the United States where she has been provisionally included among those commemorated by the American Episcopal Church. Far more of her books are in print there than in Britain and a number of American writers have written commentaries on her work. The difference may partly be due to the fact that the stylistic 'cosiness' which sometimes grated on British taste had no such impact in America.

Her major contribution in her time, even though her books on the subject have been superseded, was her initiative in restoring to the Church of England the tradition of mysticism, which, unlike the Church of Rome, it had largely neglected. Her published addresses appear to have given comfort to many, for several collections remain in print, together with *Worship*.

The crisp legal form of expression, first of her father then of her husband, both eminent lawyers, was a sobering influence on the style of her writing, protecting it from the woolliness and gush of many contemporary popular books on religion. But her writing, as Charles Williams pointed out, was the least part of her vocation, which, he said, was 'rather to be a guide, in the end a light.'[42] She herself felt that 'my particular call, such as it is, concerns the interior problems of individuals of all sorts and opinions, helping them to get out of their own light.'[43] After her death an article in the *Times Literary Supplement* observed that she never ceased teaching and never ceased learning and that she possessed insights into the meaning of both the culture and the individual gropings of the soul that were unmatched by any of the professional teachers of the time.[44] 'The final test of holiness,' she said, 'is not seeming very different from other people, but being used to make other people very different; becoming the parent of new life.'[45]

Not the least interesting aspect of Evelyn Underhill's career is how she managed to live out her religious and mystical experiences in a secular world, married happily to an agnostic husband, over whom she loved to fuss, and throwing herself into shopping sprees in Paris, or bringing her religious friends together at her parties with writers, poets and lawyers. Her outward cloak of ordinariness enabled her to break down barriers without causing controversy.[46] Very quietly she set a precedent for women in the Church of England as retreat conductor, spiritual director and teacher in theology, all the more remarkable because she was attached to no centre or institute.

Her style of life depended on privilege and domestic service; according to Lucy Menzies she never boiled a potato in her life. In careless remarks in letters on her travels, never meant for publication, she could appear unimaginative about this, by saying for example that no one who did not care for mountains could understand the Synoptic Gospels, thus ignoring how small a proportion of the English population of her time could ever afford to see the Alps. Yet she constantly pulled herself up about the exercise of privilege and was more sensitive about social conditions than her critics have allowed.

'We are sewing the miserable little patches of what we call charity and social service,' she wrote, 'to the rotten garments of our social life. Thousands of us are eating what we suppose to be the bread of life at our brother's expense.'[47]

She had reached out to all sorts of people, not only theologians and priests but students and youth groups and radio audiences. As the Secretary of a Wives' Fellowship which she had addressed remembered, 'She could steer the frail craft of human longing out into the deep waters of the spirit, with such humour and vigour, yet with penetrating understanding.' As she soothed the tense and overexcited, coaxed the self-occupied out of themselves, broadened the horizons of the unimaginative and urged on the docile and eager, the desire seemed fulfilled that she had expressed on the eve of her 17th birthday: 'I hope that my mind will not grow tall to look down, but wide to embrace all sorts of things.' Perhaps, if she has sometimes been misunderstood, in her lifetime and since, it is in part because, as Bishop Barkway said, 'She had in a marked degree the divine gift of humour which the professionally religious person finds so disconcerting.'[48]

Further Reading

There is a biography by a friend, Margaret Cropper, *Evelyn Underhill*, London, 1958, and a more critical one, *Evelyn Underhill, An Introduction to her Life and Writings* by C.J.R. Armstrong, London, 1975; this contains a bibliography of works by and about her. Of Evelyn Underhill's many books, *Mysticism*, 1911 and subsequent editions, *The Mystic Way*, London, 1913, and *Practical Mysticism*, London, 1914, are still important, as is her later *Worship,* London 1932. She also wrote studies of individual mystics, and many of her collections of lectures and articles were published. Her posthumous *Collected Letters*, London 1943, is important in itself and for an introduction by Charles Williams. Bishop Lumsden Barkway wrote an article on her in E.Underhill, *Collected Papers*, London, 1946, and Lucy Menzies contributed a memoir in E. Underhill, *Light of Christ*, London, 1944. Her collections of poems, *Immanence*, London 1913, and *Theophanies*, London, 1916, seem little read. Among recent American works are Dana Greene, *Evelyn Underhill – Artist of the Infinite Life*,

New York, 1990, and Grace A. Brame, *The Ways of the Spirit*, New York, 1990.

Notes

1. Michael Ramsey in C. Armstrong, *Evelyn Underhill*, London, 1975, pp. IX, X.
2. Valerie Pitt, 'Clouds of Unknowing' in *Prism*, Vol. III, No. 3, June 1959, pp. 7–12.
3. D. Greene, *Evelyn Underhill*, London 1991, p. 147.
4. Evelyn Underhill, *Letters*, ed. Charles Williams, London 1943; M. Cropper, *Evelyn Underhill*, London 1958.
5. E. Underhill, *A Bar Lamb's Ballad Book*, London, 1902.
6. C. Armstrong, *Evelyn Underhill*, London, 1975, p. 91
7. E. Underhill, *Letters*, London, 1945, p. 127.
8. Cropper, *op. cit*, p. 28.
9. E. Underhill, *Mysticism* 12th edition, 1967, pp. 444–7.
10. M. Cropper, *Evelyn Underhill*, London, 1958, p. 109.
11. Armstrong, *op. cit.*, p. 126.
12. Armstrong, *op. cit.*, p. 146.
13. L. Johnston in *Quarterly Review* Vol. 220 (1914), p. 220, cited in Armstrong, *op. cit.*, p. 155.
14. Armstrong, *op. cit.*, p 144.
15. Cropper, *op. cit.*, p. 68.
16. Armstrong, *op. cit.*, p. 210ff.
17. Cropper, *op. cit.*, p. 69.
18. *Ibid.*, p. 94.
19. Armstrong, *op. cit.*, p. 235.
20. E Underhill, *Letters, op. cit.*, p. 230.
21. *Letters, op. cit.*, p. 139.
22. *Letters*, p. 197.
23. *Ibid.*, pp. 152, 261, 272, 273.
24. *Ibid.*, p. 259.
25. *Ibid.*, pp. 212, 227.
26. Cropper, *op. cit.*, p. 58.
27. E. Underhill, *Practical Mysticism*, London, 1914, p. VIII–X.
28. Cropper, *op. cit.*, p. 59 ff.; Armstrong, *op. cit.*, p. 173; E. Underhill, *Theophanies*, London, 1916, p. 117.
29. Cropper, *op. cit.*, p.117.
30. E. Underhill, *Collected Papers*, London, 1946, p. 121ff.
31. E. Underhill, *Mixed Pasture*, London, 1933, p. 113.
32. G.A. Brame, *The Ways of the Spirit*, New York, 1990, p. 19.
33. Armstrong, *op. cit.*, pp. 269–70.

34. E. Underhill, *Worship*, London, 1936, p. XII–XIII.
35. Cropper, *op. cit.*, p. 166.
36. *Ibid.*, p. 177.
37. E. Underhill, *An Anthology of the Love of God*, London, 1953, p. 18.
38. Armstrong, *op. cit.*, p. 244.
39. *Ibid.*, p. 285.
40. Cropper, *op. cit.*, p. 229.
41. Armstrong, *op. cit.*, p. 291.
42. *Letters, op. cit.,* p. 24.
43. Armstrong, *op. cit.*, pp. 266–285.
44. E. Underhill, *An Anthology of the Love of God*, London, 1953. p. 17.
45. *Evelyn Underhill, Modern Guide to the Ancient Quest for the Holy*, ed. Dana Greene, Albany, USA, 1988, p. v.
46. A.M. Allchin, 'Evelyn Underhill and Anglican Spirituality.' unpublished lecture in Washington Cathedral, 1991, p. 6.
47. *Letters, op. cit.*, p. 12.
48. Armstrong, *op. cit.*, p. 285.

PART III

COMMUNITIES

Octavia Hill

Pandita Mary Ramabai

Eglantyne Jebb

Caroline Chisholm

Christina Rossetti

Evelyn Underhill

Mother Harriet Monsell, at the time of her marriage, 1839

Mother Cecile

Sister Dora

Mary Slessor and her adopted children

Florence Nightingale

Florence Nightingale

Elizabeth Fry

Catherine Booth

7

Mother Harriet Monsell (1811–1883)

*'Sisters must always be ready to leave God for God –
to leave God in devotion to seek God in those for whom
He shed His blood.'*

One of the most important consequences of the Oxford Movement was the revival, for the first time since the Dissolution of the Monasteries in the sixteenth century, of religious Sisterhoods within the Church of England. That they came to be accepted after violent initial opposition owes much to Harriet Monsell who was described by J.M. Neale, when he was seeking advice on the establishment of his own Sisterhood, as 'the most sensible woman I ever met.'[1] Though Harriet Monsell had other outstanding and spiritual qualities, common sense was perhaps that which was required more than any other for the Sisterhoods' survival in a climate of wild allegations and serious setbacks. For in the early Sisterhoods the first Superior of the Community of St Mary the Virgin at Wantage rapidly followed its inspirer, Archdeacon Manning, into the Roman Catholic Church. The Society of the Holy Trinity, of which Lydia Sellon was Superior, was bitterly attacked in pamphlets and the press; Mother Lydia was described as living in luxury whilst her Sisters were dying of their mortifications. When Neale established his Sisterhood at East Grinstead, a major riot took place at the funeral of a Sister who was rumoured to have been lured into the Community, persuaded to leave her money to it and allowed to die of neglect.

    Harriet O'Brien was born into one of the oldest families in Ireland, which traced its descent from King Brian Boru. Her father, Sir Edward O'Brien, Bart., owned the large estate of Dromoland in County Clare where she grew up with eight brothers and sisters. When her eldest brother became head of the clan as Lord Inchiquin she acquired the prefix of 'The Honourable'. Whilst the boys went to English public schools

161

and universities, the education of the girls was desultory; she used to say later that she wished that she had enjoyed as regular an education as the children in the orphanages under her care. The O'Briens were staunchly attached to the Established Church. Her father and two brothers served as Members of Parliament; one of the latter, William Smith O'Brien, led the Irish rebellion of 1848 and was transported to Van Dieman's Land; his statue now stands in O'Connell Street in Dublin as a Nationalist hero.

At the age of 28, shortly after the death of her father, Harriet married Charles Monsell. He was four years younger than herself and was studying theology after abandoning the law. Her mother only gave her consent reluctantly because of his poor health and prospects. Harriet accompanied her husband to Oxford where he completed his theological studies; there they both came strongly under the influence of the Oxford Movement and in particular of Dr Pusey. Charles Monsell was ordained, and served first as his father's curate in Derry and then as a prebendary of Limerick Cathedral. He and Harriet stood firm when a number of their Oxford friends followed Newman over to Rome. A few years after their marriage Charles' health gave way. The remainder of his life was spent in a losing fight against tuberculosis, much of it in Italy. Early in 1850 in Naples, after receiving Communion from an Anglican chaplain, he died quietly, lying on Harriet's arm. She wrote to her sister 'Let none delude themselves with the idea that the Church of England cannot train saints for glory and that her sacraments cannot support a dying hour.'[2]

Kneeling by her husband's body, Harriet consecrated the rest of her life to God's service. She had no fixed plan, but it happened that her sister and brother in law, the Rev. & Hon. Charles Harris, were at Clewer on the outskirts of Windsor, helping temporarily with the organization of a House of Mercy as a refuge for 'penitents' – former prostitutes and mothers of illegitimate children. Harriet went to stay with them and helped at the House of Mercy; when they moved to a permanent post elsewhere she remained in Clewer to continue to work.

The refuge had been set up by Rev. T.T. Carter, Rector of Clewer, with whom she was to work closely for the rest of her life. Carter had been at Christ Church, Oxford where he had been well acquainted not only with Newman, Pusey and Keble but with W.E. Gladstone; he was profoundly affected by the Tractarians. Until this time, although there were several secular 'penitentiaries' in England for rescuing 'fallen women', the Church of England was doing nothing for them. Carter's parish contained some of the worst slums in England. These, together with the presence of army barracks and of railway 'navvies', fostered prostitution. Under Carter's guidance the House of Mercy was set up and run by local ladies, but Carter was convinced that in the long run the work could only be carried out effectively by a religious Sisterhood. 'The Sister of Mercy,' he maintained, 'occupies in relation to the object of her care a totally different position from that of any paid worker, a position which implies a personal devotedness which is the truest note of Christ's love ... It influences where all the influences have failed.'[3] Gradually Harriet came to feel that this was her vocation. In 1851 she was clothed as a Sister of Mercy. In the following year she was professed in the presence Samuel Wilberforce, Bishop of Oxford, and instituted as the first Superior of the Community of St John Baptist, together with two companions.

How the Community would develop depended not only on Carter and Harriet Monsell, but on Wilberforce, who became its Visitor. Although he and Dr Phillpotts of Exeter were at the time the only Bishops who were prepared to take responsibility for Sisterhoods in their dioceses, Wilberforce, who had been seared by the defection of three brothers and two brothers in law to Rome, made firm conditions. No life vows were to be taken by members of the Community and Pusey was to have nothing to do with the place. Although Mother Harriet had been recommended by her husband to go to Pusey as her spiritual director, she accepted his exclusion, as well as the prohibition of vows so long as Wilberforce was Bishop, recognizing his feeling that 'Sisterhoods are at present an experiment amongst us: a failure at this moment might deprive us of them permanently. I therefore am bound to use every precaution to prevent their failure.'[4]

He remained nervous. 'Dear Carter,' he wrote, 'is acted on by these women far too much, and kept from heartily and with a strong English tone putting down the sentimentalism which leads to Rome.'[5] He visited Clewer for a long talk with Mother Harriet. His diary recorded that he told her that 'No one should be admitted who would not be contented with the spiritual aid of Bishop or Chaplain, else it would become a mere nest of true Puseyites. Also an absolute removal of crucifixes. Mrs Monsell approved. She said "No doubt Sister − would go if she were required to give up the crucifix." I replied that if so she was not for us.'[6]

He forbade habitual confession, telling Carter 'You must not let the soft influence of the women's souls ... make you into a *Director*.'[7] He addressed a letter to the Sisters telling them that 'Whilst the Church of England cultivated a tone of serious earnest but sober devotion in prayer, Rome appealed to the animal sensation in our nature. Whilst the Church of Rome strengthened the power of the priest over the people by making each soul subject to a Director, the Church of England endeavoured to strengthen the individual character.' He directed that Roman Catholic devotional books must not be used.[8]

Mother Harriet complied diplomatically. She ordered those Sisters who wore crucifixes to do so under their habits. If they wished to read Roman Catholic devotional books, in default of Anglican ones, they were not prevented from doing so in the privacy of their rooms. No enquiries were made as to whom they consulted about their spiritual welfare when away from the house. The Bishop as Visitor had no desire to look too closely for what he did not wish to find.

Mother Harriet's problems with Rev. T.T. Carter were of a quite different kind. Their Churchmanship indeed was similar, both having been strongly influenced by the Tractarians. Though initially he was against vows, eventually the Sisters convinced him that they were desirable. He had a low regard however for the capacity of women to manage their affairs. 'Ordinarily woman is most honoured when least exposed to public notice,' he began his Life of Harriet Monsell, and he wrote to W.E. Gladstone 'A woman cannot be recognized as a responsible authority − this is not in accordance with Scripture and natural law. There is needed an officer between the Bishop-Visitor and the Superior, acting like the Father in an R.C. Convent, who should adopt rules, see that they are kept, admit or reject Sisters in concert with the Superior and sanction all her proceedings in matters of discipline. This office I take to be the Warden.'[9]

Mother Harriet thus had to work under a much closer control than did the Mother Superiors of most other Sisterhoods. Carter appointed all male committees, composed equally of clergy and laymen, to manage the Community's affairs. Mother Harriet usually manipulated them successfully, though their caution tried her. On one occasion when the committee refused to approve a contract to build St Andrew's Hospital at Clewer because funds were not assured, Mother Harriet, as Carter recalled, 'greatly aroused,' herself signed the contract and took responsibility for collecting the funds.[10]

Upper and middle class mothers of girls who wished to try their vocations could now confidently entrust them to a Community which had the Bishop as its Visitor, a married parish priest as its Warden and the Hon. Mrs Monsell, widow of a clergyman, as its Mother Superior. If they enquired further, they were relieved to learn that entrants were not accepted without the consent of their parents and were allowed annual holidays to visit their families; also that no vows were taken and that Sisters retained the right to dispose of their private assets in their wills.

Thus the number of entrants and scope of the work increased more rapidly than that of any other contemporary Sisterhood. Only three years after the founding of the Community its huge neo-Gothic buildings were opened. Perhaps what impressed visitors most was that the care of the 'penitents' was entirely undertaken by the Sisters themselves, 'ladies' who had been gently brought up with numerous servants to wait on them. Most of the penitents did laundry work, including that of one of the Houses of Eton College, though those with weaker consitutions did needlework. All received religious instruction and each was under the care of a particular Sister who kept in touch with her when she left. After a two year course, most were found places in domestic service. Some however preferred to remain and lead consecrated lives in the House of Mercy.

As the number of Sisters increased, other Houses of Mercy came to be run, though not owned, by the Community, in Oxford, London, Devon, Salisbury and elsewhere. Mother Harriet considered however that not all Sisters had the gifts required for working with penitents. She was particularly glad to broaden the Community's scope because it had been the hope of herself and her husband, having no children of their own, to found an orphanage with a religious character. The Community soon found itself establishing an orphanage at Clewer for children who came from London. Later, other orphanages were founded in London and elsewhere. From the beginning the Sisters visited the poor in their homes. Almost inevitably from this work a convalescent hospital developed. In the same way a Ragged School was started which led to more formal teaching when the Education Act of 1870 brought elementary education for all. Eventually the work spread abroad, to New York whilst Mother Harriet was Superior and to India within her lifetime.

Shortly after her death Canon Furse, who had been T.T. Carter's curate at the time, recollected Harriet Monsell at the beginning of her work —

'No one would have described her as specially meditative, retired, profound, far sighted. She was not literary or scholarlike or imaginative ... Hers was the brightest and gayest of natures, with a quick, clear knowledge of men and manners, the sharpest commonsense, great confidence in her power of managing, which was due neither to imperiousness or intrigue, but to that ingenuousness which has neatly been described as the temper which trusts others and expects to be trusted. Her sympathy was a vast power.'[11]

Not only her background but her approach was unusual. As Carter wrote 'It would be a mistake to expect to find in Harriet Monsell one trained according to ordinary rule, and confined to the special obligations of the religious life. She was of a nature which could not have borne to be cast in a strictly conventional mould ... And indeed she had her training before she became a Sister ... of a heart and mind that had tasted of the bitterest sorrow, and in its surging depths had found the secret of an undoubting trust in God.'[12] She retained her interests in the outside world and remained 'Aunt Harriet' to her numerous nephews and nieces.

Mother Harriet's limited formal education was compensated for by a considerable ability to see to the heart of a problem and then to go ahead with what one Sister called 'the most living power I have ever come across. She would never allow discouragement'. This was the secret of the influence which she exercised over the penitents; they began to think that they must do better when they saw she expected it of them. Even when she gave a rebuke she did it in a way that would encourage.[13]

She had a very real love of liberty, accepting suggestions and acknowledging her own faults. Because her strong sense of justice was recognized, decisions which were unwelcome were more willingly accepted. Whenever a new enterprise was started outside Clewer, she would entrust considerable independent authority to its Sister Superior and would then spend much time in prayer on its behalf. She did not object to being disturbed in her prayers, and would sometimes give instructions on her knees.

Her most beautiful quality, her Sisters recollected, was her motherliness. Nothing was too trivial for her to be interested in. She spoke and wrote to her Sisters sometimes earnestly and sometimes playfully and in homely terms. 'Treat your life as a drawing,' she wrote to one. 'Place the main features right and leave the rest to God to fill in ... A peach requires mellowing: do not worry or feel it, else you destroy the bloom. Do the same with your life.'[14]

Her messages generally followed the same lines. Sisters should seek the grace of simplicity. Their lives must be practical. 'How irrepressibly practical was the life of our Blessed Lord on earth, ever ready for everyone's need, ever absent from self.' They should not seek to plan their lives. 'Plans are God's not yours. Leave them to Him and let Him gradually unfold what He would have you do ... Look at my life. I made no plans. When I sailed out of the Bay of Naples after my husband's death, I felt there was some work I must do for God ... Then he shewed me step by step what to do.' And they must not let themselves be overwhelmed by the work allotted to them. 'Another might do it better, but God has sent you to do it and no one else.'[15]

There were two frequently recurring themes. Firstly from her husband she had acquired the profound conviction that the Church of England had within its resources the power to develop both the contemplative and active sides of the supernatural life. The two must be kept in balance. 'Sisters,' she said, 'must be prepared to leave God for God,' to switch as necessary between the contemplative to the active role.[16]

The second theme was a comparison between the religious life and marriage; in both, she said, it was the first six months that set the seal on the whole life. 'At first there is fussiness and anxiety about the love being felt and understood, but as years go on love grows deeper, more satisfying, more satisfied.'[17]

In accepting a novice she not only considered with great care how she would fit into the Community and what qualities she would bring to it, but would write to the relatives to ask if they accepted the application as God's call. She was insistent that the claims of family life were as important as those of the religious life. On the occasions when it emerged that there was no vocation, she was understanding and friendly. To one young women who was leaving the noviciate she sent her blessing, adding, 'You must leave here unfettered by the restraint of the Rule. You have tried it, and it did not suit you, do not try it again. Live simply in work for God, and attached to some Church and among poor whom you can love and serve.'[18]

Mother Harriet was not only an outstanding religious Superior. She also exercised a wide influence outside her Community; Canon Furse described her as the 'nimble correspondent and quick witted adviser and generous advocate in ten thousand difficulties, and few Belgravian mothers had a lighter hand in manipulating with tenderness and skill les affaires du coeur ... No one living in the world ... was more accessible than "The Mother of Clewer". No one devoting herself to social duties was the inmate of more English homes, and the recipient of the confidences of more hearts that needed counsel and comfort. The loves of the maiden, the pleasantries of the youth, the profession of the son, the anxiety of the father, the wedding clothes of the bride, the weariness of the widow, came all in turn for their crumb of comfort, and sat at her feet to be fed from her hand.'[19]

In letters to friends outside she shows great sympathy for 'the weary nothingness, the bane of middle class girls' lives, living a life with nothing to do but that which seems self pleasing.' And yet, she says, 'Living in the world is not serving the world ... It is as much your duty to entertain in your father's house as ours to invite the outer world to our commemoration day.' Again and again she insists that a life in the world can fulfil God's purpose as much as a life in a Community. 'It matters not what our entire course is if once we give our heart to God. It may be given in home life, in married life, in the consecrated life.'[20]

'Young ladies' lives are generally so desultory or so uncharted and irregular,' she said, 'that they may need to lay down some moderate rule for their life'; sometimes she would send them meditations. She shows a large understanding of the depression which seeps into such lives. 'Formerly, dear,' she writes to one young woman, 'the struggle was to overcome temper: now the struggle is to overcome a worse enemy, dreariness,' and yet, almost paradoxically, she explains, 'I believe that a quiet, aimless life, lived in the sunshine of God's will can be bathed in light and be a gladness and a warmth and cheer to others, simply because we have become so dead to ourselves and our own will. We live but to reflect His light and give this warmth to others.'[21]

In these letters she does not evade the cruellest problems. To a man whose terminal illness has been diagnosed she writes 'Nothing anyone can do can fill the solitude of your being but God ... It is no longer now how best to do the day's work but how best to live the day's life, with all its burden of suffering and weakness, to God's glory.' 'I sometimes think we want to make too light of things,' she wrote on another occasion. 'Pain *is* pain; sorrow *is* sorrow, and God alone who sends it knows how real our efforts may be to bear that which He means us to feel very keenly.'[22]

Patience was a quality she often urged on her younger correspondents – 'Remember God always works very slowly, very surely; ... we must work as God works, not with the great strides self love would like to work with. Try little things, not great things . . . Try to do little things for God's glory without letting anyone know.'[23]

'We must speak of ourselves, if we want to help others,' she believed. 'Our experience has been given us for others, not for ourselves alone.' One visitor, who was becoming hardened under a great sorrow, remembered how Mother Harriet had welcomed her by saying 'I know just how you are feeling and I know well how it was to feel hard and rebellious when my husband was taken from me. Sit down and I will tell you all about it.' 'I could not have spoken of my grief, only she told me all about herself and her own sorrow, and so I told her all and she comforted as no one else has ever done.'[24]

Her advice to those who consulted her from the outside world went further than conduct and morals, and acceptance of suffering. 'I feel,' she wrote to one of them, 'that God has been calling you to the highest point of union with his Divine Life, and you must be very true in following. And that following is not in the outer actions of your life, although they are the bulwarks and stays of it; but it is in the inner surrender of the soul, the willingness that self should suffer, be buffeted, cut down, cease to exist − no longer "I like it," but that God wills it; that life has no will but to respond unhesitatingly to the Divine Will.'[25]

Mother Harriet's aristocratic background and Irish charm enabled her to move easily in any circles. Queen Victoria, visiting the Community at Clewer from nearby Windsor Castle, found the Mother Superior 'an excellent person' and was impressed by the fact that all was 'pretty not gloomy.' Mother Harriet was not afraid to tease her: when the Queen asked why, although her visit was private, 'all whom we meet curtsey to me,' she replied, 'But, Your Majesty, they are not curtseying to you, but to me.'[26]

In addition to the Gladstones, she was on excellent terms with A.C. Tait, the Archbishop of Canterbury, who was married to her cousin. Mrs Tait had been considerably influenced by Charles Monsell and used to say that if she had not fallen in love with her husband she would have 'become a nun and a very bad one.'[27] Tait had been born a Presbyterian. As an Oxford don he had been a strong critic of the Tractarians. As Archbishop he had caused legislation to be passed to control ritual, the unauthorized use of which in churches had led to riots and public scandal. In 1875, with most of the other Bishops, he issued a pastoral letter which exhorted the clergy to obey legitimate authority, to refrain from disseminating doctrines contrary to Holy Scripture, and from disquieting their congregations by introducing novel practices and unauthorized ceremonies.

Mother Harriet wrote to him indignantly – 'I cannot be good and keep silence. Your "Irish cousin" cannot contain the Celtish spirit within her . . . Your pastoral comes like an icicle into the hearts of your sons . . . Do please set things a little straight in Convocation and claim for the English Church her Catholic position as a branch of the primitive church.'[28]

On other occasions she wrote to the Archbishop to entreat him to allow liberty of action to the clergy as regards Confession, to urge a spirit of tolerance in relations with Rome, and to express her dismay at the closure of St Alban's Church in London because the ritualist priest, Alexander Mackonochie, had been imprisoned.[29]

The tone was not however always passionate and critical. In 1879 she wrote to Tait 'I hope you have a good cheering congress, that you decapitate Penzance, squeeze G and B in a vice until he cannot stir his little hand or foot, and tell people everything has two sides, take which you like. That is my recipe for restoring peace.' She was a frequent visitor at Lambeth Palace and at the Taits' country home; after Mrs Taits' death she invited the Archbiship to come and see her in her retirement 'when the clouds are heavy.'[30]

Eventually Carter became caught up in the ritualist controversy and was denounced to the Bishop of Oxford for illegal practices. The Bishop deplored the practices, but even more the fact that the denouncer was not a member of Carter's congregation. He refused to prosecute and was upheld by the courts. Carter however resigned as Rector of Clewer; his parishioners built him a house and he remained Warden of the Community until long after Mother Harriet's death.

In 1875 Mother Harriet's health obliged her to resign her office as Superior. Her final message was 'My one exhortation to the Sisters is not to let the sparkle go out of the Community. I love that in a life of sacrifice they should give God a joyous service.'[31] She moved into a cottage near the Community's house at Folkestone. Here her condition steadily deteriorated, but even when she ceased to be able to write she continued to dictate. There was no impatience. She read the newspapers and used in her prayers the knowledge of political problems and personal needs of which she had read. Many visitors from within the Community and outside still came for her advice. More and more her time was spent in intercessory prayer. She said now that she felt she had done a more real work for God while stuck in her chair than in all her busy active working years. 'People often waste their energies in running about doing active work,' she reflected shortly before her death, 'and think that they serve God in this way, while all the time they utterly neglect the inner life of Communion with Him. We must not rob God. We must give Him His due ... What I want to impress upon you is that you must *live* the *life*, not merely do the work.'[32]

She died in 1883. Canon Furse ended his obituary: 'No one who ever talked and wrote so much kept more absolutely free of misunderstanding and offence. And she was one of the most hopeful women in the world. With a dead pull against the stream of public opinion for 25 years of a notorious work, overtaking and overpassing prejudice at every stroke, committed to a venture of great audacity, insisting on the creation of a work absolutely new in the English Church, with no optimistic and sentimental ignoring of hard and ugly facts, she lived by hope, which is more than clinging to it; and the facility and gaiety and security of her venturous life was the beautiful product of the hopefulness of her soul. When the history of the revival of Sisterhoods in our Church is written, a golden page will be given to Harriet Monsell.'[33]

Further Reading

T.T. Carter, *Harriet Monsell – A Memoir*, London, 1884. Valerie Bonham, *A Joyous Service – The Clewer Sisters and Their Work*, Windsor, 1989 and *A Place in Life – The Clewer House of Mercy, 1849–83*, Windsor, 1992.

A.M. Allchin, *The Silent Rebellion − Anglican Religious Communities 1845−1900*, London, 1958.
The writer is indebted to Canon A.T. Allchin for sight of an unpublished lecture, 'Living by Hope − Mother Harriet and the Revival of Religious Life in 19th Century England'.

Notes

1. A.M. Allchin, *The Silent Rebellion*, London, 1958, p. 79.
2. T.T. Carter, *Harriet Monsell − A Memoir*, London, 1884, p. 21.
3. Allchin, *op. cit.*, p. 70.
4. S. Wilberforce, *Life and Letters*, Vol. II, p. 168.
5. *Ibid*, II, p. 279.
6. *Ibid.*, II, p. 167.
7. S. Wilberforce Papers, Bodleian Library, c 22, f.179 May 18, 1854.
8. *Ibid,* c 22 f174, May 19, 1854.
9. T.T. Carter, *Harriet Monsell − A Memoir*, London 1884, p. vii. P. M. Rampton, The Thought and Work of T.T. Carter of Clewer, London, Ph.D. thesis, 1985, p. 69.
10. Carter, *op. cit.*, p. 38.
11. C.W. Furse in *The Guardian*, April 4, 1883, p. 898.
12. Carter, *op. cit.*, p. 38.
13. Carter, *op. cit.*, p. 43.
14. Carter, *op. cit.*, p. 70.
15. *Ibid.*, pp. 67, 126.
16. *Ibid.*, p. 58.
17. *Ibid.*, p. 52.
18. Valerie Bonham, *A Joyous Service*, Windsor, 1989, p. 79.
19. Furse, *op. cit.,* p. 899.
20. Carter, *op. cit.*, pp. 133, 136.
21. *Ibid.*, pp. 145, 158, 159.
22. *Ibid.*, pp. 155, 162.
23. *Ibid.*, pp. 168, 172.
24. *Ibid.*, p. 173.
25. *Ibid.*, p. 160.
26. Bonham, *op. cit.*, p. 78 and oral tradition of the community.
27. W. Benham, *Catherine and Crawford Tait*, London, 1879, pp. 213−215.
28. Archbishop A.C. Tait Papers, Lambeth Palace, Vol. 99, ff 292, 1879.

29. *Ibid.*, Vol. 79, ff197−8, 1858; Vol. 94, ff86−7, 1871.
30. *Ibid.*, Vol. 99, f.191, 1879; Vol. 99, f.292, 1879.
31. Carter, *op. cit.,* p. 185.
32. *Ibid.*, pp. 207, 215.
33. Furse, *op. cit.,* p. 899.

8

Mother Cecile of Grahamstown (1862–1906)

'Sparkle ... Don't let the fun go out of the place'
Mother Cecile's last message to the Community, 1906

Among those who read Miss Lonsdale's life of Sister Dora
of Walsall was the Bishop of Grahamstown in South Africa,
A.B. Webb. It was, he reflected, a grand and beautiful life,
but it did not multiply itself. There was no continuity in it.
It ceased with the individual existence and its results were not
gathered up by any who came after.[1]

These reflections were to shape the remarkable career of
Annie Cecile Ramsbottom Isherwood who was to become
Mother Superior of the Community of the Resurrection of
Our Lord in Grahamstown and who is commemorated in
the Calendar of the Anglican Church in South Africa. She
was born in Uxbridge, near London, in 1862. Her father
was an army officer and her mother an Australian. A happy
childhood was broken first by the sudden death of her mother
when she was 8, and then by that of her father in an accident
when she was 13. She attended a boarding school until she
was 15, after which she lived with the family of one of her
father's former fellow officers and continued her education
by attending lectures and classes.

One day when she was 16 she entered by chance St Peter's
Church, Eaton Square in Kensington and heard a sermon
by the Vicar, G.H. Wilkinson, which made a profound
impression. She asked the Vicar to prepare her for Confirmation and from his instruction, she would later say, the
Christ of St John's Gospel became the great human love of
her life. She devoted herself to the social work of the parish
and went to live with other workers at the St Peter's Mission
House.

It was at St Peter's Church a few years later that she heard
a sermon which was to be of equal importance in her life.

A.B. Webb, the newly consecrated Bishop of Grahamstown
who was seeking women missionaries for his diocese, preached
on the Conversion of St Paul, taking as his text 'I was not disobedient unto the Heavenly Vision'. Cecile felt a clear call;
after seeking the advice of the Vicar, she offered herself for
service in South Africa for three years and was consecrated as
a Deaconess. Shortly afterwards she set sail, together with the
Bishop and the party of twelve women workers whom he had
recruited, who were playfully known by the other passengers
as the 'Bishop's Widows' on account of the mournful black
bonnets which they always wore.[2]

During the voyage the Bishop had an excellent opportunity
to get to know and begin to assess the capacity of each of his
recruits in light of the plan which he had in mind. He had
recently been translated from the Diocese of Bloemfontein to
that of Grahamstown which had been bitterly divided by a
quarrel between the previous Bishop and the Dean, who eventually locked him out of the Cathedral. Bishop Webb saw his
first task as one of reconciliation – but who was to assist him
in it among the impassioned partisans?

He had become convinced in Bloemfontein of the need
for religious sisters and had obtained the services of some
of them from the Sisterhood of St Thomas the Martyr in
Oxford. This Order however was unable to spare members
for Grahamstown, and in any case he had come to believe
that it was necessary for a Sisterhood to be rooted within
a Diocese, with an allegiance to the Bishop, rather than to
a Mother House in Britain. He had set out his ideas during
his visit to England in a pamphlet on *Sisterhood Life and
Women's Work in the Mission Field of the Church*.

In this he pointed out that in South Africa there was not,
as in Britain, a supply of 'disengaged women', and that it
was useless to send these out to the colony because they were
sure to be absorbed by marriage soon after their arrival; once
married they would have little time for voluntary work because
of the lack of capable servants to take care of their homes.
Yet to extend mission work both to whites and blacks it
was even more important to change the attitudes of women
than men. There were 20,000 young warriors in Zululand,
he pointed out, who would not find women willing to marry

them until they had 'wetted their spears in blood'.... 'Such as the women are, such are the homes and such the civilization and the Christianity of Society. To reach that centre is women's work'.

What therefore was needed was the establishment in South Africa and in the colonies elsewhere of 'religious communities of women, pledged in some way to work for God and the Bishop' and who would 'supply the wants of God's Honour and of Man's good.' The members would work through education, personal influence, visiting and ministering, 'even as the holy women of old'. They must be selected with great care. Women who had domestic obligations, or who were useless at home or who sought excitement or self-importance must be rejected. Only those with a true vocation, a sense of which must often be patiently awaited, should be allowed to enter a Sisterhood, after a period of probation as a novice.

The Sisterhoods would be to the Church what the Staff College was to the Army. They would demonstrate an idea in practice and would be a safeguard against Romanism. Each would be under the rule of a Mother Superior and the spiritual direction of a Warden in Holy Orders. The Sisters, sitting as a Chapter, would elect their Mother Superior, but the nomination must be approved by the Warden before the appointment was made by the Bishop.

The essence of the plan was that the Sisters would be 'handmaids to the Bishop.'[3]

On arrival in Grahamstown, Cecile found herself helping to clean the pro-Cathedral and organizing Mothers' Meetings. It was a dull start, and to future novices she would confess that she had felt that 'nothing might come of this, there was so very little work at first.' But she did what she was asked to do with devotion, charm and constant good humour. To the Bishop it became clear that although she was only 21, she was the woman he needed, and he asked her to start a religious community, eventually to be known as the Community of the Resurrection of Our Lord. In 1884 first Cecile and then two others were clothed as novices. The Bishop found a property for the Community, happily called Eden Grove, where the three novices lived, together with two or three lay workers.

From the beginning the Community's main work was educational. A day school for children of middle class whites was started as St Peter's School. Then a Good Shepherd School was arranged at Eden Grove for children of the poorer classes. Here, Sister Cecile wrote ruefully, 'Our first and only pupil taught me missionary patience. If she had never learnt, it was equally certain I had never taught, and our first educational efforts were certainly sown with tears.'[4] Next there was the beginning of an orphanage: at that time there were no Children's Homes or workhouses, so waifs and strays were deposited in the prisons. A small orphanage and industrial home was therefore started where a simple education, including instruction in domestic work, was given.

The main source of finance was Sister Cecile's income, but the Community were very poor, as most of this went to pay off the mortgage on Eden Grove. The only two chairs were in the room in which visitors were received; the Sisters and their pupils sat on packing cases. If a visitor stayed for a meal one of the novices or workers had to do without it. A single pair of strong boots and one large cloak had to be shared in turn. Once, when there was no money at all in the house, an African priest brought five shillings. 'But we are doing nothing for your people,' the Sisters protested. 'No, but you will,' he replied.[5]

Sister Cecile never lost faith that prayer would pull the Community through. The most essential building, a chapel, was erected, paid for by Sister Margaret in memory of her mother; now whenever an emergency arose Sister Cecile would remark 'we must use our knees.' Gradually funds were raised by appeals in Britain and the work was extended. Hitherto the Sisters had cared mainly for white children. In 1886 a school for those of mixed race was started by them in Port Elizabeth. There they also established a Refuge for 'penitents', mostly former prostitutes, and their babies. By 1887, in addition to three lay workers, there were five novices in the Community, including a trained teacher and a nurse, but the latter died whilst nursing heroically in a fever epidemic. Bitterly though the Community felt the loss, Cecile comforted them by saying 'No Community can be really founded until one of its members has gone to be a living stone in Paradise'.

It was in this year that she was professed as a Sister, but in 1888 her health broke down and she was sent to England to recuperate. Whilst there she visited and was warmly welcomed by the Sisters of the Community of St John Baptist at Clewer, where she later sometimes sent her own Sisters for special training. But she could see, as she explained later, that 'though we want to copy the truth, simplicity and reality and faithfulness of the Rule at Clewer, we must not forget that it could never be reproduced here. Sisters are for the Church, not the Church for Sisters, and the Church here is not ready for that; so day by day we have to learn what He would form and mould us into'. Her brother and sister shared the widespread prejudice in England against Sisterhoods as 'Romanistic' and refused to meet her, but she recruited eleven new workers and brought them back with her to Grahamstown.

On her return the orphanage needed her urgent attention, for children were being sent to it from all over the Province, whether there was room for them or not. She had to spend long hours in the lobbies of the Cape Parliament to buttonhole members as they passed through and urge them to make provision for the abandoned children who were in the jails. Sometimes her activities were more exciting. A Malay woman who had sold her child repented whilst she was dying in hospital and asked Mother Cecile to rescue it. Armed with a magistrate's order and escorted by a policeman, she seized the child and, tucking it into the voluminous sleeve of her habit, bolted with it to the railway station, pursued by a mob.

The increased membership enabled new initiatives to be taken. Nursing staff were provided by the Community to enable a children's ward to be opened at the Port Elizabeth Hospital. In Grahamstown a boarding school was started for the children of the railway workers who were frequently transferred.

Mother Cecile had always wished the Community to work among African girls. 'The attitude about natives and native work makes my blood boil,' she wrote. 'We certainly in the Church can never do enough to make up for the great wrong our white race has brought to them'.[7] The Sisters started a school for Xhosa children in the Herschel District on the borders of Basutoland. This did not prove viable, as the parents were very poor. Another school for African girls was therefore started in Keiskama, closer to Grahamstown. A number of the Herschel girls followed the Sisters there to continue their training in industrial work or as pupil teachers.

In 1893 the new Superintendent General of Education in the Cape Colony, Dr Thomas Muir, appealed at a public meeting in Grahamstown for help in forming a teachers' training school for the Eastern Province, so that certificated teachers might be found locally, instead of being brought from England. Mother Cecile was at the meeting and within a few days presented Dr Muir with a plan, which he accepted, for the establishment by the Community, in close collaboration with the Government, of a Teachers' Training College. Although this was eventually to become their most important undertaking, a number of the Sisters were at first reluctant; they wanted to concentrate on teaching poor children, the poorer the better. Mother Cecile won them over to recognise that at this stage it was more important for the Community to train women teachers, British and Boer together, in a religious environment than to teach children themselves.

Many of the pupil teachers came from lonely farms and upcountry villages where there was little opportunity to attend church services. They would be at the College during the three most formative years of their lives, and would return to teach in places where the teacher's was often the only civilising influence. The College was thus established on a residential basis, and the nearby St Bartholomew's Church Primary School was taken over to provide opportunities for practical training. For the rest of her life raising money for this project became Sister Cecile's greatest burden, since the Government could not contribute to the capital or staffing costs because the College was specifically Anglican.

In 1899 there was a serious threat to the College. Dr Muir, who was a Presbyterian, addressed another public meeting in Grahamstown at which, although he expressed admiration for the work done by the Sisters, he pointed out that the buildings at St Peter's were quite inadequate; the Government however could not legally make a grant for the repair and extension of religious premises. He suggested therefore that the people of Grahamstown should come forward with a scheme to establish a non-denominational college into which St Peter's would be merged. The Government would then be able to pay for the capital and much of the recurring costs. The idea appealed to many nonconformists, though it was made clear by the Community that they would have to withdraw from teaching if such a scheme went forward. At a subsequent public meeting a resolution in favour of Dr Muir's proposal was defeated by one vote.

Mother Cecile, who had been in England when the crisis arose, returned to handle a fraught situation with characteristic skill and sensitivity. She persuaded the Government and the nonconformists to accept an arrangement by which the Sisters would continue to own and run the College, but nonconformists would be represented on its Governing Council. Further, Ministers of all denominations would be allowed to instruct their members in religion on the College premises. The Community undertook to pay for the extension of the building and to strengthen the teaching by bringing out a Cambridge graduate as the first male Principal. Not without difficulty Mother Cecile persuaded her own Church authorities to accept these arrangements, which were quite unorthodox in an Anglican College at the time.

The scheme worked well. Both Dr Muir, who later became Minister of Education in the Cape Government, and the nonconformist Ministers, through their membership of the College Council, came to be Mother Cecile's firmest supporters. She, however, was obliged to devote even more of her time to money raising.

The Community was sorely tested by the Boer War. Parents of girls in the Training College were fighting on both sides. Grahamstown was at one time surrounded by the Boers, and the Sisters took on extra tasks in nursing soldiers, far more of whom were dying of enteric fever than in action. But not a lesson in the College was missed. In 1900, in the middle of the War, 56 candidates were presented for the State Examination for Teachers, of whom 53 were successful.[8]

Once the War was over, Mother Cecile saw that the College had an even more important role in reconciling the Boers and the British. The older generation might never be able to forget and forgive, but a new generation could learn to overcome prejudice by working together.

In 1904 Dr Jameson, the Provincial Premier, attended the prize-giving ceremony, at which he praised Mother Cecile's broad and tolerant view of other religions as well as the attitude to race which the College was inculcating under her influence. 'She recognised in her large minded way', he said, 'that the only way to get rid of race feeling was to begin at the bottom'.[9]

Two aims had been set for Mother Cecile by Bishop Webb − the first was to forge the new Community into an instrument for God; the second was the organisation of an educational programme, inspired by the Anglican religion, but in close collaboration with the government, which would reach out to all races. We have seen how she set about the second task. When she died there were 236 students at the Training College; they included not only South African girls but those who had come out from Britain, often at the expense of the South African Emigration Society; Mother Cecile considered that it was much better for the immigrants to take their training in local conditions than in Britain. There were 47 Africans in the Industrial School, and 145 children in the orphanage.[10] The latter were very dear to Mother Cecile, who had herself been an orphan; she eventually succeeded in persuading the Government to acknowledge its responsibility to make provision for them also elsewhere in the Colony, so that waifs and strays were no longer committed to jail.

There were now 81 Sisters and novices, all selected and admitted by her as Mother Superior. How she discharged her first task, the development of the spirit of the Community, can be illustrated from the letters which she wrote to them when she was in England or from Grahamstown when they were out in the field. In these she often quoted from the Bible and Book of Common Prayer but seldom from any other book. There is no evidence in her letters of the influence of Saints or mystics.

She guided her novices and Sisters but did not seek to press them into a mould. 'Every nature ought to be allowed to unfold like a flower', she said, 'for different souls reflect different sides of our Blessed Lord's life'. Thus the Community reflected unity in diversity, and she would deliberately seek out new entrants who could bring new gifts. She was incapable of taking an unintelligent view of persons or things, or one that was unjust or unsympathetic; nothing that others cared about did she hold lightly. As for her rule over the Community, 'I do believe intensely', she wrote, 'in loving truly, *expecting* the best, praising when one can. Then when there is need for reproof there is, to the person reproved, the knowledge that personal pain has been given not only to our love but our ideal for them'. She rarely rebuked and generously forgave, but could be severe about waste, particularly of writing paper and soap.

Despite the setbacks and the financial anxieties, the Community was a happy one. 'People will only understand vocation', she said, 'when they see Sisters full of humble, loving, and unselfish joy'. She had the knack of drawing everyone into a conversation, and was a kindly tease.

The novitiate, she knew from experience, 'brings out rightly all the faults of character; and novices want infinite love and patience'. She told them firmly that 'there can be no measuring of the future ... The very essence is the acceptance of uncertainty in all the earlier stages of any true vocation'. Their start must be 'total renunciation and unceasing prayer ... Bring each person, each difficulty to Him; then really pray; then do what seems best, and then dismiss it and go on to the next.'

The object of the Community, she told its members, was to glorify Christ, firstly by the power of prayer and secondly by the power of sacrifice, in body, soul and spirit. In time they would come to think less and less of self 'because we realise that so much less remains of life for us to give to God and our neighbour; a wonderful joy comes in because the heart, giving all, is empty, to be filled with the peace of God'.

She urged 'quiet definite meditation on the life and character of Christ and then the bringing of our life and character, words and thoughts side by side with His'. But 'self knowledge will come from the Holy Spirit, not from your own introspection'. They should remember that 'as the end of religious life we are not Sisters for the sake of the beauty of our own life or character (that is only a means to an end) but pleasing God by being and doing'. She dwelt much on the need for patience and acceptance of God's will, even when its purpose was not understood. 'God,' she said, 'does not put us in the world to put the world to rights, but to do His will in our own little corner of it ... 'Tarry thou the Lord's leisure, be still'. He cannot work on us if we are all in a fuss'. 'It does help me so when I am impatient to fix my mind on the patience of God and on the love shown by Christ which won't take account of dullness or stupidity or perverseness, which has anticipated disobedience or gainsaying, which is not baulked by a failure or two, which goes on as if it had not failed at all ... and yet hides the disappointment and buries the bitterness.'

She reminded her Sisters that they could not excuse their sins by attributing them to their circumstances. 'God allows our environment. When we accept this humbly, and out of our failures learn to cry to God himself, our deeper life of prayer begins.'

'Sorrow', she said, 'comes for our own edification. Care is always to be cast on God'; but she did not always find it easy to do so herself. There was a loneliness in the life of a Mother Superior which often oppressed her. She became sore, she confessed, at not having a shoulder to lean on, 'and that makes one hard and bitter'. Her humility struck all who met her. In her letters she revealed her own struggle with her pride and temper. To one of her lay workers she said, 'I write and speak as one to whom our Lord has forgiven much ... If ever He has allowed me to serve Him in any little bit done for you, ask that it may come back in the gift of the really humble childlike heart to me, will you, dear?' 'The smashing up of all my plans', she wrote in 1901, 'has given me, I really believe, a deeper trust in God's eternal plan' certainly many things that don't go my way have ceased to fuss me a bit'. She constantly reminded herself as well as others 'how by the daily thwarting of our hopes and our plans we learn obedience by the things we suffer'.[11]

From these letters we may learn how the family which she had created saw her. Those outside it recognised not only her spirituality but, in spite of, or perhaps because of, her lack of formal education, her genius as an organizer. Michael Furse, the Bishop of Pretoria, considered her the ablest woman he knew. Rev. Eric Bodington who was Warden of the Community for some years and thus particularly close to her, described her genius as not so much an original one, but of the receptive, fertilizing kind. Ideas, he said, did not so much spring up in her mind, but were met by her in search of them. 'She had a quite noteworthy power of critically examining them, and assimilating from them what was going to be of service to our needs, and finally administering in such a way as to get the best result from them.' Bodington considered that this receptivity was sharper than it would have been had she been 'highly educated, and consequently more theological but less religious in the truest sense.'[12] It was probably no accident that he picked on this quality, for it was receptivity rather than original thinking which Bishop Webb had outlined in his book as the most desirable quality in a Sister. Cecile had no Mother Superior or Novice Mistress to instruct her, and it was thus the Bishop who was the most formative influence on her character.

Somewhat in the same way as she picked up, selected from and refined ideas thrown out by Bishop Webb, who was a notable religious leader but an erratic administrator, similarly on the Government side she responded to Thomas Muir, a man from a very different religious persuasion, but whose horizons were broad like her own. For she was determined to bring all her educational work into line with that of the State and to accept its standards and certificates of efficiency. Whilst he had started with a Presbyterian and bureaucratic suspicion of Anglo-Catholic teaching orders, her charm, ability and commonsense eventually caused Muir to press her to produce more and more teachers and warmly to support her fund raising campaigns.[13]

Her charm and empathy struck all sorts of people: as Eric Bodington described his first meeting with her: 'Her manners were perfect. They were the finished manners of a woman of the world, with just perhaps a touch of the purposed kindness of the Saint ... As she took us round her premises, she radiated an atmosphere not only of love and happiness but of life and distinction over the dullest details of the work ... It was impossible to be dull where she was.'[14]

Someone who called himself 'one of her frivolous, worldly friends' remembered how 'Her great attraction was that nothing was too bad for her. She entered into every bit of one's life and one could tell her anything, sorrows, joys, faults, and she sympathised with everything and always saw the amusing side of everything too, with that dear, dear twinkle in her eye'.[15]

This attraction, this magnetic influence drawn from her personal religion, and in particular from her constant study of the Gospel of St John, she was aware of as a dangerous asset. 'Above all', said Bodington, 'she dreaded exercising undue or unfair influence on any young generous soul so as to be the means of persuading her to make a great sacrifice of life in the world, when God had not called her to it'.[16]

Canon Scott Holland, who both raised money for her in England and visited the Community in South Africa, noticed that 'In all she had bearing on her soul the racial burden of South Africa. She recognised as inevitable the immense predominance of the Dutch in the Colony and took the full value of their deep and tenacious virtues ... She laboured to open out her educational training to the Dutch, feeling passionately that any tendency to shut up an institution to English use only served to intensify the division of the races. Hence she was not afraid to strain a little the limitations inevitably set on her work by its being based on the Catholic worship and truth in South Africa.

She was like nobody else in the world ... The whole thing lived through her; hardly anyone could come near her without passing under her sway; she possessed an incomparable charm which was blended with singular intellectual capacity'.[17]

'It would be such a relief to be delivered from the constant raising of funds', Mother Cecile sighed in 1904. But there was to be no relief. A visit to Grahamstown by Joseph Chamberlain, the Colonial Secretary in 1903, did indeed result in more Government aid. Yet the strain seemed unending. Even at the opening ceremony of the new building, Dr Muir spoke of the need for yet more teachers and for new colleges to produce them; a further extension was necessary if St Peter's was to maintain its place.

To and fro to Britain therefore Mother Cecile went. The Bishop would not allow her to return to St Peter's until financial targets were reached. How much depended upon her personally was indicated in a speech made on a fund raising occasion in London by the eloquent Canon Scott Holland:

Here we have Mother Cecile. Here *is* a personality. Here is actually a thing that is succeeding. Everything is growing, as hard as it can. Here is an institution of the Church which is governed by a policy which really has a mind. The whole of this great work is hanging on Mother Cecile just now until it be created and made, as it were. It will never really be created and established, and laid out on strong lines except by the inspiration she gives it.'[18]

In the end, her colleagues and biographers believed, it was the inexorable pressure and anxiety of fund raising which killed her. At the end of 1905 she became seriously ill and was sent to England for treatment. The doctors advised that if she took a long rest a dangerous operation might be avoided; but she could not refrain from speaking at meetings on behalf of the College and its finances. She now had to undergo the operation, which proved fatal. Before it she murmured a brief message to the Community. Whether by accident or recollection, it was similar to that of Mother Harriet: 'Peg away ... Sparkle.' When she was asked what the last word implied, she said at once with her old bright smile, 'O, not to let the fun go out of the place.'

The cycle was complete. Her funeral took place at St Peter's Church, Eaton Square, where her spiritual adventure had begun. She had died so young that the two men who had inspired it, Bishop Wilkinson and Bishop Webb, were present, together with the Archbishop of Canterbury; and the service ended with the hymn which she had requested for her Confirmation in that same church, 'O Jesus, I have promised.'

Further Reading

Mother Cecile in Africa, Foundress of the Community of the Resurrection of our Lord, compiled by a Sister of the Community, London (SPCK) 1930, is particularly valuable for her letters and for the tributes to her which it contains, but it says nothing about her early life. The gap is partly filled by Sister Kate in *Mother Cecile*, London, SPCK, 1922, and by Margaret W. Robins in *Mother Cecile of Grahamstown*, London, 1911.

Margaret Cropper's *Shining Lights*, London, 1963 contains a chapter on Mother Cecile as does *A Bundle of Memories* by H. Scott Holland, London, 1915. *Sisterhood Life and Women's Work* by the Rt. Rev. A.B. Webb, Bishop of Grahamstown, London, 1883, is invaluable in setting the scene for her work.

Notes

1. *Bishop A.B. Webb, Sisterhood, Life and Women's Work*, London 1883, p. 74.
2. Sister Kate, *Mother Cecile*, London 1922, pp. 1–6.
3. *Bishop A.B. Webb, op. cit.*
4. *Mother Cecile in South Africa* by a Sister of the Community (M.C.S.A.), London, 1930, p. 4
5. *M.C.S.A., op cit.*, p. 13.
6. M. Cropper, *Shining Lights*, London 1963, p. 145.
7. *M.C.S.A..*, *op. cit.*, p. 45.
8. *M.C.S.A.*, *op cit.*, p. 157.
9. *M.C.S.A.*, *op. cit.*, pp. 136–7.
10. M.W. Robins, *Mother Cecile*, London 1911, p. 46.
11. The quotations from Mother Cecile's letters are all quoted from *M.C.S.A.*, *op. cit.*, pp. 229–295.
12. *M.C.S.A., op. cit.*, p. 198.
13. *M.C.S.A.*, *op. cit.*, p. 198.
14. *Ibid.*, p. 193.
15. *Ibid.*, p. 191.
16. *Ibid.*, p. 192.
17. H. Scott Holland, *A Bundle of Memories*, London 1915, p. 242.
18. *M.C.S.A.*, *op. cit.*, p. 89.

PART IV
LOCAL SAINTS

9

Sister Dora of Walsall (Dorothy Pattison) (1832–1878)

'Do not look upon nursing in the way they do so much nowadays as an art or science, but as work done for Christ. As you touch each patient think it is Christ himself and then the virtue will come out of the touch to yourself. I have felt that myself, when I have had a particularly loathsome patient.'

Sister Dora to her pupils, *c.* 1875

In the centre of Walsall in Staffordshire is a statue which claims to be the earliest in England to commemorate a woman other than royalty. The original figure, unveiled in 1886, was of marble, but this was eroded by the polluted atmosphere of the Black Country and in 1957 was replaced by one in bronze. Around the plinth, like that of Nelson in Trafalgar Square, incidents are depicted, though not of battles but of Sister Dora's life among the victims of a blast furnace explosion and a colliery disaster, and on the wards of Walsall Hospital.

The early life of Dorothy Pattison, later to be known as Sister Dora, could have provided a model for a novel by the Brontës. She was the daughter of the Rev. M.J. Pattison, Rector of Hauxwell in Yorkshire. His eldest child, Mark, was to become famous as a man of letters and Rector of Lincoln College, Oxford; there followed ten daughters, of whom Dorothy was the youngest, and finally another son, Frank. The Rector and his wife were Evangelicals, whose religion could be summarized as fear of God's wrath and faith in the Atonement. Rev. M.J. Pattison was an Oxford graduate who immediately after his ordination had been Chaplain to the Duke of Leeds at whose table he had been accustomed to dine, amiably addressed by his patron as 'Chancellor'. This experience was the origin, according to his son Mark, of 'his

191

social aspirations . . . he liked to live with gentlemen and know what was going on in the world . . . he must have read Debrett at that time more than the Bible.'¹ With marriage and a growing family however he had to exchange this agreeable existence for the obscure country living of Hauxwell in Yorkshire where he was profoundly bored, lacking any vocation for pastoral work. His frustration and black moods grew, until two years after Dorothy's birth he suffered a total mental breakdown and was placed in a private asylum. Although he was released after a few months, he never forgave his wife for having him confined. He resumed his duties but remained morose and suspicious, from time to time bursting into violent rages directed at his family.

Whilst Mark was sent to Oxford, the girls were educated at home. They were trained in domestic work, such as sewing and preserving fruit and vegetables, and they visited the deserving poor to whom they were encouraged to give away their own lunches. For a time the elder sisters ran a school for the village children. They had little social life. One of their main interests was to follow the brilliant career of Mark at Oriel College, Oxford, where, under the influence of Newman, he became a fervent Tractarian; he continued to be one after he was ordained and elected a Fellow of Lincoln College, Oxford. The girls at Hauxwell emulated him enthusiastically; they recited the Monastic Hours, beginning with Prime in the early morning and creeping out of bed to hear Compline at half past ten; by day they sewed surplices for their brother and read the tracts of the Oxford Movement. In their father two of his most powerful feelings, pride in Mark and horror of Roman Catholicism, now clashed. 'You are all a pack of infidel schoolgirls with a Romish priest at your head,'² he exploded. The next four years were almost intolerable. Mark was forbidden to visit the Rectory. For several months the elder girls were confined to their bedrooms, where Tractarian books were smuggled up to them by their younger sisters. The village school which the girls had started was closed down by the Rector to prevent 'the propagation of error.'

Mr Pattison's loathing of the Mass caused him to forbid any celebration of Christmas − 'the termination of the word being so papistical.' Mrs Pattison's religion comprehended a blind obedience to the Rector both as husband and ordained Minister; she shewed no sympathy to her daughters.

Very early Dorothy felt her vocation to be a nurse. When she was 12 there was an epidemic of scarlet fever in the village and the girls' visits to the poor were suspended. Dorothy however visited an old woman and, finding her alone, washed her and nursed her until she died in the night. She was not allowed to return home but was sent direct to the seaside with her old nurse, lest she spread the infection.

When Dorothy was 16, Mark was at last allowed to visit his family again. The girls were puzzled to find that after Newman's departure to Rome their adored brother had abandoned Tractarianism and was set on a path which was to lead him away from religious belief altogether. His interest now was in teaching the Classics, and for the next twelve years he directed Dora's reading by correspondence. In 1858 she visited him in Oxford in the Long Vacation, helping him by writing to his dictation and copying out references. Now he shared with her the new liberalism and rationalism in religion which he was to express in *Essays and Reviews*.

Among the Rector's quirks was a determination that none of his daughters should marry. Nevertheless Rachel escaped to become the wife of a farmer, Robert Stirk, whose brother was a suitor for Dorothy's hand. At the same time Dorothy was more attractively wooed by James Tate, a schoolmaster in Richmond nearby. Tate however failed to stand up to the opposition of the Rector. The unofficial engagement was broken off, then renewed, though Tate was forbidden to enter the house, where Dorothy felt obliged to remain and nurse her ailing mother. The Rector now behaved in a manner which his daughters could hardly bring themselves to forgive. Mrs Pattison had money of her own which under her Will was to be divided among all her daughters. In her final illness the Rector attempted to bully her into cutting out of her Will the daughters who had married without his permission; on this one matter however she would not yield. On her death bed she had only two wishes, to see her absent children and to receive Holy Communion. Both were denied; the Rector refused her the Sacrament unless she would alter her Will at his dictation, and she died without receiving it. To his Tractarian daughters this abuse of priestly authority for vindictive personal ends seemed a final blasphemy.[3]

Dorothy now no longer felt obliged to remain at home. Although at times she longed to be in love and devote herself to marriage, at the age of 29 she put aside both her suitors and went to become the sole teacher in the village school at Woolston in Buckinghamshire. Here she lived in a cottage attached to the school, employing no servant and delighting in her freedom. There were about thirty children, nearly all under 10, to whom she taught the Liturgy and Catechism as well as the three Rs. She loved to take them out on sunny days and share their delight in animals and flowers and a roll on a haycock, or in winter to tell them stories.[4] Yet much as she enjoyed teaching she continued to hope to become a nurse. In the evenings she would visit sick villagers and sit through the night with the seriously ill or dying. Now she returned to her religious reading and overcame the doubts sown by her brother. The only way open to her at that time to obtain nursing training was through one of the recently established Anglican women's orders; to the indignation of her father, she became a novice of the Sisterhood of the Good Samaritan at Coatham, taking the name of Sister Dora.

This Anglican Sisterhood, the only one in the north of England, had recently been founded by a wealthy widow, Mother Theresa Newcomen, with a young Cambridge graduate, Rev. John Postlethwaite, as her Chaplain. The Sisters, whether professed or associate, took no vows and were free to leave the order and to marry. The Sisterhood had established the first Cottage Hospital in England at Middlesborough, as well as a convalescent home and a home for children on the sea nearby at Coatham.

Dorothy's sister Frances also entered the Sisterhood, whose members retained their private incomes; those of Dorothy and Frances were very small, and they were thus largely dependent on the community. Sister Dora, like other Associates, started in the kitchen, washing, baking, scrubbing and blackleading. She was taught to make a hospital bed and the Sister in charge would dump the sheets and blankets on the floor if there was the slightest imperfection. The thoroughness of this domestic training scandalised both her snobbish father and her first biographer, but was to prove invaluable to her as a nurse. The religious observances throughout the day, Prime, Terce, Sext, Nones and Vespers, were later practised by her whenever possible. The words carved above the door of the convalescent home became her favourite text. 'Inasmuch as ye have done it to the least of these my brethren, ye have done it unto me'. Whenever later critics would object that her patients, whether brawling men, drunken women, or thieving children, were not deserving, she would answer '*Whatever* they are, "inasmuch" holds good'.[5]

Wise old Sister Mary taught her a lesson which she was to repeat to her own pupil nurses, how to overcome repugnance at terrible cases of wounds or disease: 'As you touch each patient think it is Christ you touch, then virtue will come out of the touch to you'. From Sister Mary, with whom she worked in North Ormesby Cottage Hospital, she acquired also the habit of saying a brief prayer at the bedside of each patient.

Even within the Sisterhood she experienced her extraordinary power to charm and influence. 'Everyone is so kind', she wrote, 'that I am only afraid that I shall get spoilt'. Her spirits were high. One day she could not resist vaulting onto a donkey in her habit and eventually was thrown, suffering bruises whose origin she had to disguise. The novice's habit with its long black dress, white apron, and frilled muslin cap suited her perfectly. Many years later she confessed 'I never could have joined one of those Sisterhoods who make themselves hideous frights with bibs and bands across their foreheads.'

It was in 1865 that Sister Dora first came to Walsall. Nine miles from Birmingham it was a town of collieries, blast furnaces, ironworks and leather factories. It had no hospital until 1863, when a boy of twelve had his arm torn off in a hide splitting machine and a small girl whose legs had been shattered by a chain in a coal mine died whilst being transported to hospital in Birmingham. Money was then raised to open a small Cottage Hospital, 'to furnish in cases of accident surgical aid and trained nursing.' The surgical aid was provided by the doctors of the town on a voluntary basis. Nurses were much harder to find, but a successful appeal was made to

Mother Theresa to send two of her Sisters. When Sister Mary fell ill, Dora, although still a novice, was sent to replace her.

Walsall had a reputation for roughness. Wild hordes had stoned John Wesley and refused to let him preach. More recently there had been fierce clashes between local people, who were nominally Protestant, and Roman Catholic Irish immigrants. Margaret Lonsdale, one of Sister Dora's pupil nurses and her first biographer, described the town where she came to work with its 'forests of chimneys which vomit forth volumes of smoke and fierce tongues of flame, its steaming polluted streams, its rows of red brick houses, begrimed inside and out with dirt, crowded with men, women and swarms of blackened people. At night, the blinding glare of blast furnaces, the snorting of engines and the ponderous thud of steam hammers bewilder the senses.' The men had great muscular strength, acute intellect and narrow minds. 'They too often spend their high wages on buying luxurious food and a quantity of spirituous liquor for their own consumption ... and the claims of their wives and children are often disregarded ...' As for the women, 'drunkenness and immorality are scarcely looked upon as a disgrace ... A stranger is invariably treated as an intruder until his good intentions are proved ... but their gratitude towards those who do them a good turn is unbounded.'[6]

Dora, who had been so bored with the country life of a vicar's unmarried daughter, delighted in the rough vitality of the place. Walsall Hospital, it was said, came to be her home, its committee a sort of composite husband to be served and cajoled, and its patients above all her children.

Sister Dora had only been in Walsall for a month when she caught smallpox from the outpatients. She was quarantined in a room which always had the blinds down. A rumour spread that this room had been turned into a 'Popish oratory with an idol of the Virgin Mary, with a crown on her head'. Protestants demonstrated outside, throwing horsedung and mud at the window, and crying out against 'idolators and Papist bitches'.[7]

The Sisterhood, in order to help to finance its charitable work, supplied nurses for private cases, whose fees were paid into the general fund. When she recovered, Sister

Dora was sent to nurse a rich old lady. She summed up the experience ... 'An uncommonly unpleasant time I had of it, what with the mad old lady who was fond of me, and the relatives who were jealous of me, and the footman who took me for a servant and would make love to me'.[8] She disliked her comfortable work on private cases, and the Pattison family felt humiliated because she was treated as a servant. Somehow she arranged to be sent back to Walsall after six months.

Shortly afterwards an incident greatly helped to overcome local opposition to, and suspicion of, the Sisters. One night when Sister Dora was visiting a patient in the town a young miner called out 'There goes a Sister of Misery!' and hurled a stone which cut her face. A few days later he was seriously injured in a coal pit and was brought into the hospital. Sister Dora recognised him and gave particular care to nursing him. As she later told the story, when he was recovering, she found him gently sobbing. 'Sister', he said, '*I* threw that stone at you'. 'Oh', she replied, 'did you think I did not know that?' 'What', he asked, 'you knew me and have been nursing me like this?' 'You see', Sister Dora recollected, 'it was his first practical experience of good returned for evil, and he did not know what to make of it'.[9]

As the Sisters came to be trusted, the number of outpatients greatly increased, and in 1867 the hospital moved to new premises. Here something else happened which enhanced Sister Dora's reputation as the news of it spread. The doctor in charge had a well justified dread of infection; in most accident cases of crushing or compound fracture he would therefore amputate the limb. The patients mostly survived, but with no prospect of finding work and no future for themselves and their families except the workhouse. As Sister Dora checked the dressings, the amputees would mutter 'You might as well have killed me.'

One night a young iron-worker was brought in whose arm had been caught and twisted in a revolving machine. Dr Burton took a quick look and prepared to operate. The patient seized Sister Dora's hand, crying, 'O Sister, save my arm for me; it is my right arm.' She looked at him with that concentration which made it seem as though she could see through a wound to the state of circulation beneath, and said 'Doctor,

I believe I could save this man's arm, if you would let me.'
Grumpily Dr Burton agreed, muttering 'But it's *your* arm,'
and that if gangrene led to the patient's death it would be her
responsibility, not his.

For three weeks, Sister Dora nursed the patient night and
day, frequently changing the dressings. Rest, free drainage
and the absence of strong antiseptic chemicals saved the limb.
The doctor forgave her. The patient spread the news through
Walsall and became known as 'Sister Dora's arm.'[10] Now she
began to be called out at any time to mend a limb broken in a
drunken brawl or to dress the burns of a scalded child. Gradually, her reputation spread beyond Walsall. In 1872, when the
Pelsall coal pit was flooded, 22 men and boys were cut off.
Among the women and children waiting at the pit head a journalist saw her − 'a form glides among the hovels in the pelting
rain, over the rough bank and through miry clay, now ankle
deep', as she persuaded the mourners to return to their homes,
'her face radiant with kindness and affection'.[11]

Sister Dora was described by those who wrote about her
shortly after her death as having deliberately chosen to devote
herself to good works, preferring this life to that of wife and
mother.[12] In fact, having taken no vows, she was not immune
from personal romance. Towards the end of her life indeed
she declared 'If I had my life again I would marry, because
a woman ought to live with a man and be in subjection'.[13]

Both Miss Lonsdale and Miss Ridsdale refer discreetly,
naming no names, to her relationship with a doctor whom her
later biographer, Jo Manton, identifies as Dr John Redfern
Davies, an adventurous character who had served as a surgeon
in the American Civil War and now helped out at the Walsall
Hospital. He shared Sister Dora's love of the poor and was,
says Miss Lonsdale, 'the only person she had ever met who
could understand her strange imaginings and longings ... She
suddenly seemed to throw to the winds all considerations, save
the satisfaction of this passionate attachment'. But Davies was
a humanist and disciple of Darwin and Huxley; he had no sympathy with the religious inspiration of Sister Dora's work.

Torn between her feelings and her faith, she consulted the
Vicar of her local Church, who 'urgently entreated her to
pause and consider what she was about, for although her

friend could give her the intelligent sympathy and support for which all her life she had craved, either her own faith would not suffice to stand against the power of this man's intellect, or else she must suffer the misery of seeing him, with whom her life was to be passed, differ from herself on subjects which she considered the most momentous of all ... He pressed her to draw back while there was yet time'.[14] After weeks of anguish of mind she broke off the engagement, conscious that 'she had treated her lover with the utmost unfairness' and caused him to think meanly of her principles and conduct.[15]

John Redfern Davies resigned as surgeon and died shortly afterwards in an accident. The professional lessons of his advanced teaching in medicine and surgery remained with her. Taking the advice of her Vicar, she threw herself even more vigorously into her work, visiting the homes of smallpox victims with, says one contemporary, 'scarcely veiled longing for some hope forlorn enough to throw away her life upon'.[16] When the two other Sisters fell ill and were withdrawn, Dora became Sister in charge of the hospital where there was now no regular doctor; medical care was provided on a rota system.

She thus had a free hand. She reorganised the kitchen to provide nourishing food instead of the hospital 'low diet'. Curtains and carpets were ruthlessly discarded and walls and floors scrubbed fiercely. She made the beds herself morning and evening.

With the Hospital Committee, composed mostly of tradesmen and clergy, she had little trouble. When asked to attend she would remain standing with her hand resting on a chair; a younger member of the Committee said that the way she stood and looked you in the face reminded him of a Greek goddess, such as Athena giving her instructions to Ulysses.[17]

When a new Acting Surgeon, John MacLachlan, was appointed, he left Sister Dora to deal with the outpatients except those whom she referred to him. The success of this partnership, which lasted until Sister Dora's death, was perhaps based on an affinity of opposite characters: 'Where she was dashing, impulsive and imaginative, he was steady and firm. He had a dry sense of humour which pulled her wilder flights of

200 Far Above Rubies

fancy sharply back to earth. He regarded religious feelings with tolerant amusement ... There was nothing remotely romantic or sentimental about their relationship.'[18]

Dr MacLachlan was so impressed by Sister Dora's abilities that he advised her to go to Edinburgh University and qualify in medicine and surgery, as Sophia Jex Blake was then doing. She refused, finding in nursing a deeper satisfaction than that which the intellectual interest of medicine might offer.[19] Though surprised by her decision, since there was no resident surgeon he taught her himself, beginning with anatomy and surgery, and then to carry out all the duties of house surgeons and dressers.

MacLachlan admired her dexterity. 'Apart from her excellence as a nurse and a manager,' he wrote after her death, 'there was something fascinating in the charm of her manner, so playful and winning in all her ways,' and yet 'her glorious nature, physical and mental, was marred by undisciplined impulse. Her character would have been best formed by marrying a man who would have dominated her, and she would have shone subdued.'[20]

In 1872 the work became too much for Sister Dora to handle alone; there were more than 2,000 outpatients and 200 inpatients. She therefore persuaded the Hospital Committee to invite 'lady pupils' to come for training, and henceforth there were always two or three of them on the wards. She taught them to observe each patient, every change in his face, voice or attitude. 'If you cannot observe', she told them, 'you had better give up being a nurse, for it is not your calling, however kind or anxious you may be'.[21] Some of the lessons which she passed on seemed to have been learnt by her instinctively, for they were far ahead of their time. Thus cases of burns were treated for shock before their wounds were dressed, and she gave mouth to mouth artificial respiration.

She demanded from applicants complete dedication. 'This is not an ordinary house, or even hospital', she said, 'all who serve here, in whatever capacity, ought to have only one rule, love for God, and then I need not say love for their work. I wish we could use and really mean the name "Maison Dieu".'[22] 'Don't forget your prayers', was her advice to her pupils, 'Do get all you want and don't have any troubles that you do not tell me'.[23]

Some of Sister Dora's pupils, such as Louise MacLaughlin in the Balkan Wars, were to have brilliant careers. Another pupil, Margaret Lonsdale, who was her first biographer, was critical of her. She accused Sister Dora of jealousy, of a constant tendency to yield to an unworthy dislike of those who showed symptoms of ability to fill her place; and of therefore gathering around her 'second and third and even fourth rate workers, from whom it was impossible to choose when a substitute was wanted.'[24] This is a serious indictment, but Margaret Lonsdale had a carping nature; later she was to get into trouble whilst working at Guys Hospital because of her public criticism of its nursing methods; she seems to have had an angular character. Sister Dora herself recognized that she was sometimes impatient with her nurses. 'I was anything but forbearing, dear, I was overbearing,' she wrote to one of her former pupils on her death bed.[25]

Nothing did more to establish the legend of Sister Dora than her conduct in the smallpox epidemic of 1875. At first she fearlessly went out to visit the patients in their homes. Then an Epidemic Hospital was opened, but no one would enter it. 'Leave us alone: we would rather die at home,' the sufferers would say. When the smallpox ambulance appeared, patients with streaming pustules were hidden in upstairs rooms, and remained to infect every member of the family. The wards at the Walsall Cottage Hospital at this time were relatively quiet and could be left in the care of the pupil nurses. Sister Dora sensed that, if only there were someone at the Epidemic Hospital whom working people would trust, they would allow members of their families to enter it; she volunteered to go herself and was proved correct. For the next six months she ran the Epidemic Hospital alone except for an old Irish workhouse nurse and a porter, both of whom were often drunk. Dr MacLachlan visited every day. For the first month Sister Dora never set foot outside, and there was only one death. 'Is not this a glorious retreat for Lent?' she wrote to a friend. 'I can have no idle chatter.'[27] As the epidemic diminished she would go out herself in the ambulance to seek out the remaining cases and bring them in. Now she was able to return to the Walsall Hospital each day to take the outpatients clinic. She received the thanks of the Mayor and Corporation, but Rev. John Postlethwaite on behalf of the Sisterhood complained sharply to the Hospital Secretary because she had absented herself from the Cottage Hospital without his consent. Sister Dora thereupon resigned from the Sisterhood. She continued to wear its uniform in modified form, but on her rare holidays now felt able to lay this aside, particularly when she went swimming and skating.

Another page of the legend was Sister Dora's work in the worst catastrophe in Walsall's history, when the furnace burst at the Birchills Ironworks. Fourteen men were buried under a torrent of molten metal. Sister Dora immediately arrived to direct the lifting up of the screaming men and their removal to the hospital, where they were set down on the floor, more like charred logs than human beings. Little was then known of treatment for burns. The smell of decaying flesh in the ward was so appalling that even the doctors were overcome, but Sister Dora remained there day and night. She did not conceal from the patients the approach of death; instead she talked quietly and simply of her faith in an after-life, and when they had lost consciousness followed them with her prayers. Of the twelve injured men who reached the hospital, ten died. One of the survivors, who was six months in hospital, remembered Sister Dora silently going round the ward in shawl and slippers at two in the morning to check the dressings. 'It did you good', he said, 'even to look at her'.[28]

Her dedication to her patients now seemed total. She had a bell placed above her bed and at night, when summoned by a patient, could be dressed and on the ward in three minutes. She liked to do as much as possible herself; she would wash the patients, make their beds, serve the meals and read prayers in the wards. She was, as one patient remembered, 'a great tucker up.'[29] In the outpatients room she dressed wounds, set fractures and extracted teeth. After tea she would talk to patients individually; then a pupil nurse played the piano, and hymns were sung heartily whilst she did the washing up. She would carry frightened children around with her and take them into her bed. Her patients noticed that whatever her troubles she would always enter the ward with a face like sunshine. 'She could make you laugh even if you were dying,' [30] said one Irishman.

She never seemed to forget a face, and her patients became her friends for ever. She gave the men nicknames and persuaded them to wait on one another. On her parents' death she inherited a small income. Out of this she would buy tools for former patients to enable them to work again; she would visit them in jail, or would pay for tickets to enable them to emigrate. She was content to live from day to day, delighted to have been granted these opportunities of service. 'Everyone has been so good and kind,' she wrote to a friend, 'I think, and I say this in all humility, I have learnt to love God more. Eternity has become real.'[31] And on their side the former patients never forgot her. A number of them who were railway men built a small open carriage which they presented to her together with a pony in the hope that she would 'take the air'. She found it invaluable when visiting patients in their homes.

Gradually a cult grew up around Sister Dora and her almost miraculous power of healing, as it had done round local Saints in the Middle Ages. Her relics, a cup, a glove, a letter, a nurse's belt or scissors were treasured for years by their owners. Her picture hung in countless Walsall homes; little ragged dirty orphans would run up to her in the street, tugging at her gown and holding up their faces to be kissed.[32]

Sister Dora did not disguise the face that her religion was the main spring of her work. In her last years, by intense contemplation, she said, 'she seemed to see Jesus face to face as she went about her duties.' To an observer she appeared to lead 'two lives inseparably blended. The outward life one of hard incessant toil; the inner, constant communion with the unseen world.'[33]

Every morning and evening she said prayers on the stairs. On Sundays there was a service and tea to which former patients were invited. After a sermon by a clergyman, Sister Dora would give a talk. She insisted to her pupils on the absolute necessity of constant private prayer, to which she attributed her remarkable powers of healing. Margaret Lonsdale severely recorded Sister Dora's doubts regarding the inspiration and authenticity of the Holy Scriptures. 'Her main stumbling block,' she said, 'was

the acuteness of her intellect, and the complete surrender of
it was her only possible escape from infidelity.'[34] As a later
biographer was to observe however, 'Miss Lonsdale frequently
slips her own scanty garment of thought over the elusive spirit
of Sister Dora.'[35]

Her unorthodox religion puzzled many people both before
and after her death. Her friend Richard Twigg, the High
Church 'Apostle of the Black Country,' asked her if she used
the love and admiration which surrounded her to win souls
or to satisfy her need for power.[36] She was indeed sometimes
overwhelmed with regret that hours had been wasted when
souls had not been led to Christ, but her reticence in refusing
to press any particular kind of religion on her patients was
one of the reasons why they loved her.

After her broken engagement with Redfern Davies Sister
Dora almost became an ascetic. Sometimes she would go to
her room at the normal time, but deliberately avoid sleep
by sitting on the floor, singing softly to herself the hymns
which she called the dearest companions of her solitary life;
her servant next door could often hear her praying late into the
night. Food, like sleep, was a grudged necessity; she seldom
ate a meal uninterrupted.

Ellen Ridsdale in her memoir of Sister Dora, published in
1880, described her as 'one of those noble Christian workers
who God did not make happy wives but set them apart with
their own full and joyful consent as nurses of the sick and
poor.'[37] Sister Dora's character was not this simple. Her last
romance was hidden from her contemporary biographers.
Over 50 years after her death a plumber and a decorator
working in a large house in Walsall each found a packet
of letters in her hand addressed to Kenyon Jones, one of
the owners of the Birchill Ironworks. These were eventually
deposited in the Walsall Local History Library. From them
emerged the pathetic story of her last love. Kenyon Jones
was 14 years her junior. His visits to the hospital had commenced when he brought fruit, eggs and wine for his injured
workers. He designed and had made in his workshops a set of
overhead pulleys to lift the helpless patients. Then he came
every evening whenever the furnaces of his works were not
at full blast. Sister Dora could look out of the window and

tell from the height of the flames whether to expect him. He was a tall, handsome extrovert and there are no signs in the letters of the intellectual affinity which everyone had noticed between Sister Dora and Dr Davies ten years earlier.

Now Sister Dora became the prisoner of her own legend as the Guardian Angel of Walsall. They exchanged photographs; but either had to meet in secret or by arrangement through apparently accidental encounters in church, at schoolchildren's treats, and yeomanry manoeuvres, or in trains. Sister Dora was now out of the hospital more than she had ever been before. Then one evening she forgot her promise to visit a patient far out of town. When she went next morning a woman rushed up and cried 'Too late, Sister Dora, too late!' She plunged from exaltation to the depths of self blame.

The relationship cooled. Jones's family appear to have deplored his relationship with a much older woman. Soon afterwards he made a business journey to South Africa. When he returned he neither wrote to nor visited Dora. One evening when they found themselves next to each other at a concert he did not speak to her.[38]

In 1877 Sister Dora consulted a specialist outside Walsall who diagnosed cancer of the breast, which at that time was considered an inevitably fatal form of disease since it was bound to disseminate through the body. She told no one and declined an operation which could only postpone death and might leave her without the strength to continue to work. She seemed now to throw herself into her duties with an intensity and urgency even greater than before. One night, nursing a child with diphtheria on whom an emergency operation had been performed, she put her mouth to the tube and deliberately cleared it by sucking the diphtheric mucus.

The relationship with Kenyon Jones was renewed. They found a way to catch a glimpse of each other each morning; as his train took him to work it passed within a few feet of the hospital; if Dora stood in the window, her face, framed in its white cap and collar, showed up clearly against the dark house. Now that she knew that she would soon die, though he did not, she felt less conflict between love and duty, or worry about the difference between their ages.

Not long after Sister Dora's illness was diagnosed, the premises which were being used whilst a permanent hospital was being built became infected and had to be closed down. For the first time since she came to Walsall she found herself with free time.

She used it courageously by going to London to observe Lister's new methods of antiseptic surgery. Before her health finally broke down she ordered equipment for an antiseptic operating theatre for the new Walsall Hospital. On her return to Walsall she collapsed; a small cottage was rented for her where she remained until she died. Her insistence on secrecy about her condition was to be described harshly by Margaret Lonsdale – 'There was a wilfulness about her determination, which neither her own lonely agony nor the distress which she must have known she was causing her family could shake. She showed on her deathbed the same proud and wilful reticence, the same determined following of her own way at all costs, which marked her character so strongly in days of health and strength'.[39]

A more sympathetic witness wrote of her on her deathbed – 'Her sorrow was that she could not realise God's presence more, and her fear was lest she should seem impatient. She spoke most decidedly against the idea that we need anyone to go between the soul and Christ, and I shall never forget her bright beautiful smile as she listened to the words 'He that believeth on me hath everlasting life', saying 'That is just what I want'.[40] She lived long enough to approve the name of her successor and to arrange to give thirty pairs of warm gloves as Christmas presents to the cabmen and porters of the parish.

She was visited by Kenyon Jones until she wrote him a last pathetic note – 'My darling, I dare not see you, it agitates me so much. I feel almost it might kill me. I am sure it only distresses you to see me in such a state and I cannot prevent it ... Oh Kenyon, you must not fret or grieve for me – I think I shall soon lay down the Cross and must exchange it for a crown'.[41] On Christmas Eve, when she felt the approach of death she told those around her to leave the room, saying 'I have lived alone. Let me die alone'. A few hours later she was dead.

She had asked that her funeral should be as plainly and quietly conducted as possible. The bearers of her coffin were railway workers whom she had nursed. The procession was headed by the Mayor and Corporation, physicians and surgeons, the Bishop and other worthies; but as it reached the cemetery it was joined by hundreds of Sister Dora's poor patients and their relations who pushed past the police and flocked round the grave. Because the huge crowds delayed the burial, Sister Dora's coffin was joined by four others from the workhouse. Thus the service was read over all five coffins together and some of the many wreaths which had been sent for Dora were placed on the paupers' graves.

Her brother Mark did not attend. 'I shall not go to her funeral,' he wrote, 'as I should be sadly out of place among those Sisters and long-coated hypocrites.'[42]

There were various plans to commemorate Sister Dora. The Vicar of Walsall raised money for a memorial window in the parish church which illustrated the seven qualities of mercy. A portrait was painted and hung in the General Hospital. Margaret Lonsdale offered to give the royalties of the biography to endow a Sister Dora Convalescent Home; the Town Council and Hospital Committee indignantly refused however to accept money earned by a book which had described the people of Walsall as 'uncouth' and 'half civilized', so she paid for the convalescent home to be built herself and became its first Matron.

The former patients of 'Our Sister Dora' wanted her to live not only in their hearts but in the minds and eyes of their children for all generations to come, and decided to put up a statue of her. Slowly over seven years £1,200 was raised, mostly from works' collection boxes. The statue was unveiled by the Mayor in 1886. Margaret Lonsdale did not dare to appear in public, but kind Dr MacLachlan allowed her to watch the ceremony from his house, behind drawn curtains.[43] In Sister Dora's honour, for the first time on such an occasion, ladies were invited to a banquet. They could thus share in the indignation with which local speakers defended the reputation of Walsall and Sister Dora against Miss Lonsdale's strictures, the pathos with which a lady soloist sang 'The Lost Chord', and the cheerfulness with which the band played extracts from

Rigoletto. Sister Dora would have been delighted that this was also the first occasion on which Protestant and Roman Catholic school children were entertained together; 6,000 of them were each allowed two buns. Everyone went away happy except the non-conformist Ministers who complained that they were given no place in the procession.

Shortly before her death, Sister Dora told Samuel Welsh, 'When I am gone many absurd tales will be circulated about me. I desire however that nothing should be written about me; quietly I came among you and quietly I wish to go away.'[44]

This prohibition, as we have seen, did not prevent Margaret Lonsdale from writing a biography which appeared two years after Sister Dora's death and rapidly went into many editions. Its criticisms of Sister Dora's character caused much indignation locally. Ellen Ridsdale, a Methodist friend of Sister Dora's later days, wrote an 'anti memoir' defending her from the charges of being restless, arrogant and jealous. The *Walsall Observer* pointed out many sensational passages in the Lonsdale book which were quite untrue. No Irish mob, it said, had ever stormed the hospital mortuary to recover the corpse of an Irishman which Sister Dora was dissecting: the suggestion that she had to serve as a protector of local clergymen whilst they walked among their parishioners was insulting and absurd; it was ridiculous, too, for Miss Lonsdale to maintain that Sister Dora had no one of her own social position with whom to measure her intellect, for she had doctors and Ministers of several denominations among her friends.[45] Margaret Lonsdale remained recalcitrant in her prefaces to successive editions of her best seller. Sister Dora's Life, she declared, 'has not been written to please the Walsall people, nor is her memory private property.'[46]

It may be that the fact that the biography was critical as well as admiring gave it its great appeal with the wider public. Here was a subject whose noble work was depicted as only achieved through painful and not always successful control of the kind of weaknesses which the readers felt in themselves. A flood of articles and little books poured out, intended as devotional aids and Sunday School prizes, each trying to find something new to add, however slender the basis for it. An American lady absurdly described Sister Dora's father and mother as 'ideal parents' and rebuked the young Dorothy for foxhunting ('cruel, cowardly and no fit tragedy for a girl to witness') and the mature Dora for 'doing her work with that don't care manner that denoted mental unrest.'[47] Others compared her not only to Old Testament heroines such as Jepthah's daughter and Esther, but to Lady Godiva and Grace Darling.

Above all, her religious affiliations were warmly disputed after her death. Miss Lonsdale in her first edition stated that Sister Dora looked upon the Ritualist Movement with unfeigned astonishment, not unmixed with amusement, but had sought to become a Roman Catholic; in her second, however, she printed a letter from a non-conformist Minister denying that Dora 'had become a pervert to the Romanist schism.'[48] She was always anxious to try anything new, commented Miss Lonsdale, especially if it were in the sensationally religious line. Ellen Ridsdale maintained that she had felt most at home among Methodists. The prolific Evangelical author Jennie Chappell, who called Sister Dora 'A wingless weekday angel,' managed to get in a dig at the Anglo-Catholics by describing her as having been 'crushed and helpless in the hands of a harsh Mother Superior,' adjectives which must have astonished her former patients.[49]

The popular Anglican Church historian and author of *Onward Christian Soldiers*, Rev. Sabine Baring-Gould, used her memory to chastise not only the follies of Roman Catholic Saints but Latin peoples in general, when he somewhat incongruously included a chapter on her in his book *Virgin Saints and Martyrs* in 1900. He found in her 'the highest type of the Christian life, the hidden life of the soul, combined with that outer life devoted to doing good to suffering and needy humanity.' By contrast, he said, the Order which St Clara had founded was 'void of commonsense and good principles,' and St Theresa's energy 'was directed to no better purpose than that of a squirrel in a cage, so that her followers were reduced to a general level of incapacity by giving them nothing to do.' Musing on this contrast, he reflected comfortably that 'the Latin races seem doomed by God to go down, and His hand is manifestly extended to bless and lead on the great Anglo Saxon race.'[50]

There was one friend however who had worked with Sister Dora thoughout her time in Walsall, the Hospital Secretary, Samuel Welsh, himself a Baptist, who in two articles published some years after her death, truly reflected her accommodating, comprehensive attitude to religious denominations. 'As she predicted,' he wrote, 'many idle and absurd tales have been circulated concerning her, but these representations have arisen from misconceptions of her sublime character and noble nature, which enabled her to rise above petty denominational distinctions and narrow sectarian jealousies, for her great soul seemed to have anticipated that larger platform which is wide as the spirit itself, that city of which the Apostle speaks, in which no visible temple could be discovered.'[51]

Further Reading

The best biography is Jo Manton, *Sister Dora* (London 1971). Among contemporary Lives the most important are the controversial *Sister Dora, A Biography* (London 1880) and other editions, by Margaret Lonsdale, and Ellen Ridsdale *Reminiscences of Sister Dora* (London 1880), which was written to refute it. The Walsall Library has published an illustrated pamphlet, *Sister Dora* (1988), containing her letters to Kenyon Jones.

Notes

1. J. Manton, *Sister Dora*, London 1971, p. 27.
2. Manton, *op. cit.*, p. 51.
3. Manton, *op. cit.*, p. 123.
4. *Ibid.*, p. 138.
5. Manton, *op. cit.*, p. 160; *ibid.*, p. 158.
6. M. Lonsdale, *Sister Dora*, London 1880 (4th edition), pp. 27–28.
7. M. Price, *Inasmuch As*, London 1952, p. 5.
8. Lonsdale, *op. cit.*, p. 34.
9. Lonsdale, *op. cit.*, p. 31.
10. Manton, *op. cit.*, pp. 189–191.
11. S. Baring-Gould, *Virgin, Saints and Martyrs*, London 1900, p. 378.
12. Ridsdale, *op. cit.*, p. ix.
13. Manton, *op. cit.*, 200.
14. Lonsdale, p. 77; Manton, pp. 194–9.

15. Lonsdale, p. 77
16. Manton, p. 207.
17. Lonsdale, p. 253.
18. Manton, p. 222.
19. Manton, p. 230.
20. Manton, p. 235.
21. Manton, p. 252.
22. Manton, p. 255.
23. Manton, p. 257.
24. Lonsdale, p. 138.
25. Manton, p. 252.
26. Manton, p. 285.
27. Lonsdale, p. 145.
28. Manton, p. 297.
29. Manton, p. 220.
30. Lonsdale, p. 67.
31. Manton, p. 227.
32. Manton, p. 245.
33. Manton, p. 277.
34. Lonsdale, *op. cit.*, p. 42.
35. M. Price, *Inasmuch As*, London 1952, p. 3.
36. Manton, *op. cit.*, p. 274.
37. E.E.M. Ridsdale, *Sister Dora*, London, 1880, p. ix.
38. Manton, *op. cit.*, p. 322.
39. Lonsdale, p. 220.
40. Lonsdale, p. 235.
41. Walsall Chronicle No. 10 *Sister Dora*, Walsall, 1988, p. 42.
42. Manton, p. 278.
43. Manton, pp. 342−8.
44. Samuel Welsh in *General Baptist Magazine*, London, 1889, p. 272.
45. *Sister Dora, A Review*, reprinted by Walsall Observer, 1886, p. 9.
46. Lonsdale, *op. cit.*, 4th edition, 1880, preface.
47. Forence Burleigh, *Sister Dora and Her Work*, London, 1890, pp. 7, 8, 13.
48. Lonsdale, *op. cit.*, 2nd edition, p. 235.
49. Jennie Chappell, *Four Noble Women and their Work*, London, 1898, p. 102.
50. S. Baring-Gould, *Virgin Saints and Martyrs*, London, 1900, pp. 399, 314, 346.
51. Samuel Welsh in *General Baptist Magazine*, 1889, pp. 224 and 268.

10

Mary Slessor of Calabar
(1848 – 1915)

'All work for others is first of all discipline for our-
selves. God cannot give success (what is success?) in our
best aspirations because we cannot bear it ... God will
work out the purpose by another way though, for with
Him there is no waste, so no desire or prayer is lost.'1
Mary Slessor to Thomas Hart, 1912

No-one who had not been baptized either as an Anglican or
Roman Catholic was included among the people commemorated
in the ASB in 1980. If others come to be admitted, a strong
candidate will be Mary Slessor who is already treated as its
particular saint by the City of Dundee. Not only are her an-
notated Bible, diaries and even spectacles on permanent display
in the Museum there, but a stained glass window traces the
whole career of the mill operative who became, as the lettering
proudly relates, 'the White Queen of Okoyong.'

Mary Slessor was born in Aberdeen in 1848 and baptized
into the United Presbyterian Church. Her father, a shoe-
maker, lost his job because of his drinking, and in 1859 the
family moved to Dundee where the mother and girls could
find employment in the textile mills and the father obtain
casual work when sober. Mary was only 11 when she entered
Baxter's Mills as a half-timer, working six hours a day as a
weaver and six hours in the mill's school.

The happiest day of the week was Sunday when, as Mary
recalled, 'We would as soon have thought of going to the
moon as of being absent from a service.' Here in the Presbyterian Church the shame of Robert Slessor's brutal and
noisy Saturday evening conduct and the dreariness of the mills
could be forgotten. The most fascinating services were those at
which a missionary would preach about the romantic work of

212

the Presbyterian Mission in Calabar in West Africa. At home the Slessor children would play at missionaries and preach to their toys, and it was always hoped that John, the surviving son, would join the Calabar Mission. Mary was in her teens when she experienced a religious conversion as an old widow gathered some of the girls off the streets round her hearth fire and told them that if they did not repent of their sins and believe in the Lord Jesus Christ their souls would burn in the flames for ever.

Now she became active in Home Missionary work, Temperance Meetings and Sunday School teaching. She was often menaced by roughs and acquired the courage and skill which would serve her well in Africa, where, tiny though she was, she had no difficulty in throwing a drunken man to the ground.

For fourteen years she worked in the mill to support her family. Propped on the loom were the works of Milton and Carlyle and those of Philip Dodderidge which she read with particular diligence, though discouraged by her inability to meditate, which he maintained was necessary for the soul. When her father died she installed her mother in a shop. Then her brother John died and Mary resolved to go to Calabar in his place. She was 27 however, before her two sisters were in secure jobs and she was thus freed to offer her services, inspired by the news which had just reached Scotland of the death of her hero David Livingstone.

In 1875 she was accepted as a teacher for Calabar by the Foreign Mission Board of the United Presbyterian Church. After a three months' training course at Edinburgh, which she later described as too bookish and insufficiently practical, she sailed for West Africa. As she watched the cargo of gin and rum being loaded, she wryly exclaimed 'Scores of casks and only one missionary![2]

At the time of Mary's arrival in 1876 Calabar, which is now part of Nigeria, was not under European rule, though in a British sphere of influence. It had once been an important slaving port where the coastal chiefs had traded slaves brought from the interior for spirits, guns, cotton cloth and the brass rods which served as currency. With the abolition of slavery palm oil became the main export. The Calabar Mission had been established in 1846, in a spirit of reparation for the evils of the slave trade, by the Presbyterian Rev. Hope Waddell, who brought with him from Jamaica as assistants the descendants of slaves who had been shipped from Calabar. The missionaries had been welcomed by the chiefs for the English education which they provided and which helped them to deal with the foreign traders. A dictionary and books in the Efik language had been prepared. The object was not so much to evangelize the people as to raise a native agency to do so, for the climate was so fatal to Europeans that the shipping lines sold no return tickets.

The Europeans in the Mission numbered four ordained missionaries, with four men and four women teachers; there was one ordained African and eighteen African agents. The work was mainly confined to the coast. Whilst church attendance was large, membership was not, for this would have involved the abandonment by the local people of the practices of polygamy and ownership of slaves, which were unacceptable to the church. Among other customs on which the missionaries had little influence were the ceremonial execution of scores of dependants and slaves when a chief died, trial by ordeal, and the murder of twins and widows. Great power was exercised through its masked agents by a secret society, the Egba. In 1878 the British Consul made a treaty with the coastal chiefs, imposing penalties for human sacrifice and the death of twins, but this had no effect inland.

Mary, barely five feet tall, with her red hair cut short like a boy, seemed younger than her age, climbing every tree within miles of the mission, often returning too late for meals, which were smuggled up to her room by a missionary host who was less strict than his wife. She started work as a teacher in Duke Town, the mission's headquarters. Her early letters read strangely in light of her later career. 'This land is dark', she wrote home in 1877, 'and to us dry, and parched. The surrounding heathenism has such a depressing influence and the slow progress (which is the result of utter debasement) makes one heartsick. O for a heart full of Jesus and to love these perishing ones for His sake! For one cannot love them for their own, at least some of them. You may *read* or *hear* but to *see* the state of society is sickening'.[3]

She rapidly acquired a remarkable fluency in the Efik language. In the afternoons, when teaching was finished, it was her duty to visit women in the town, dosing ailments, instructing in housecraft and needlework, vaccinating against smallpox, and counselling. She was also sent to visit the Mission Stations, travelling by river and on foot through the forest, and found the rural people more congenial than the more sophisticated population of the town.

Partly, perhaps, as a result of her lack of formal education, particularly in Presbyterian theology, she took a broad-minded view of local beliefs and customs and acquired an unusual understanding of them. The local people, she was often to insist, were not irreligious; they believed in God but were troubled by their belief in evil spirits. On this first tour of duty she suffered severely from fevers and went on furlough in 1879.

The European lifestyle of the missionaries irked her, and she longed to work among 'the untouched multitudes'. On her return she asked to be posted away from Duke Town and was put in charge of the work in Old Town, three miles away, as well as that in two neighbouring villages. Now commenced her practice of living entirely on local food, at first because this enabled her to send part of her salary home and later because it brought her closer to Africans.

From Old Town she supervised schools, dispensed medicines, trained teachers and visited villages to preach. She became an intrepid traveller, fearless of leopards on the trails or of crocodiles on the river, always keeping her canoeman and carriers singing. It was now that she began to adopt the children who were later to accompany her everywhere, even to Scotland when she went on leave. Most of them were twins, who were always considered as offspring of evil spirits and abandoned, if not murdered. Others were orphans of slave mothers who had died. She stayed in harems where her tact and cheerfulness often helped to improve the treatment and condition of wives.

In 1883 she was again invalided home, taking with her a six month old twin who was baptized in Scotland with the name of Janie and accompanied her when she lectured to raise money for the Mission. At the end of her leave she had to remain in

Scotland to support her mother and invalid sister; it was only after three years' absence that she was able to arrange for their care, and was thus free to return to Calabar. Some of this time was spent in obtaining experience at Exeter Infirmary for her dispensary work. Shortly after her return her mother and sister died. 'Heaven', she declared, 'is now nearer to me than Britain and no one will be anxious about me when I go up country'.[4]

She persuaded the Mission to allow her to settle inland among the Okoyong, a Bantu tribe who had no direct contact with Europeans and were not bound by the coastal treaties which in principle banned slavery. Arriving with her five black children, she was welcomed by Chief Edem as well as by his sister Ma Eme who had herself survived trial by ordeal when her husband died. They allowed their yard to become a sanctuary for the women and children whom she rescued and protected, and they became her firm supporters. In the Okoyong region, though she moved from village to village, she was to remain for fifteen years. She had to start by clearing the ground to build a house and school with her own hands. She taught in the simple way in which she had been instructed in Scotland through alphabet, numbers and Bible stories.

A crisis arose with the accidental death of the Chief's son, upon whom a heavy log fell when he was building a house. Men and women from the village where this happened were seized and assembled to be sacrificed so that their spirits might accompany him on his way. Mary stood guard over them. She decked out the corpse in a European suit and added yards of silk, placing a plumed hat on his head, rings on his fingers and an umbrella and silver-handled whip in his hands. To embellish the ceremony, she organized a magic lantern show. Gradually and grudgingly it was accepted that the dead man could be buried thus with sufficient dignity, and the prisoners were released.

A visiting Scottish carpenter, Charles Ovens, who had come up from the Mission headquarters to help Mary construct her church, house and school, wrote on his return a detailed account of this episode which was published by the *Mission Record* in Edinburgh. He described too how Mary would box a drunkard's ears or topple him over, how she would step between opposing forces in a brawl to persuade them to lay down their arms and stack them on her verandah, and portrayed her in another mood gently caring for the sick and orphans.

What established Mary's status with the Okoyong was not so much her dramatic interventions in preventing mass sacrifices and trials by ordeal as her success in commercial diplomacy and in ending their isolation. She organized and accompanied a delegation of their Chiefs, very reluctantly unarmed, to a conference at Creek Town where her friend King Eyo agreed to allow them to sell their palm oil. They were particularly impressed by the respect with which their own 'White Ma' was treated by the King and coastal chiefs.

In 1891 Britain established firmer control over the region, now known as the Oil Rivers Protectorate, under a Commissioner and Consul General, Sir Claude MacDonald. Courts were established in the settled districts and twelve young men were brought out from Britain to administer the up country districts. Mary advised Sir Claude, who was a Scot and Presbyterian, sympathetic to the Mission, that the Okoyong would not tolerate an unknown official being stationed among them or the rapid introduction of new laws. He thereupon appointed Mary herself as Vice Consul and magistrate, somewhat to the consternation of his superiors in Whitehall, long before women were eligible to serve as magistrates in England.

In this capacity she presided over a court which tried cases according to native law, except insofar as this was repugnant to civilised practice. She used her authority sparingly. 'After all', she said, 'we are foreigners and they own the country, so I always try to make the law fit in, while we adjust things between us'.[5]

She would try cases all over Okoyong, sometimes knitting, sometimes with a child on her knee. The cases were mostly concerned with lands, debts, thefts, and stealing of wives and children. Her conduct was unorthodox. On at least one occasion she lambasted a Chief with his own umbrella for lying. It was said that a woman never lost a case in her court.

Her fame spread not only through the *Mission Record* but the writings of Mary Kingsley, the explorer and anthropologist, who stayed with her and was deeply impressed with her understanding of superstitions and needs, and, in particular, with how she handled an attempt to murder twins which occurred during her visit. Mary Kingsley described her as 'a very wonderful lady ruling as a veritable White Chief over the entire Okoyong district ... Her knowledge of the native, his language and way of thought, his diseases, his difficulties, and all that is his, is extraordinary and the amount of good she has done no man can estimate ... Okoyong was a district regarded with fear by Duke and Creek Town natives. It was given, as most of the surrounding districts still are, to killing at funerals, ordeal by poison, and perpetual internecine wars. Many of these evil customs she has stamped out and Okoyong rarely gives trouble to its nominal rulers, the Consuls in Old Calabar, and trade passes freely through it to the sea ports'.[6]

British District Officers from neighbouring districts would visit her to profit from her knowledge and understanding of customs. They would observe how she made palavers easy to settle because she could represent to each side accurately what the other party wished to convey. Often these young men would pour out their troubles as to a mother or sister, though a few resisted her spell and accused their colleagues of 'Mariolatry'. She in turn enjoyed their visits, finding them more understanding and less contemptuous of local institutions than the missionaries.

Visitors' accounts and her diaries give an idea of her daily life. She observed none of the European rules of health, walking barefooted and bareheaded, and drinking unboiled water. On Sundays she would preach to between eight and twelve meetings in different villages. On weekdays, if she was not in court, she could be found cutting bush, sawing boards, cementing or vaccinating, always helped by her adopted children. Or she might be receiving visitors with all sorts of problems, nursing sick babies, dosing patients, or teaching in school. Having no alarm clock, she would tie a rooster to her bed to wake her. From her bed, strings were also tied to the hammocks in which rescued baby twins were sleeping, so that she could rock them at night. She received whoever came to see her with informality, whatever their rank. Senior Government Officials were teased and addressed as 'laddie'. Her adopted son Dan remembered how she made a visiting District Officer repair a fence, playing tricks with him and untying his work.[7] Her work as a missionary was lonely, for very seldom was there a visit by a Minister to celebrate Communion or carry out baptisms.

On one of her visits to Calabar Mary met Charles Morrison, a new recruit to the Mission. They had much in common, particularly a love of books. Though she was 42 and he was 24, they became engaged to be married, on the understanding that both would work in Okoyong. But Charles was a highly qualified teacher whose services were of considerable importance in training future African teachers and missionaries in the school in Duke Town. He would have had little scope in the bush. Mary, on the other hand, refused to be transferred back to Calabar. 'If God does not send him up here then he must do his work and I must do mine where we have been placed', she declared. Charles was invalided home in any case, and died shortly afterwards, whilst seeking to restore his health in Canada.[8]

Mary disliked administrative duties and was by nature a pioneer. When the Okoyong shifted west she moved with them to Akyap which became their capital. Then in 1900 the British administration sent a military expedition to Itu against the Aro tribe to put down slave traffic and abolish the Long Juju through which it was manipulated. Mary regretted the need for the expedition. If only her Mission had been able to send in more workers, she believed that the Aros could have been reformed. As it was, they sought her help in the peace negotiations. After the troops left she moved to Itu taking her 'bairns' with her. Her Mission could not or would not finance the new work, so she renounced her furlough to Scotland and used the money which would have been spent on it to pay for this. She found the slavers, deprived of their livelihood, anxious to 'learn book' and turn over to legitimate trade.

She proposed to her headquarters a new way of working by which bands of African Church members might travel and teach in their own neighbourhoods, supervised by visits from Christian European traders. She put little stress on the firm educational foundations and permanent buildings considered essential by her colleagues. She was in disagreement with most of them too when she maintained that pioneer work was best done by women, who caused less alarm than men; African chiefs told her, she said, 'Ma, we don't want a man; we want a woman like you to come and teach our girls to read and sew and wash and know God's Book'.[9]

Eventually she persuaded the Mission authorities to establish a medical station at Itu, as a strategic point where the Cross River divides. The District Commissioner of Itu, Charles Partridge, was a Fellow of the Royal Geographical Society who had studied both theology and anthropology at Cambridge. He and Mary worked in a close partnership, based on mutual respect. He persuaded her to become Vice President of the Itu court − effectively she was President, as the titular President was the District Commissioner himself. The court was composed of herself and three Chiefs. As in Okoyong, most of the cases concerned land, debts and possession of women. Often when litigants were fined she would give them work in the Mission compound which would enable them to pay.

The Government's annual report recorded the District Commissioner's success in getting husbands of twin-bearing women to take back their wives, by summoning the husbands for desertion and non-support; it added 'The result is a sign of the civilizing influence worked through the Court by that admirable lady, Miss Slessor'.[10]

After Partridge was transferred, Mary was rebuked by a new District Commissioner for trying a case which he considered should have been referred to himself and she sent in her resignation. Her long letters to Partridge after his transfer, describing the decline of administration under his unworthy successors, are preserved in the Dundee Museum. Though he did not often reply, when civilization advanced and roads improved he sent her a bicycle.

Refreshed by home leave in 1907, Mary returned with two European helpers who took over her station and enabled her to move once more in order to set up a women's industrial training centre. Long experience had convinced her that the problems of the women were economic. They had no status except as dependants, and were exploited by men as labourers, carriers of kernels and oil, and boilers of nuts. If they were not attached to some man, they could be insulted or injured with impunity. She saw the solution as the establishment of centres where unattached women could support themselves by farming and industrial work.

She was now situated five miles from the road and was without visitors, mail or supplies for weeks at a time. She was reduced to reading the newspapers that lined her boxes, until, she said, she had memorized the names of all the hotels in Europe from the advertisements.

By now she was almost a legend. The Governor General of Nigeria, Sir Frederick Lugard, visited her and recommended her for a decoration. His brother Edward, in the Colonial Office, felt 'a great lump in my throat as I read her life story' and reflected on 'the long years of not quiet, but fierce devotion – for they say she is a tornado – unrecognized and without hope of, or desire for, recognition.'[11]

In her last years she was seldom well, plagued by boils and quite bald; she had to be pulled around in a bathchair. She sometimes became rather irascible; her diaries however show no despondency, only frequent thanks for the opportunities she has been given. 'God is very good to me' she exclaims, when Sabbath congregations are full, or as she opens a parcel of goodies from friends in Scotland.

The difficulty she had felt on her arrival in loving the 'debased' Africans had long since been overcome. 'How decent and clean and fine mannered they are' her diary records in 1912. As for their religious capacity, she wrote to a fellow missionary in the same year, 'the native feels deeply but cannot express it in ordinary language, or in ordinary times. He never gushes; the training and the slavery which still holds them in all its traditions and national habit of life make them a deceitful people in the ordinary affairs of life, but in the soul work I have not found deceit.'[12]

One biography of Mary Slessor describes her as 'half hoyden and half saint.'[13] A hoyden she remained all her life: the girl who had climbed trees became an old lady who felt no embarrassment in greeting British officials and missionaries as she sat on the roof carrying out repairs and wearing nothing but her chemise. With one visiting inspector from the Mission she had such a fierce quarrel that she stormed out of the room. When they next met at supper, she said no more about the matter but simply put her tongue out at him. She retained too her fascination. A crew of European contractors working on the roads nearby forswore drink on Christmas Day for the pleasure of having supper with her, and even they sensed the saint beneath the hoyden.

Mary Slessor's religion is quite as interesting as the work which it inspired. Although she recollected that as a girl Hell fire had driven her into the Kingdom, she found it a kingdom of love and tenderness and mercy, and never sought to bring anyone into it by shock.[14] Fear is not worship, she said, nor does it honour God.

When a new arrival at the Mission asked what she should do, Mary told her 'You've just got to *be*, and the doing will follow.' Her own faith was robust, grounded on Bible reading and prayer. It was easier to believe, she said, than to doubt. She read the Bible three times a day, pencilling comments in the margin such as 'God is never behind time,' 'Christ was never in a hurry,' and 'Blessed is the man or woman who is able to serve cheerfully in the second rank.' Sometimes she was puzzled by a verse but 'trusted God with all I do not understand.'

Although she found that praying was harder than doing, she felt her life to be 'one long daily, hourly, record of answered prayer,'[15] not only her own, but those of her friends in Scotland and elsewhere for her. It was this that gave her the ability to endure.

'I am just surrounded by love,' she wrote, 'Christ is here and the Holy Spirit, and if I am seldom in a triumphant or ecstatic mood, I am happy and satisfied in His love.'[16] As Daniel, who slept in her room when a child, remembered, 'She went to bed late, tucked up the babies and would remain awake on the bed repeating a psalm or verse or humming one of her Efik hymns, written by herself. In moonlight nights she would remain for hours gazing straight into the moon, and calling to God for help, courage and resource.'[17]

The secret of all failures, Mary believed, was disobedience. 'All work carried out for others is first of all a discipline for ourselves,' she wrote to her colleague Thomas Hart in 1912, 'God cannot give success (what is success?) in our best aspirations because we cannot bear it ... God will work out the purpose by another way though, for with Him there is no waste, so no desire or prayer is lost, though it does not run through our chosen and small channel.'[18]

Despite the fame which she achieved, she remained remarkably humble. In a letter to 'Dear friends and fellow workers' in 1908 she described how unworthy she felt to have her work valued at a much higher rate than she felt to be true ... 'To be trusted notwithstanding and prayed for and rejoiced over and gifts given in order to help and cheer ... makes me tremble and even keeps me from sleep.'[19]

The radiance and the thankfulness for the privilege of her work remained until the end. She struggled on until the beginning of 1915 when she died, surrounded by her adopted children. Her last words were in Efik as she prayed, 'O God release me soon.' The funeral in Calabar was impressive. Schools and offices were closed and police lined the streets. To some it was not an occasion for mourning. Old Ma Fuller, the missionary from Jamaica, who had welcomed Mary on her first arrival, exclaimed 'I don't know when I enjoyed anything so much; I have just been near Heaven all the time.'[20]

She had led exactly the life to which she had aspired as a girl in Scotland, listening to the sermons about Calabar. She was supremely conscious of the privilege of being able to do so. Her afterthoughts on the marriage which never took place are not known, for she destroyed most of her personal papers when she was dying. But towards the end she wrote 'I'm a witness to the perfect joy and satisfaction of a single life, with a tail of human ragtag hanging on behind.'[21]

Further Reading

W.P. Livingstone, *Mary Slessor of Calabar*, London, 1916 is a main source, as the documents on which much of it was based were destroyed in the war. The most useful subsequent Life is C. Christian and G. Plummer, *God and One Redhead – Mary Slessor of Calabar,* London, 1970. There are numerous short Lives, some written for schools. There is an excellent chapter on her in C. Oliver, *Western Colonial Women in Africa*, London, 1982. Some of her letters and diaries, as well as ms accounts of her by her foster son Daniel Slessor, are in the Dundee City Museum and the Dundee Public Library.

Notes

1. M. Slessor – T. Hart, 6 July 1912, Dundee Museum ms 1984–272.
2. W.P. Livingstone, *Mary Slessor of Calabar*, London, 1916, p. 20.
3. M. Slessor to 'Maggie', 17 April 1877, Dundee Museum ms 1984–259
4. C. Christian & G. Plummer, *God and One Redhead*, London, 1970, p. 51.
5. Christian and Plummer, *op. cit.*, p. 119.
6. Mary Kingsley, *Travels in West Africa*, London, 1965 edition, (originally published 1897), p. 74.
7. Memories of Daniel Slessor, 1948, Dundee Museum, 1984–273.
8. Christian and Plummer, *op. cit.*, p. 77 ff.
9. Christian and Plummer, *op. cit.*, p. 136.
10. *Ibid.*, p. 149.
11. M. Perham, *Lugard*, Vol. 2, London, 1956, p. 397.
12. M. Slessor – T. Hart, 6 July 1912, Dundee Museum ms 1984–272.
13. Christian and Plummer, *op. cit.*, p. i.
14. Livingstone, *op. cit.*, p. iv.
15. The Mary Slessor Calendar, London, 1919, pp. 9, 11, 30.
16. Livingstone, *op. cit.*, p. 163.
17. D.M. Slessor, MS, Reminiscences of Miss Mary Slessor, 1958, Dundee Central Library D 8380 E.
18. M. Slessor – T. Hart, 6 July 1912, Dundee Museum, ms 1984–272.
19. M. Slessor, 'Dear Friends,' 20 May 1908, Dundee Museum, ms 1984–259.
20. Livingstone, *op. cit.*, p. 340.
21. Christian and Plummer, *op. cit.*, p. 177.

PART V

QUESTIONS AND REFLECTIONS

11

Three Queries – Elizabeth Fry,
Florence Nightingale, Catherine Booth

Although Josephine Butler was the only British post-Reformation woman to be commemorated in the ASB, two others, Elizabeth Fry and Florence Nightingale, were included in the draft calendar which was circulated by the Liturgical Commission in 1976. The records do not explain why their names disappeared later. Both women were so greatly esteemed in their time that it seems appropriate to devote some attention to them. A third name, equally celebrated, which was sometimes mentioned in the discussions, was that of Catherine Booth, who was born a Methodist, became a Congregationalist and then, together with her husband, founded the Salvation Army.

Elizabeth Fry (1780–1845)

The work of Elizabeth Fry was to be an inspiration to many women of the next generation who sought an active role in the relief of suffering and improvement of social conditions. Yet her life was full of disappointments. After a brief period when she was influential, the British Government rejected her policies for penal reform. The Society of Friends accused her of neglecting her children and of social snobbery. Her husband's bankruptcy seriously limited her sphere of action. All but one of her ten surviving children left the Society of Friends.

She was born a Gurney, in a Norwich Quaker family respected as bankers but considered somewhat frivolous by stricter Friends. She was the fourth of twelve children. As a girl she wavered between the natural attractions of country balls and a search for religious direction until at the age of 18 she experienced a conversion and became a Plain Friend. Henceforth every morning she woke up to examine what service God demanded of her that day; in her journals and letters 'you' now became 'thee' and 'first month' and 'second month' replaced 'January and February'. She adopted Quaker dress, though elegantly, her brown silk shawl being trimmed with ermine. She occupied herself by running a small school for poor children. At the age of 20, after considerable hesitation, she married Joseph Fry. The Frys were a stricter and less wealthy family than the Gurneys but the marriage was on the whole fortunate. Joseph, a tea trader and small banker, was easy going, even indolent, but devoted to his wife; although he sometimes grumbled, he was usually prepared to stay at home and look after the children when she was away on her frequent missions.

The marriage at first involved living in London above the business; Elizabeth was expected to entertain the many Frys who used the house as a base when they came to the city. She disliked this arrangement, for all her life she hated and despised domestic duties. She found life less uncongenial when the family moved to the large country house in Essex which Joseph inherited and where they employed twelve servants. She was on excellent terms with the Anglican vicar, in consultation with whom she ran a girls' school. Yet she was not happy. At 28, as she looked back on eight years of marriage which had produced five children, she had a heart, she wrote in her journal, ready to wait as a servant for divine orders, but they did not come – 'Instead of being as I had hoped, a useful instrument in the Church militant, here I am, a careworn wife and mother, outwardly nearly devoted to the things of this life.'[1]

In 1811, however, she was acknowledged as a Minister in the Society of Friends: this was to be highly important for her career. For it was as a Quaker Minister that she was able to travel without her husband, investigating social problems and organizing committees to deal with them. She discovered a facility for extempore prayer which was sometimes an embarrassment to her family, as when on the occasion of an inaugural dinner for a branch of the British and Foreign

Bible Society, in the presence of several clergymen, she suddenly knelt and prayed aloud for thirty minutes while the wine and dessert were kept back. Occasionally she would travel to preach at Friends' Meetings.

It was only in 1816, when she was 36 and had nine children, that she started the work among the female prisoners of Newgate Jail, in the City of London, which was to make her famous. The attention of the Friends had been drawn to the disgraceful conditions in Newgate by a visiting American Quaker, Stephen Grellet, a few years earlier and in 1813 Elizabeth Fry and Anna Buxton had made a visit to take clothing to the prison for the babies born there. Now, when her regular visits began, she found about 300 women, some sentenced to death, some not yet tried, crowded together with their children and infants, cooking, eating, cursing and fighting. With courage and inspiration her first appeal to the prisoners was to cooperate in the organization of a school for the children. Having obtained their agreement, she was told by the prison governor and sheriffs that her plan was impossible because no room was available. This official resistance caused the prisoners to ally themsleves with Mrs Fry and to give up one of their own cells for the school; they were encouraged by her to elect as teacher an educated young woman who was imprisoned for stealing a watch.

Now Mrs Fry turned to the more formidable task of reforming the prisoners whose confidence she had won. She expressed her 'concern' to the Society of Friends and set up a Ladies Committee of eleven Quaker women and one Anglican clergyman's wife. With the characteristic Quaker belief that God is in every man and woman and that decisions which affect groups should be taken by consensus rather than by authority or vote, she persuaded the female coiners, forgers, thieves and prostitutes to agree to their own severe rules of conduct. They unanimously voted to engage in needlework, knitting or other employment, to be divided into classes and to listen to a portion of Scripture read to them each day by one of the lady visitors. They promised to renounce begging, gaming and quarrelling, and they chose their own monitors to maintain order. Basic to the success was the organization of remunerated work for the prisoners; Mrs Fry arranged for the sale of the articles which they produced. The ladies set up a little shop where the prisoners could spend their earnings on tea, sugar and haberdashery. The Committee also supplied clothes for the women and their children.

The Lord Mayor of London, accompanied by members of the Corporation, was now invited to pay a visit and they were astonished to see prisoners who had recently been described as wild beasts quietly sewing and knitting whilst Mrs Fry read a chapter from the Bible to them. At the end of the Napoleonic Wars unemployment had led to a soaring crime rate. Parliament and the Press were alarmed. Mrs Fry and her work thus aroused wide interest. Ministers of religion of all denominations, politicians and foreign diplomats came to see the astonishing transformation. The American envoy commented that Mrs Fry in Newgate was the greatest curiosity in London. Maria Edgeworth was captivated by the voice and manner of the lady who she said had done the most good of any woman of her age.[2] Hundreds of people came up to her after meetings or visited her − business men, writers, the nobility, politicians and former prisoners. She agreed to sit for her portrait, because, she explained, the artist might otherwise be spending his time in low public houses.

Mrs Fry revealed in her journal her delight most of all at her reception by the nobility. At Knowsley, the home of the Earl of Derby, she records 'I was summoned into the grand drawing room ... the servants were open mouthed. Lady Derby and I walked in first, arm in arm, the rest followed − I should think there were in all about a hundred assembled.'[3]

As she became a household word, Mrs Fry was transformed from being a prison visitor into a penal reformer. She hated capital punishment, and, though it drained her emotions, would pray with and comfort condemned women in Newgate up to the moment of their execution. Prisoners who were condemned to death, often for thefts of small sums or for forgery, were deliberately seated by her in the front row at her prayer meetings. Politicians and members of the nobility who came to see the spectacle found it harder to take an abstract view of capital punishment when they found themselves facing and praying with women about to be hanged.[4] In an attempt to save one of her women from execution for forgery, she involved both Prince William and the Governor of the Bank of England, thus alienating the Home Secretary, Lord Sidmouth. She learnt from the experience and was more diplomatic with his successors.

As her work in Newgate became established, Mrs Fry, usually accompanied by a relative, visited other prisons in Britain, travelling also as a Quaker Minister, and setting up committees of lady visitors. When she entered a new prison her approach was always the same. She would face a suspicious gathering of women prisoners and ask them if they wanted to turn from what was wrong and be visited by ladies who would sympathise and help them to lead better lives. One by one they would vote rules for their conduct similar to those in Newgate. Then Mrs Fry would read the parable of the Prodigal Son and kneel in prayer. Her prayer, said one observer, 'was beyond words – soothing and elevating . . . I felt her musical voice to be like a mother's song to a suffering child.'[5]

In 1818 she was asked to give evidence before a House of Commons Committee on London Prisons, an unprecedented honour for a woman. At the Committee's request she described the methods of her prison work, whose most important features, she explained, were the provision of employment, for which the prisoners were paid, and the supervision of women by female jailers instead of men.

She was warmly praised by the Parliamentary Committee for her work. But as for the Society of Friends, 'The prudent fears which the *good* have formed try me more than most things,' she noted sadly. Accused of neglecting her family, she wrote in her journal in 1817, 'O that I could prosper at home in my labours as I appear to do abroad.'[6] One by one her children grew up to marry outside the Society of Friends, and each time she felt obliged to refuse to attend their weddings.

In one respect Mrs Fry's success in drawing attention to the scandalous conditions in jails were self-defeating. In 1823 Parliament made the prisons the responsibility of local authorities; the latter were obliged by law to provide an adequate diet and clothing to prisoners and to employ a paid turnkey instead of warders who lived on fees and bribes. The Justice of the Peace would seldom agree to allow access by the Ladies

Committee because they might see and report that the new conditions were not fulfilled.

Elizabeth Fry's interests were not confined to prisons. As she travelled she inspected lunatic asylums also. She set up homes for discharged prisoners and 'naughty little girls.' She provided libraries for coastguards. One of her important achievements was to improve the conditions of women who were deported from Newgate to Australia. By practical demonstration she showed that if the women were brought to the convict ships in cabs, instead of on foot and in irons and pelted by the mob, they would be easier to handle. She persuaded the authorities to allow them to take small children with them and to build a barrack for their accommodation on their arrival in Sydney. The Ladies Committee provided them with materials for work on the voyage and Mrs Fry visited, encouraged and prayed with them on board before they sailed.

She was sensible and far-sighted. When she visited Ireland with her brother Joseph in 1827 they drew up a report for the Lord Lieutenant in which, presciently, they urged more intensive cultivation so that if the potato crop failed wheat would be a substitute. Twenty five years later the Attorney General for Ireland told Parliament that 'a better State Paper was never produced.'[7] For Mrs Fry care of the poor was a religious duty, laid down in the Scriptures. She devised a scheme for Brighton, which was emulated elsewhere, by which district visiting societies were set up. Their members encouraged the poor to save and visited them in their homes, rewarding thrift and relieving distress.

Elizabeth Fry was also a pioneer in the training of nurses. The German Pastor Fliedner was inspired by her to start his institution in Kaiserswerth for training Protestant Deaconesses who nursed the sick; here Florence Nightingale was to be trained. In England itself Mrs Fry drew up plans for a school for uniformed Protestant Sisters of Charity who were trained at Guy's Hospital in London and then lived in a Nurses Home in the city, tending the poor of the parish. Several of the 'Fry Sisters' accompanied Florence Nightingale to Scutari.

In 1827 came personal disaster. Elizabeth's husband Joseph, as she soon noticed after her marriage, was neither as capable nor as hard-working as the Gurneys. He was also extravagant, impulsively buying a picture by Rembrandt or Canaletto whatever the state of his finances. His business and bank were once saved by loans from the Gurneys, but now in an economic depression his bank stopped payment and he was declared bankrupt. The Gurneys salvaged his tea business and employed him to run it on a salary, and Elizabeth received an annual allowance from them. Houses, land and furniture however were confiscated by the bailiffs. Pathetically, Elizabeth's small nephews and nieces sent her their pocket money to buy back a few of her personal possessions. Joseph was disowned by the local Quaker Meeting. Elizabeth did not cease to attend, but was sometimes told that she would not be welcome when she proposed to continue her visits around the country as a Minister.

Further unhappiness came when the Government rejected her approach to penal reform. Elizabeth Fry was primarily concerned with moral reformation of the individual. The Whig Government which came into office in 1832 on the other hand was motivated by a 'scientific' approach to deterrent punishment. From America they adopted a policy of solitary confinement under which conversation between prisoners was strictly forbidden; Pentonville Prison was built to implement this. Mrs Fry, who had advocated supervised group work by day and separation of prisoners only at night, was appalled by the new policy. She regarded solitary confinement over a prolonged period as having a devastating effect on the personalities of uneducated people, from which many of them never recovered.

A report by Government Inspectors on Newgate, published in 1835, could hardly fail to acknowledge the good motives of Mrs Fry and her ladies, but attacked their methods because they 'diminished the necessary gloom of a prison and mitigated the punishment that the law had sentenced the prisoners to undergo.'[8] In 1835 Elizabeth Fry told a Committee of the House of Lords that 'There is more cruelty in prisons that I have ever seen before.'

Humiliated by the bankruptcy, and with her policies for penal reform rejected in England, Mrs Fry turned in her later years to spreading her ideas on the Continent, to which she made five visits between 1838 and 1843.

On her first visit she was accompanied by her husband and daughter Kate, but wore them out. Her energy was formidable. Even on landing, seasick, at Boulogne, she would preach at her hotel to the staff and the landlady's relations. On later expeditions she usually took one of her brothers, a couple of young and admiring nieces, and sometimes a weighty Friend. They travelled in a handsome coach provided by the Gurneys, followed by a van full of victuals and tracts.

The party would visit jails and lunatic asylums and hold religious meetings with whatever Protestant groups they met along the way. Introductions provided by Prince Albert, as well as Mrs Fry's international reputation, opened the doors of all institutions which the party wished to visit. Wherever she went she was received by sovereigns and their ministers. In her journals she gives a lively account of her advice to kings and queens, who seem to have behaved with considerable aplomb when she knelt in prayer and blessed them; it is unfortunate that she seldom records their replies. On her first visit to Paris she created a sensation when she preached to a thousand women inmates of the St Lazare prison on the parable of the Prodigal Son, asking them if they would like ladies to visit and sympathize with them; not only the prisoners, but the jailers were in tears. There was general astonishment that her message could be so moving, even through an interpreter. She warned the French upper classes boldly about the bad example of their theatre-going and late hours but was warmly received by King Louis Philippe. To the French Prime Minister, the scholarly Guizot, she urged that the universal circulation of Scripture was the one means capable of controlling the power of sin.

In Belgium she had two meetings with the King, 'who held out both hands to meet me,' she recorded; she spoke to him of the brutal conditions in some of his prisons and gave him improving books.[9] She told the King of Holland after her inspection that she hoped his reign might be marked by prisons becoming means of reformation of prisoners, as well as by the provision of religious education for the lower classes and the liberation of slaves in Dutch colonies. She followed up with a letter to his Minister of the Interior, urging her usual recommendations: for the female prisons, women as warders and the use of Ladies Committees; for the lunatic asylums an interest in the mental recovery of the inmates instead of incarceration and neglect. 'And has the King', she persisted, 'attended to the question of scriptural education for the lower classes?'[10]

In Denmark she was shocked to find Baptist Ministers in solitary confinement for preaching their faith. When she saw the King she quoted Luther in favour of religious toleration and obtained their release. She lectured the Queen of Hanover 'on the difficulties and temptations to which rank is subject' and the obligations on royalty to take an interest in Bible Societies and prison reform.[11]

It was with the Prussian royal family that she had her greatest success. On her first visit she described her work among prisoners in England and knelt down to ask a blessing for the King, the whole state, and prisoners in the dungeons. The King was fascinated, and later corresponded with her frequently on the reforms which he was introducing. When he visited England, he came to hear her read to the prisoners in Newgate and afterwards was entertained at her house to a lunch which she described as 'handsome and fit for a King, yet not extravagant.'[12]

Mrs Fry did not neglect the royal family in England itself. She conversed with Queen Victoria on religious subjects, regretting (rather strangely) that she was 'under so much High Church influence.' Seated next to Prince Albert at a Mansion House dinner, she offered advice on how to manage the royal nurseries and on the infinite importance of a holy and religious life, leading on to the condition of prisons at home and abroad. She does not record any remark by the Prince.[13]

From the somewhat complacent accounts of these visits in her letters and journals, an impression could be given that Mrs Fry's approach to royalty was remarkably unsophisticated. Yet from the letters she later received it is seen how effective she was. As a result of her pleas prisoners were unchained and provided with employment and healthier prisons were built and heated in winter. New Committees were created whose members visited prisons and brought humane attitudes to them.

No gleam of humour breaks into Elizabeth Fry's journals, written in the pious idiom of the time, and it is not easy to understand how she exercised her extraordinary personal influence. Even her sister Louisa seemed puzzled by it as she wrote to her son, 'Catholics, Protestants, high and low, learned and ignorant, are drawn to your Aunt by a sort of witchery.'[14] The captain of a steam packet which picked her up in a storm from a rowing boat in which she was returning from a visit to a convict ship wrote 'To see her was to love her, to hear was to feel as if a guardian angel had led you.'[15] In several accounts her preaching is described as 'magic'.

When Elizabeth Fry died at the age of 65, a thousand people attended the funeral in the Friends' burial ground in Barking. Religion, she had written in her journal, 'has been anything but bondage to me, but has brought me a delightful freedom.' Through exercising that freedom she brought comfort to thousands and eventually, after her death, her humane approach to prisoners and lunatics prevailed. Yet the price of her freedom was considered in her lifetime by many critics, including several of her children, to have been neglect of family duties. Indignation among Friends was exacerbated when the Inner Light led her to banqueting with Kings and Lord Mayors.

After her death two of her daughters however, wrote a memoir, mainly consisting of careful selections from her letters and journals, which portrayed her as a saint. Whatever was disconcerting was suppressed. When, much later, biographers read diligently through the forty four volumes of her journals, a more complex character emerged. A recent biographer sums up – 'Through her personal courage and involvement men and women all over the world have been enabled to recognize in the prisoner behind the bars their own face. For her signal achievement was to acknowledge the humanity of the prisoners and to consider their individual needs ... She had the gift of touching people's hearts by her own deep religious feeling and her passionate concern for good.' Yet, the same writer continues, 'she was proud, selfish and ruthless ... ready to sacrifice her family at any time for the cause.'[16]

The verdict seems somewhat harsh. The frustrations caused by all the unplanned – perhaps unwanted – births were severe for 19th-century women with a call to the service of God and their fellows. She was keenly aware of her faults and weaknesses. 'How deeply, how very deeply,' she confided to her journal, 'I fear the temptation of ever being exalted or self conceited.'[17] It would be interesting to know whether her name was removed from the list of those recommended for commemoration in the ASB of 1980 because of her weaknesses or simply for the technical reason that she had never been baptized.

Notes
1. J. Rose, *Elizabeth Fry*, London, 1980, p. 58.
2. Rose, *op. cit.*, p. 117.
3. Rose, *op. cit.*, p. 106.
4. *Ibid.*, p. 95.
5. *Ibid.*, p. 106.
6. Rose, *op. cit.*, pp. 108, 100.
7. Rose, *op. cit.*, p. 131.
8. Rose, *op. cit.*, pp. 158, 160.
9. *Memoirs of the Life of Elizabeth Fry by her two daughters* London, 1847, p. 357.
10. *Ibid.*, II, 399.
11. *Memoirs*, II, 404.
12. *Memoirs*, II, 428.
13. *Memoirs*, II, 437.
14. Rose, *op. cit.*, p. 131.
15. *Memoirs*, Vol. I, p. 441.
16. Rose, pp. 204–5.
17. *Ibid*, p. 71.

Florence Nightingale (1839–1910)

Of all the women who may be considered for commemoration, the claims of Florence Nightingale are perhaps the most difficult to assess. She was hailed as a saint in her lifetime by the common people, who she consoled in their distress. Yet no one was more critical of the methods by which she achieved her aims than herself. 'You take the Cross and use it as a club,' she admonished herself in her journal. ' . . . I have never been Thy servant. I always seek my own glory, not Thine.'[1]

Her career is so well known that it may be briefly summarized. It was only possible because she came from a wealthy and well connected family. An enlightened and dilettante father gave Florence and her sister Parthenope a very broad education, teaching Latin and Greek to them himself, as well as French, Italian and German. The family moved between their two country seats and a London house, with long journeys on the Continent of Europe.

Mrs Nightingale and Parthe expected Florence to enjoy the kind of social life which would lead to a brilliant marriage. She however was sure from an early age that she wished to lead a life of service and to train as a nurse. At the age of 29, though much attracted to him, she refused to marry Richard Monckton Milnes, conscious that marriage would interfere with the kind of work she felt called to do and also that 'until a married woman can possess property there can be no love.'[2] Her mother and sister repeatedly prevented her by hysterical scenes from training in what they considered to be the disgusting profession of nursing. In her frustration and misery she came to regard family life as the worst of all tyrannies. Eventually however she managed to undergo training with the Protestant School of Deaconesses at Kaiserswerth in Germany and with a Roman Catholic Order in Paris. Further, through reading reports and through correspondence, she acquired a very wide knowledge of hospital and public health conditions.

In 1853, when she was 33, her father at last overruled her mother, gave her an income, and allowed her to become head of a private nursing institution for sick governesses in London. Here her administrative talents at last found scope. In a few weeks the institution was modernized and reformed, as she manoeuvred her committee of titled ladies and her committee of gentlemen. 'I do all by intrigue,' she admitted.[3] She also made time in an epidemic to nurse cholera cases outside the institution.

In the following year the Crimean War broke out between Britain, France and Sardinia on the one side and Russia on the other. Despatches from the correspondent of *The Times* at the front, W.H. Russell, described the appalling suffering of the British wounded due to lack of adequate arrangements for their care. The medical services of our French allies were far superior, he reported, and he asked, 'Why have we no Sisters of Mercy?'

In this situation Florence Nightingale's qualifications seemed to Sidney Herbert, the Secretary at War to be unique. At his request she went out at a few days' notice with a group of nurses to the base hospital at Scutari. On arrival the party was informed by the Army Medical Officers that their services were unnecessary. With great restraint Miss Nightingale confined her nurses to scrubbing floors and making bandages until, after the Battle of Inkerman, the numbers of sick and wounded were so great that the authorities had to seek their help. It was now that Florence Nightingale became famous through letters which the wounded wrote home, as 'the Lady with the Lamp', who never let anyone who came under her eye die alone, who held the hands of patients during amputations and seemed to have a special power to soothe them, and who sat up for half the night, writing to their relatives. Her achievements as an administrator and reformer had a far wider effect. Whilst army hospital equipment and rations were mislaid or could not be unpacked because the purveyors lacked instructions, Miss Nightingale used the Times Fund which was at her disposal to buy whatever was necessary locally in the vast market of Constantinople. She was the only person with money at her disposal and authority to spend it.

Through her direct correspondence with Sidney Herbert she caused a Sanitary Commission to be sent out which found that the huge death rate in the Scutari Hospital was due to defective sewers. Once Scutari had been cleansed, supplied and reorganized, she took in hand the hospitals in the Crimea itself. She also set up recreation rooms for the troops, and provided them with books and games, incurring reproaches from senior officers that 'She was spoiling the brutes.'

Florence Nightingale returned to England haunted by her memories of the way in which the British Army had destroyed itself; far more men had died from unnecessary or untreated disease than in action. 'O my poor men who die so patiently,' she wrote, 'I feel I have been a bad mother to you, coming home and leaving you in your Crimean graves, unless truth to your cause can help to teach the lessons which your deaths were meant to teach us ... I stand at the altar of the murdered men, and while I live I will fight their cause.'[4]

With the support of the Queen and the Prime Minister, Lord Palmerston, she brought about a Royal Commission on the health of the Army; she chose its Chairman, Sidney Herbert, and most of its members, coached its witnesses and largely dictated its report. In her own evidence she showed that the death rate in military barracks in England was twice that of the civil population. She saw to it that the recommendations were not pigeon-holed but immediately implemented through four Subcommissions, each chaired by Sidney Herbert. When Herbert became Secretary for War she drove him into an attempt to reform the War Office itself and to abolish its system of endless minuting which delayed all decisions. Although his doctor said he was dying, she brushed the verdict aside and expressed her contempt when he resigned with the task unaccomplished; on his death shortly afterwards she became sick with remorse.

She now turned to sanitary reform in India, starting by sending out questionnaires to three hundred Indian stations. She soon recognized that the British Army's health could only be satisfactorily improved if similar plans were also made for that of the civil population among whom it lived. This led her into studying and making proposals about irrigation works and land reforms which could finance health programmes. She had a passion for statistics. She seldom left her house. Viceroys, Secretaries of State and Generals came to her to be briefed; files were sent to her from the Ministries.

In her honour a Nightingale Fund had been set up during the Crimean War. She used this to support a school at St. Thomas's Hospital which produced a new kind of nurse with a high ideal of her profession. She read the reports on the probationers every month and showed them great kindness, inviting them to stay for a few days in her house when they needed rest. Among her many other interests were a new kind of layout of hospitals in pavilions, to prevent the spread of infection, and workhouse reform.

The success of her campaigns was due to her flair for sensing where power lay, her ability in using information extracted from experts, and the clarity and forcefulness with which she could state her case. She was sustained by a moral conviction that she was right, and in her hand was the seldom-used weapon of her enormous public prestige. Her tactics varied. When the Liberals were in office she could take a firm line. When the Tories came in she described herself as 'frightening, intriguing, soaping or going on all fours.'[5]

She was able to charm and inspire experienced administrators, soldiers, and sometimes even politicans. She was also a bully who overworked her associates remorselessly and never spoke to them again if they felt obliged for the sake of their families to leave her exacting service. She maintained that organized blunders do more mischief than crimes and that indifferent and organized carelessness was far more hurtful than sin. 'Of all the human sounds,' she said, 'I think "I don't know" the saddest.'[6]

Her earnestness was relieved by a caustic humour, so that Gladstone was castigated as 'a most unsanitary brute'; Lord Shaftesbury, she said, 'would have been in a lunatic asylum if he had not devoted himself to reforming lunatic asylums'; the inept Generals and Medical Officers who received the K.C.B. after the Crimean War she described as 'Knights of the Crimean Burial Grounds.' Her humour was not always sardonic. Soldiers from the Crimea remembered her as 'full of fun and life, when she talked with us, especially if a man was a bit downhearted.'[7] Young children loved to be with her.

In her loneliness she was apt to dramatize her situation. 'Did it ever strike you,' she asked a friend, 'how if Christ had to work *through* Pilate he would have done? ... Christ was betrayed by one but my cause has been betrayed by everyone.' In other moods she would reflect on her faults and describe herself as a vampire.[8]

In 1889 Florence Nightingale wrote to Benjamin Jowett that she could never remember a time when mystical or spiritual religion had not been the main question of her life. 'The two thoughts God has given me all my life have been − first to infuse the mystical religion into the forms of others (always thinking they would show it forth much better than I) especially among women, to make them "hand maids of the Lord". Secondly to give them an organization for their activity in which they could be trained to be "handmaids of the Lord" ... When very many years ago I planned a future my one idea was not organizing a hospital but organizing a religion.'[9]

This religion was of an unusual and personal kind. Both her parents came from Unitarian families. Her mother found Anglicanism more suitable to her social station; Florence was thus brought up in the Church of England of which she always remained a loyal, if quizzical member, though she was tolerant of all faiths which issued in good works. She admired the Roman Catholic Church for its attractive saints, its businesslike methods and the useful role which it gave to women: but though when young she sometimes stayed in its religious houses, she felt no compulsion to submit to a Church which would insist on telling her what she should believe. Like Joan of Arc (as she recollected) on four occasions she heard voices calling her to a life in God's service. She read and pondered on the mystics, in particular St John of the Cross and St Teresa of Avila, but declared that the 'mystical state is the essence of common sense: the ecstatic state is unreal and should not be at all.'[10]

She regarded herself as a mystic but not a contemplative. She saw the purpose of every experience as increased action. Religion, she maintained, 'is not devotion but work and suffering for the love of God ... It is not knowing doctrine but bearing fruit that He desires ... It is a religious act to clean out a gutter and prevent cholera: it is not a religious act to pray (in the sense of asking).'[11] And, as the sardonic mood took hold, she asked 'Is there anything higher in thinking of one's own soul than one's dinner?'[12]

Confined for many years to her rooms by her weak heart and nervous condition, her only recreation apart from her cats was theological and metaphysical speculation. Cautiously encouraged by Benjamin Jowett and J.S. Mill, she wrote an enormously long book, privately printed, called *Suggestions for Thought to the Searcher of Truth among the Artizans of England*. In this she developed a natural theology which could come to terms with the discoveries of science and which, to her friend Jowett, appeared to combine a spirituality based on the writings of the saints of the Early Church with 19th-century rationalism. Its message was that though the essence of God was a mystery, the character of God was knowable. The universe was governed by divine laws which could be discerned by experience, research and analysis. Evil had been placed in the world as a challenge to man. Discovery of the divine laws, and consequent doing of God's will, would lead to communion with God; education through mistakes lay along the way. God's laws in the social sphere could be ascertained by statistics, the study of which thus became a religious service.[13] The conflict between love of God and love of self was to be resolved through work. Every man and woman was called both to be a saviour and a servant.

At times she felt desperately cut off from God. She wrote to Jowett in 1865, 'I think if I had felt God loved me I could have borne anything, but I never could feel it,'[14] Later, partly because of Jowett's liberal and soothing influence, she became more confident and could instruct her probationer nurses to treat old people in workhouses 'like those to whom comes the love of Christ,'

Florence Nightingale was described by Lytton Strachey as treating God as 'a glorified sanitary engineer'. She reminded herself indeed that 'I must remember that God is not my private secretary' and admitted 'O Lord even now I am trying to snatch the management of the world out of Thy hands.'[15]

When she was young she was embittered by the Church of England. 'I would have given her my head, my hand, my heart,' she wrote. 'She would not have them. She did not know what to do with them. She told me to go back and do crochet in my mother's drawing room, or, if I were tired of that, to marry, and look well at my husband's table.'[16] In her mature years and in a lighter mood she would cry, 'From Committees, charity and schism, from the Church of England and all other deadly sins — from philanthropy and all the deceits of the devil, Good Lord deliver us.' She would prefer, she said, to work in Hell, to save the poor living bodies, rather than be shut up with Bishops and Deans in Heaven.[17] Nightingale nurses however were instructed to pray together twice a day and to attend services of the established Church on Sundays.

In her old age Miss Nightingale became quite benign, venturing out to stay in the country with her sister, now Lady Verney, and writing sentimental letters to her young Nightingale nurses. When she was 78 she was visited by the Aga Khan and reported, 'A most interesting man, but you never could teach him sanitation ... I told him as well as I could all the differences, both in town and country, during my life. "Do you think you are improving?" he asked. By improving he meant believing more in God.'[18]

Florence Nightingale's achievements in bringing about reductions in suffering and deaths and a caring attitude to people whom society had despised are outstanding. It is not easy to see how, in a time when a woman was unable to sit in Parliament or become a senior civil servant, they could have been realized except by her kind of ruthless methods of intrigue, flattery and bullying. She herself, whose first interest was in religion, may however have pondered towards the end of her long life the Aga Khan's question. She had improved the world but had she in doing so come closer to God?

Should the Church of England, which she teased, but in which she felt comfortable, join the Anglican Church in Canada and the American Episcopal Church in commemorating her? Perhaps the authors of the ASB were right in deciding in the end that it was more appropriate to leave her to be honoured as a secular heroine. For as Benjamin Jowett, though he loved her dearly, said, she was a very violent lady.[19]

Notes

1. F.B. Smith, *Florence Nightingale, Reputation and Power*, London, 1982, p. 199.
2. *Ever Yours*, Selected Letters of Florence Nightingale, ed. M. Vicinus, London, 1989, p. 288.
3. *Ibid.*, p. 74.
4. *Ever Yours, op. cit.*, p. 164; F.B. Smith, *op. cit.*, p. 73.
5. C. Woodham Smith, *Florence Nightingale*, London, 1950. p. 447.
6. *Ever Yours, op. cit.*, p. 202; E.T. Cook, *Florence Nightingale*, Vol. 1, London, 1913, p. xxiii.
7. Woodham Smith, *op. cit.*, p. 589.
8. *Ever Yours, op cit.*, p. 5; Woodham Smith, *op. cit.*, p. 231.
9. Cook, *op. cit.*, Vol. II, p. 366.
10. Woodham Smith, *op. cit.*, p. 525.
11. F.B. Smith, *op. cit.*, p. 184; *Ever Yours, op. cit.*, p. 3.
12. Cook, *op. cit.*, Vol. I, p. 488.
13. Cook, *op cit.,* Vol. 11, p. 396.

14. *Ever Yours, op. cit.*, p. 264.
15. Lytton Strachey, *Eminent Victorians*, London, p. 171; Woodham Smith, *op. cit.*, p. 529; Cook, *op. cit.*, Vol. II, p. 244.
16. Woodham-Smith, *op. cit.*, p. 98.
17. Cook, *op. cit.*, Vol. I, p. 135; F.B. Smith, *op. cit.*, p. 183.
18. Cook, *op. cit.*, Vol. II, p. 405.
19. Quoted by Jan Morris in *Oxford Book of Oxford*, Oxford, 1978.

Catherine Booth (1829 – 1890)

No woman before her, wrote her friend and admirer, the journalist W.T. Stead, exercised so great a religious influence in her time as Catherine Booth.[1] She also did as much as anyone in her century to obtain recognition of the capacity of women to teach, to organize and to command. The women in the Salvation Army tended to be better educated and come from a superior social background than the men. Because of Catherine Booth's own unique position there was never any barrier to the promotion of women to any rank. She confidently sent out her Hallelujah Lasses as missionaries into the roughest pubs in England's cities and her daughter Kate into the workers' bistros of Paris.

Catherine Mumford was born at Ashbourne in Derbyshire, though the family later moved to London. Her father was a carriage maker and Methodist lay preacher, and her mother, who taught her at home, was so rigid in her morals that Catherine was not allowed to learn the French language lest it lead her to corruption. The conversion of the world was a favourite topic of family conversation. At the age of 17 she became suddenly conscious of being saved. She never in her life had a day free of pain from spinal curvature and other ailments, but her enforced leisure gave her the opportunity to read the Bible through eight times before the age of 12 and to acquire a wide knowledge of theology. She threw in her lot with the reforming Methodists, then with the Congregationalists. When she fell in love with William Booth at a party where he recited *The Grog-Seller's Dream*, the future General was a pawnbroker's assistant. She guided his studies, drafted his sermons when he became a

Congregationalist preacher, and strengthened his determination not to be confined to a circuit but to preach at large and found the Salvation Army, despite the insecurity which this caused to his family.

Catherine and William were both 26 when they married. They had seven surviving children, all of whom, except the invalid Maria, Catherine dedicated to God and the Army. At home she sat at the head of the table. She insisted on implicit obedience from her children from their fourteenth month and whipped them when they were disobedient. In their presence she would pray that she would lay them in their graves rather than mourn for one who turned from Christ.

When he was 7 she demanded of her son, 'Willie, you must answer me, will you give your heart to God, yes or no?'; he bravely replied 'No.' Yet a few months later he came forward and squeezed on to the penitent form along with other children.[2] When another son, Bramwell, as a teenager felt no call to preach, she turned on him fiercely, 'Your name should have been Bramble not Bramwell ... I hope the Lord will make you so miserable everywhere and at everything else that you will be compelled to preach.'[3] It was however a happy family. Her husband adored her. She knew how to encourage him and he how to calm her. Friends remembered him arriving like a hurricane, scattering children right and left as he rushed into the kitchen to share new ideas with her.[4] Children, she said, could no more grow up without love than a plant without sun, and Sundays were joyful occasions for picnics and excursions.

In her earliest pamphlet Catherine asserted the Biblical evidence for equality between men and women and the right of women to teach religion and to preach; she attacked the contemporary system of education of women as training them to an imbecile dependence on others. But it was only at the age of 30 that she was suddenly, and to William's surprise, inspired to preach. Shortly afterwards she occupied his pulpit for nine weeks whilst he was ill. When the Salvation Army was formed she preached to the middle class in the West End whilst William spoke to the masses of the East End. She was a moving preacher with a beautiful presence and a voice, said an American visitor, 'like a silver bell across a still lake.'[5] She would lose all sense of time, preaching for between one and two hours and afterwards spending as long guiding those who came forward to the penitents bench. The financial contribution which her work brought in was probably more important than that of William though neither of them took much thought for the morrow.

It was Catherine who designed the Salvation Army's flag and uniforms and gave teetotalism a prominent part in its programme; William had been used to take an occasional glass of port for his digestion.

She enjoyed, and was inspired by, visiting the poor – the more depraved the better. A sinner was the subject of great compassion, but once converted was strictly controlled. Conversion must lead to restitution, even if this led to prison. Like her husband she tended to see the worst in those who did not instantly obey them. She urged her friends to expel their sons from home if they either got into debt, could not account for money, or came home after 10.30 p.m. Her granddaughter and biographer comments that whilst William was the demagogue, she was the teacher, and, in her less happy moments typically the governess, who could not resist laying down the law, and imposing a rigid Victorian discipline not only in her family but in the Army.[6] She advised that reading novels was un-Christian and maintained that thousands of people had been ruined by reading Voltaire. She warned against levity and, still worse, buffoonery. She was indeed earnest and humourless but was saved from fanaticism by her humility, sense of unworthiness and dependence on divine grace. Towards the end of her life she told one of her daughters-in-law that she regretted that she had not got more happiness out of life – 'I advise you,' she said, 'not to be such a slave to daily work as to have no time to love one another, to make each other as happy as possible.'[7]

Her theology was conventional and orthodox. People were prevented, she believed, from being saved not from want of faith, but want of obedience. After a great struggle she considered herself dead unto sin. From childhood she was on speaking terms with the Devil, and this was a constant tonic in supplementing her belief in God. She had a passionate sympathy with all who were suffering, animals as well as people.

When she was 59 and at the height of her influence as the Mother of the Army cancer was diagnosed. She would not submit to an operation or take opiates but lived on for two years, slowly dying in public. Her bouts of pain were alleviated by news of the Army's victories, and unknown to her a stenographer, hidden behind a screen, took down all her words. Among the last was regret that she had not been able to do something for the prisons and asylums. Each of her children had to promise her on her death bed to be faithful to the Army. Perhaps she pressed them too hard; after her death three of them resigned and Eva was to help to lead a successful coup against Bramwell, who had succeeded William as General.

When she died 36,000 people filed past her coffin, draped with the flag which she had designed; through its glass front she could be seen with her arm resting on her favourite picture of the General, who in his tribute declared, 'The guides and authorities of other religions are all Fathers; only in the Salvation Army has a woman been chosen to lead the way.'[8]

It would be difficult to exaggerate the influence for good of Catherine Booth in her joint leadership of the Salvation Army. Its message and the workers whom she trained helped thousands of outcasts of society in the worst of the slums to a better life. But her humourless, uncompromising style might make her an uneasy companion among those honoured in the ASB.

Further Reading

Elizabeth Fry

The most useful modern life is J. Rose, *Elizabeth Fry* (London, 1980) but *Memoirs of the Life of Elizabeth Fry from her Journals and Letters* by her two daughters (London, 1847) is still essential.

Florence Nightingale

C. Woodham Smith's *Florence Nightingale* (London, 1950) is the most useful biography though that by F.T. Cook, from which much of it is drawn *(Life of Florence Nightingale*, London, 2 vols, 1913), remains indispensable. A selection of her letters has been published as *Ever Yours*, edited by M. Vicinus and B. Nergaard (London, 1989). Lytton Strachey's chapter in *Eminent Victorians* (London, 1918) can still amuse. Nancy Boyd, *Josephine Butler, Octavia Hill, Florence Nightingale*, (London, 1982) is interesting on her religion. F.B. Smith, *Florence Nightingale, Reputation and Power* (London, 1982) is somewhat hostile.

Catherine Booth

W.T. Stead, *Mrs Booth of the Salvation Army* (London, 1900); C. Bramwell Booth, *Catherine Booth – The Story of Her Loves* (London, 1970). Whilst the above are the most readable, there is also a massive uncritical three-volume *Life of Catherine Booth* (London, 1893) by her son-in-law, F. de L. Booth-Tucker.

Notes

1. W.T. Stead, *Mrs Booth of the Salvation Army*, London, 1900.
2. C. Bramwell Booth, Catherine Booth – *The Story of Her Loves*, London, 1970.
3. *Ibid.*, p. 342.
4. *Ibid.*, p. 168.
5. *Ibid.*, p. 423.
6. C. Bramwell Booth, *op. cit.*, p. 358.
7. *Ibid.*, p. 415.
8. F. de L. Booth-Tucker, *The Life of Catherine Booth*, Vol. III, London, 1893, p. 434.

12

Some Other Worthies

The writer's choice of the ten women to whom individual chapters have been devoted has inevitably been subjective. Many other names are likely to occur to readers with either a general or specialized interest in the history of Christian women and of various movements in which they were involved in the 19th and early 20th century. Some of those who may deserve further consideration are briefly treated in this chapter.

Elizabeth Gilbert

The women who pioneered social causes in the 19th century were often the wives, unmarried daughters and widows of clergymen or of university teachers. Among them was Elizabeth Gilbert (1826–85) who lost her sight at the age of three and devoted her life to setting up institutions for providing training and work for the blind. At a time when even kindly and intelligent people would pray that a blind child would 'be taken to Heaven,' her father, who was Principal of Brasenose College, Oxford, and later Bishop of Chichester, insisted that she be brought up just like her sisters, with the aid of reading devices which he pioneered. Her whole life was given to showing that blindness, though a great privation, was not necessarily a disqualification. Strongly supported by W.E. Gladstone both, he said, as a political economist and a Christian, she set up workshops and libraries for the blind, and developed forms of employment for them. Not only her eyes but her throat were affected and she was in constant pain. Yet when a friend told her that she was working herself to death, she replied 'Why, I am working myself to life,' and she used eagerly to look forward to the end of each month, so that she could share in the great paean of praise to God in the Psalms which are appointed for the thirtieth evening.[1]

Josephine Butler

Little need be said here about Josephine Butler (1828–1907) as she is already commemorated in the ASB and is the subject of a chapter in the present writer's *Alternative Saints*. Although she was born into a notable reforming family, the Greys, the particular causes to which she felt compelled to devote much of her life, the repeal of the Contagious Diseases Act and the prevention of organized prostitution, were utterly repugnant to her and she adopted them reluctantly: 'like Jonah,' she said, 'I fled from the Lord.' It was her clergyman husband who sustained her, thus incurring considerable unpopularity in the Church of England.

Josephine Butler came to believe that, in every cause which is God's, failures and disappointments were inevitable before success was achieved. She had a great capacity for prayer towards a God whom she felt to be intimately involved with the hopes and suffering of the world and who gave a programme and plan of action: it took more courage, she said, to be alone with God than that needed to meet human opposition. She loved the memory of the Saints and wrote lives of Catherine of Siena and of Pastor Oberlin.

She was fortunate in a husband who was generous, unambitious and much in advance of her time in his view of the rights and status of women. Her sons too willingly served as assistants and secretaries in her work.

Ellice Hopkins

One of the most attractive 19th-century women ever to take up an unattractive cause was Ellice Hopkins (1836–1904). Gifted as a poet and natural scientist, she reluctantly came to devote most of her time and energy to exposing and trying to diminish the casual exploitation of working class women and children as prostitutes by men of the upper classes. As she ruefully declared 'Nature has made me a singing bird, but man has made me a sewer rat.' In summer however, when she took a holiday and returned to her poetry, 'I resort to the original type. The whiskered snout sharpens to a golden bill and the squeak becomes a song.'[2]

She was born in Cambridge where she was educated at home by her father, a mathematics tutor. She was brought up as a member of the Church of England, as she recalled, 'in all the refined and intellectual life of a university which I sometimes think more than any other separates one from the life of the people.'[3] At a very early age she preached an evangelical and emotional Christianity to groups of working men, an exercise which she later regretted. After her father's death she settled in Brighton with her mother. There, with great initial repugnance but encouraged personally by Florence Nightingale, she embarked on rescue work, visiting prostitutes in their homes in the mornings. Her scientific and mathematical training kept her emotions under control, and the statistics which she published were so startling that they were a considerable factor in the Government's decision to make it a criminal act to keep girls of under 16 in a house of ill fame.

She then embarked on a nationwide campaign, addressing meetings of men, asking them to form Guilds or Societies for protection of women and children against prostitution. She sought to give the men 'a more aggressive form of purity, for mere self restraint will never fight the battle.' 'I did not come to help them,' she pleaded, 'but to ask their help in a battle I found too hard for me.'[4]

At Oxford, with the aid of Canon Scott Holland, she was received with great sympathy by a meeting of undergraduates. At Edinburgh University on the other hand the audience crowed like cocks, whistled like parrots and caterwauled like cats; prayer or hymns were impossible, and they would not allow the men on the platform to address them. Yet once Ellice Hopkins got up, as Scott Holland recalled, 'She held them. She mastered them ... Her language was always effective and finely chosen, but at times she would rise to passages which entranced. Then at such times the weakness of her physical frame added power by contrast to the emotional tension'.[5] In the long run her warmest support came not from the upper, middle or university classes, but from the workers, notably the pitmen and artisans of Yorkshire and Durham. 'The real cancer in our nation', she declared, 'is the aristocracy who have transferred the "not" in the Commandments into the Creeds. Their empty headedness and their intense vulgarity, I declare, irritate me as much as their coarse profligacy'.[6]

She raised money for numerous refuges and training homes for women and girls. Her work, as compared to that of Josephine Butler, was more preventive than remedial. She was a devout High Church Anglican, but with a dislike of ritual. Christianity, she considered, was not a speculative system but only life rightly seen and rightly ordered. She had a horror of sentimentality and preferred the deeply moving Psalms of David to the hymns of her day, many of which she found far too sunny, pure and unclouded for her struggling soul to breathe and live. For a time she became melancholy and discouraged, with a sense that God was cruel – 'He paid me with blows and set my trembling hands to do work which they could only bungle over'. Her depression however was overcome 'when I think that God has left me with this delightful faculty of acquiring knowledge', and she cheered herself up by writing articles on carnivorous plants and other botanical questions for the *Contemporary Review*.[7]

She was helped too by her keen sense of fun. Once, on holiday, she was picnicking in a field when she went to sleep over a long folio poem of a most depressing character which had been sent to her by an admirer. The manuscript was thus eaten by a cow, but she wrote truthfully to its author that it had been 'eagerly devoured and inwardly digested by a disciple'. She took on everybody. Attacking medical men who maintained that prostitution was necessary, she poured scorn on 'the superstitious credence which the British mind is apt to accord to what a doctor says, even when it conflicts with the dictates of our conscience', pointing out that the medical profession had been wrong in prescribing bleeding and alcohol for their patients and flogging as a remedy for mental illness.[8] She told Dr Barnado that his advertisements for his homes were 'flashy and claptrap', signing herself, 'your faithful, but odiously candid friend'.[9]

In the end her exertions brought about the collapse of a frail constitution. In her last years she was a permanent invalid, though remaining 'the confidante of many troubled souls, with a touching belief in human possibility'.[10] She left no journals, diaries or record of her soul's growth and so it must reluctantly be concluded that there is probably an insufficient basis on which to put her name forward for commemoration. Yet she may still be remembered for a few of her poems, some of which are pertinently moving in a generation which shares her sense of guilt at the suffering caused by the thoughtlessness of the human race not only to its fellows but to animals and to the environment, as in 'Life's Cost':

> I could not at the first be born
> Without another's wailing pain,
> Another's loss must be my gain ...
>
> Since then I cannot live a week
> But some fair thing must leave the daisied dells,
> The joy of pastures, bubbling springs and wells
> And grassy murmurs of its peaceful days,
> To bleed and reek
> And die for me to tread life's pleasant ways.
>
> I cannot sure be warmed or lit
> But men must crouch and toil in tortuous caves,
> Bowed on themselves, while day and night in waves
> Of blackness wash away their sunless lives.
>
> With gems I deck not brow or hands
> But through the roaring dark of cruel seas
> Some wretch with shuddering breath and trembling hands
> Goes headlong, while the seasharks dodge his quest.
> Then at my door he stands
> Naked with bleeding ears and heaving chest.'[11]

Catherine Marsh

A more robust character, Catherine Marsh (1818–1912), was best known as the champion of the navvies, the rough, rootless and despised men, often Irish, who constructed the great railway systems of Victorian England. She was the daughter of the Vicar of Colchester. Her mother died when she was a child and she continued to live with her father in Leamington and then Beckenham, on happy terms with his second and third wives. After his death she lived with a niece and her clergyman husband.

From an early age she helped in the daily round of parish work and engaged in hospital visiting, but she prayed that God would show her a more substantial form of service. Her prayer was granted when in 1853 3,000 navvies arrived in Sydenham to re-erect the Crystal Palace which had housed the Great Exhibition in Hyde Park. Two hundred of them were lodged in Beckenham. Catherine held prayer meetings for them, chivied them into church, provided hot food for them in winter, and looked after their belongings. She fearlessly intervened to separate them from fighting with each other and with the police, visiting them in prison and sometimes obtaining their release. She came fully into her own when the Government recruited them to go out to the Crimean War as an Army Works Corps: she provided them with religious cards and tracts, took care of their savings, and wrote their Wills. She went on board the ships which were to take them to the Crimea and gave them games and puzzles to break the monotony of the voyage. Many died of disease during the War but the survivors came to see her on their return, bringing little gifts of foreign coins, charms, stones and even live pigeons.

What she wrote about them was as important in raising the reputation of a despised and feared class as what she did for them personally. Her book *English Hearts and English Hands or The Railway and the Trenches* portrayed them lovingly and individually. She described the long hours which they were made to work by the contractors, how they were dismissed if they refused to work on Sundays, and how they had no shelter or boards to sit on in the rain when they ate their lunches. She declared that they were treated worse than stagecoach horses. She aimed, she said, 'to draw out the higher and nobler feelings of the less favoured classes; setting themselves gently, patiently, steadfastly to work to eradicate the notions of distrust, suspicion and envy too generally entertained by the poor towards the rich.'

She had many other causes and was a prolific writer. She gave religious talks to groups of chimney sweeps, dressmakers, shop assistants and policemen, and held Bible readings for Cambridge undergraduates. She visited the sick and dying in cholera epidemics, when, together with Mrs Gladstone and the wife of Archbishop Tait (popularly known as the Three Catherines), she set up homes for orphans of the epidemics and convalescent homes for the adult survivors.

She corresponded on social questions with Lord Shaftesbury, and J.A. Froude and with Gladstone, who patiently invited her to breakfast when she wrote to rebuke him; for her ardent Protestantism made her a fierce opponent of Irish Home Rule and of legislation to enable Roman Catholics to hold high office. However she knitted a bed jacket for the Grand Old Man in his last illness; he thanked her and hoped that they would meet again when they had both put off earthly garments and put on the garment of righteousness.

She was given to impulsive little acts of charity, such as a gift of a goose to a crossing sweeper, or intervention on behalf of a deserter being arrested at Waterloo Bridge. She believed in Eternal Life for horses, particularly her own which, she predicted, would 'follow the Glorious King when He rode out from Heaven.'[12] She was aware of her hastiness and when her niece read her letters out to her before despatch would exclaim, 'This is too teachy ... That will never do, it is too like a tract.' She always dressed in soft colours and rich materials, for she maintained that those who dwelt much with the poor should have as much respect for them as for the rich. She went nowhere, she said, where she could not have met Christ on earth, shunning theatres, opera and racecourses, but was happy to dine with publicans and sinners.[13]

She lived to a great age, steadily pouring out elevating books and tracts such as *Ready, Onward and Upward* and *Still Upward*. When she died the Bishop of Durham wrote of the 'power of one who might have done notable things in other fields, if God had not concentrated her whole thought and will upon the unsearchable riches of Christ,' and the Archbishop of Canterbury declared, 'Such a life requires a Te Deum, not a Miserere.' She had, said an obituarist, 'an arresting power. The most worldly could not but be moved by the benignant presence, the absorbing desire to gather in such as shall be saved.'[14]

Susanna Meredith

Not infrequently the lives of these energetic Victorian women, especially among Evangelicals, are marked by a note of inflexibility, even of harshness. Susanna Meredith's biography is subtitled 'Record of a Vigorous Life'. Born in Ireland in 1823, she learnt Latin, Hebrew, French and German. Married to a physician at the age of 19, she then studied medicine with him. Only 27 and childless when he died of cholera, she moved to London to live with her mother and sister and devoted herself to working with and for female prisoners, giving them breakfast when they were released from jail and finding them employment. Then she organized the care and training of children and criminals. She became an authority on the treatment of women prisoners and visited jails all over Europe and U.S.A. She was very pious, and organized Bible study on the Second Coming alongside prison mission work, as well as medical care of the poor, both in London and in the Near East. Noticing how generations of law breakers could be traced among prisoners, she became preoccupied with the Law of Moral Heredity and advocated that the children of criminals should be taken away from them and educated by the State in special institutions both 'as an effective form of punishment' to the parents and to break the chain of corruption. She even urged that children born in workhouses should be taken away from their mothers and brought up in similar State institutions.[15]

Sarah Martin

At a humbler and local level worked Sarah Martin (1791–1843), who became a prison visitor in Yarmouth shortly before Elizabeth Fry went into Newgate. Baptized in the Church of England, her parents died when she was a child and she was brought up by her grandmother, a glovemaker. In her autobiography she recalled how at the age of 12 she 'discovered an indescribable aversion to the Bible and a bitter prejudice against spiritual truth and read much trash from the circulating libraries'. She was apprenticed to a dressmaker at the age of 14; when she was 19, after reading the 9th and 11th Book of Romans, 'I saw Salvation to be entirely of Grace, I was made free'. She began to learn much of the Bible by heart, visited the poor in the workhouse and read the Scriptures and led services in the jail.[16]

She was shocked by the idleness and lack of occupation of the prisoners. The doors were simply locked on them and their time was given, she said, to gaming, swearing, playing and fighting; she settled down, in her spare time, to find them occupations. She gave materials for clothes-making to the women, and bones to the men for carving spoons and buttons; she taught both men and women to read and write. She saw that they needed to give as well as to receive, and took books to be covered and had little garments made for the children in the workhouse. When the prisoners were discharged, she tried to find them jobs and collected a fund to furnish them with the tools of their trade, even with a donkey. Though poor herself, she refused to take a salary for her work, for she believed that if she did so her influence with the prisoners would be lost.

She was an admirable person, but her concern was entirely with people and their needs, not for the reform of institutions; indeed she reported to the Prison Governor on the conduct of individual prisoners.

'She seemed,' says one of her biographers, 'to live beyond herself, entering so strongly into the trials and sympathizing so deeply with the feelings of others as to make them her own.'[17] For the most part the prisoners were smugglers, pickpockets, brawling sailors and prostitutes, and she preached to them God's mercy. When they told her 'We don't want religion, we want victuals,' she relates that 'I took pains to show them that religion, which enforced justice, industry, etc., brought plenty, and in the absence of its principles there was want and destitution.' This could seem either bland or harsh in the England of the Industrial Revolution and the Game Laws. She had no sense of humour and wrote her own funeral service, to be read to the prisoners, for whom 'to reflect upon my removal may help you to consider the uncertainty of your own life.' It is appropriate that she should be commemorated by a window in her local Church, but, though she was the subject of several lives in the mid 19th century, she hardly seems a saint for our times.

Angela Burdett-Coutts

At the other end of the social scale was Angela, Baroness Burdett-Coutts (1814–1906). No contemporary did more in such a variety of ways to increase the sum of human happiness. At the age of 23 she unexpectedly inherited £2 million from her banker grandfather's second wife. In Britain she used her fortune to build low-cost housing, schools, churches, and markets and provided drinking fountains for people and animals. She was a benefactor of fishermen and costermongers. She established industries to relieve distress in Ireland and was a founder both of the National Society for the Prevention of Cruelty to Children and the Royal Society for the Prevention of Cruelty to Animals. In the Empire overseas she endowed Bishoprics and built churches and church schools in Canada, Australia and South Africa.

She was raised to the peerage and was the first woman to be given the Freedom of the City of London. Having turned down many avid suitors, at the age of 67 she married her 30 year old secretary. She is buried in Westminster Abbey. Though she was a religious lady and gave much of her money to excellent causes, enough remained to support her in her mansion in Piccadilly in a style which can hardly be supposed to have inspired others to sanctity. It is perhaps as difficult for a rich woman as a rich man to enter the Kingdom of Heaven.[18]

Hannah Kilham

All the 19th-century women mentioned so far in this chapter remained members of the Church of England. An unusually determined and imaginative career was that of Hannah Kilham

(1774–1832) who progressed from Anglicanism through Methodism to the Society of Friends. She was born Hannah Spurr, seventh child of 'respectable tradespeople' of Sheffield. She grew up in the Church of England and was educated in a boarding school where 'she made so much progress in the study of grammar as to displease her master who thought her overstepping the bounds of female province'. At the age of 22 she resolved 'to give herself to God.' She joined the Methodists in love feasts and band meetings and visiting the poor. Two years later she married Alexander Kilham, the leader of those Methodists who had seceded from the main body, demanding a more democratic control, after the death of John Wesley. They had only been married for eight months when Kilham died, worn out by his exertions, leaving her with his daughter by a former marriage and later with her own daughter, born after her husband's death, who died whilst still an infant. Hannah earned her living by running a day and boarding school for girls which she endeavoured to make 'a home of interest and happiness'. Dissatisfied with the outward exuberance of Methodists, she joined the Society of Friends in 1803 and took part in many Quaker good works, such as the organization of schools for the poor and visiting the elderly. Troubled by the way in which the attention of children was confined to the history of wars and slaughter and the rise and fall of empires in distant places, she wrote history textbooks which were more concerned with the happiness and well-being of mankind.

Her school prospered, but gradually she began to feel a call to wider service. She was a passionate opponent of slavery. At first she wished to organize a mission in the West Indies for the education and betterment of the negroes. Then she turned to the question of the education of the children of liberated slaves who were settled in Sierra Leone. Her originality lay in her determination to arrange and reduce to letters their languages. She persuaded the Friends to take care of two Africans, selected by her from the crew of a merchant ship in London, whilst she learnt from them, and wrote vocabularies of, the Jaloof and Mandingo languages.

She was diverted from this work in 1822 when she was sent to Ireland by the British and Irish Ladies Society to organize famine relief after the failure of the potato crop. Her reports and letters were understanding and practical: she was concerned not just with relief but with provision of spinning wheels, flax and wool so that mothers could provide clothing for their families and earn income. She cooperated amicably and effectively with the Roman Catholic clergy in organizing schools and libraries.

This broad experience had equipped her well when at last she sailed for West Africa in 1823 with two male and one female companions together with the two African seamen who had been her teachers. They started a school in the Gambia for boys and girls, mostly mulattoes and children of slaves. There was little sympathy among European merchants for their efforts to produce grammars and dictionaries of African languages and use them as a medium of teaching; they preferred to converse with the natives in a kind of barbarous broken English which was amusing because of the grotesque blunders. Hannah also visited Sierra Leone where she made considerable progress in recording languages. In July 1824 she returned to England with two of her European colleagues to consult with Friends about the continuation of her work. One colleague however died on the voyage and another only survived a few weeks more in West Africa. The first school had collapsed.

Undaunted, Hannah made a second visit in 1827, this time to Sierra Leone where she remained for a few months 'taking sketches' of 25 African languages. In light of the high death rate of Europeans in what was then 'the White Man's Grave,' she now planned that schools should be established for Africans in England where they might have a Christian and general instruction. She also suggested that neither European nor African missionaries should be allowed to despise active labour but should be trained in surgery, carpenter's work, gardening, book-binding, and other skills.

In 1830 she made her third and longest visit to West Africa, where she persuaded the Governor of Sierra Leone to allow her to take charge of children rescued from slave ships in a boarding school which she set up in the village of Charlotte outside Freetown. The school was to promote three objects, an experiment in teaching English through African languages, the care of liberated children, and the training of teachers. Here, with no Europeans nearby, she told her friends not to think of her life as a mournful exile but as one delightfully relieved from any extreme care and crowned with the sense of infinite kindness and tender mercy. Happily translating, teaching and training teachers, she would occasionally emerge in Freetown to pick up more children rescued from slaves by ships of the Royal Navy, and to intervene with the Government on behalf of apprentices, who were often still treated like slaves.

Her restless spirit ranged over broader horizons. Was she to feel a call to Russia or even China? At least she should visit Liberia to investigate the condition of the liberated American slaves. In 1832 she did so, and arranged for some of the children of influential Liberians to be sent to England for their education. She died at sea, on the voyage back to Sierra Leone. Shortly after her death her devoted stepdaughter published her journals. In these the successive influences of Anglicanism, Methodism and Quakerism can be seen on a nature prone to introspection, but effective and cheerful in action. She was progressive in her educational methods, believing that children have a quick sense of right and wrong and may be greatly injured by a tart dictatorial policy. She was eminently practical in her approach to social problems among the poor in England and Ireland. In Africa she concerned herself with improved looms and encouragement of small industries whose products might be traded in the interior. She believed that Africans were 'as susceptible of improvement as the people of other countries, had they fair and just measures afforded to them', though she had no illusions about their brutal treatment of their wives in their unimproved state. She lived alongside them happily in the last period of her life. She was persistent in leading an imaginatively useful Christian life despite the tragic loss of a young husband and only child, and was in many ways much in advance of her time.[19]

Mary Carpenter

Few did more good than the Unitarian Mary Carpenter (1807–1877) who successfully campaigned for reformatories and industrial schools to be set up for juvenile delinquents who, until her time, had been committed to, and corrupted in, ordinary jails. As an example to others she herself ran a voluntary reformatory school, making it as like home as possible and giving the children pigs, rabbits and fowls to keep. Unlike Catherine Booth, she did not believe that a child should have its will broken, but that it should be taught to govern it wisely. However she accepted the conventional wisdom of the day, as Mrs Fry did not, that the first stage of adult imprisonment should be solitary confinement on a penal diet. Once her reforms had been enacted by the British Parliament, she went to India at the age of 60; there through her close links with the Brahmo Samaj and good relations with officials she achieved considerable improvements in female education, reformatory schools and in regulation of child labour in the cotton mills.[20]

By the late 19th century as many British women as men were serving as Christian missionaries abroad. Their lives have received inadequate notice. In the bibliography of Bishop Stephen Neill's authoritative *Christian Missions* (London 1965) 86 biographies of individual missionaries are listed; but only five of these are of women — Pandita Ramabai, Mary Slessor, Lilias Trotter, Mary Bird and Ida Scudder. The first two are the subjects of chapters in this book. Ida Scudder was an American medical missionary in India who died after 1950.

Lilias Trotter

Lilias Trotter (1853–1928) came from a well connected Anglican family. One brother was Vice Master of Trinity College, Cambridge; another was Consul General in Beirut and a K.C.M.G. She was a talented artist and a favourite pupil of Ruskin, who called her 'St. Lilias.' When she began to undertake social work with the Y.W.C.A. however he told her that her sense of colour was becoming debased under the conditions of her life, and mourned her loss as probably the only person who could help him in his chief difficulties and lost ways. 'Am I not *bad* enough? Am I not *good* enough? Am I not whatever is enough to be looked after as well as those blessed Magdalenes?'[21] he asked, in his perpetual unsuccessful search for perfect feminine sympathy.

But now at a missionary conference Lilias was swept away by a call to evangelize in one of the most difficult parts of the world, North Africa. With two other women she went out at the age of 25 to start the Algiers Mission Band. They lived in Arab style, working among women and children. Few women were converted and some of these were snatched away by relatives, were drugged, or even died by poison.

Lilias loved to travel to villages in the desert. She not only spoke but wrote tracts in parables which were read by people who would not have dared to attend her meetings. Her evangelistic work was opposed not only by the Muslim clergy but by the Jesuits and the French authorities. It is difficult to know exactly what she achieved. She was an able and far sighted leader, but also a mystic, some of whose writings were aimed at the Sufis, the Muslim mystics who she hoped might provide a bridge between Christianity and Islam. Her life was one of vision and prayer; her favourite phrase was 'The glory of the impossible.' Her friends remembered her as a saint with two special qualities. The first was her restfulness. 'She was still and created a stillness,' one of them said. Another remarked, 'She is beautiful to feel near. I love the quiet of her.' Secondly, her happiness in her religion was unfailing. The pages of the Song of Solomon were worn through in her Bible. 'I wish she could laugh more,' she said of a new colleague, 'but she'll shake free. They always do.'[22]

Mary Bird

Mary Bird (1859–1914) also devoted her life to the difficult – almost impossible – task of converting Muslims to Christianity. She was the daughter of a parson and related to Archbishop Sumner and William Wilberforce. She started by working among factory girls in Liverpool and went out to Persia with the Church Missionary Society (CMS) in 1891. There was no woman doctor with the mission, and though she had no medical qualifications she found herself unable to avoid treating, with the aid of textbooks, the many women and children who came to see her. She had a special liking for treating neurotic and mental cases and seemed to possess an unusual power to do so. She had not been trained as a teacher either, but had a flair for linking her message to objects around her – a flower, a leaf, a falling snowflake. She had no fear of travelling in areas which were the haunts of brigands because, she said, she had put herself under God's protection. She never believed that foreigners could evangelize a nation. All she hoped was that a few Persian women would be converted and trained to teach the next generation. When her sister married she had to interrupt the work for eight years to care for her elderly mother in Liverpool; though her heart was with her Persian women, she accepted this task patiently as a different form of ministry. On her mother's death she returned to Persia to die of typhoid.[23]

Lydia Sellon

Neither social nor missionary work were altogether new kinds of activity for women, but a third form of religious expression became open to Anglican women in the 19th century for the first time since the Reformation. In the 1840s, largely on the initiative of Dr Pusey, Anglican sisterhoods were established, twenty years before communities for men came into being. Pusey's own chosen vessel was Lydia Sellon (1822–1876) who became the Foundress of the Society of the Most Holy Trinity. Though her father was a naval commander, one of her grandfathers, her brother, and her sister's husband were all clergymen. Her biographer describes her as 'excessively plain but pleasing in manner.' She first worked as a laywoman running schools in the poor areas of Devonport. When Dr Pusey called for a Sisterhood, her father gave land and built a chapel, and the Bishop of Exeter, who was the sole epis-copal supporter of the Tractarians, gave his permission for a Sisterhood of Mercy to be established. Pusey was its spir-itual director and designed its dress. The Sisters were free to visit their relatives or to withdraw from the community. Under the rule the only expulsions were for scandalous gossip. The Sisters attended chapel four times a day. Their main activities were education of sailors, soldiers and orphans and visiting the sick and emigrants on ships. At the age of 29 Lydia Sellon became Lady Superior and was addressed as Dearest Mother, though she was younger than most members of the community.

Pusey said that Lydia Sellon would have made a Bishop had she been a man, and Wordsworth wrote a sonnet to her. The Sisters were widely praised in the national press for their work in a cholera epidemic, but there was carping from the Low Church and dissenters. In 1852 on Pusey's advice an enclosed order was formed which led a life of mortification, contemplation and intercessory and liturgical prayer. The Benedictine spirit in which the Sisterhood began was now overlaid with the tradition of military obedience of Ignatius Loyola. There were secessions to Rome; when the foundation stone of a new convent was laid, a Protestant mob pelted the Sisters with potatoes and plates and drenched them with ale. One Sister's health gave way under the austerities which she undertook, and several pamphlets were written attacking the community for practising confession and corporal penance. The Bishop of Exeter withdrew as visitor because he considered the Superior's claim to be 'Spiritual Mother and Mother in Christ' extravagant and objectionable. The Bishop of London protested at Mother Lydia's interference with the correspondence of one of her nuns with her mother. The reputation of Mother Lydia and the Sisterhood revived however when they provided nurses in the Crimean War.

Eventually the Order moved to its permanent home at Ascot, built with a legacy from Dr Pusey's mother. He made frequent visits there and toured French religious institutions with Mother Lydia, after which they visited the Holy Land and also stayed together in Malvern. This behaviour was criticised and there were defections from the community. There is little doubt that Lydia Sellon was imprudent in subordinating herself to Pusey's extravagances; he suggested that nuns, for example, who enjoyed flowers should be asked to give them up as a mortification.[24] Yet despite her autocratic ways and errors of judgement she may be remembered as the pioneer of Anglican Sisterhoods who taught her Sisters to treat the poor with respect and to seek to bring beauty into their lives.

Emily Ayckbowm

Another foundress who ran into strong opposition was Emily Ayckbowm (1836–1900); described by the Archbishop of Canterbury, Dr Benson, as 'the most comically audacious Mother in the universe.' The daughter of an Anglican Rector in Chester, she founded in 1863 the Church Extension Association, consisting of ladies who in their spare time did church embroidery, illuminated texts, and collected and mended old clothes for poor parishes. Out of this lay group emerged the Community of Sisters of the Church, an active order based in Kilburn, London, whose object was to serve and bring to Christ the poorest of the poor, though under its rule striving for holiness took precedence over the work. Emily Ayckbowm was the first Mother Superior, from 1872 until her death.

The Sisterhood's main activities were in caring for children and in obtaining second hand clothing which was sold to the poor at very low prices. In the 1890s attacks on their work and methods developed on several sides. The Charity Organization Society accused the Sisters of working in an unsystematic way and in particular of taking in illegitimate children for payment, without making enquiries, as well as keeping no proper accounts. About the same time complaints were made by fourteen seceding Sisters that Mother Emily seldom consulted the Council of Sisters, that there was no Visitor to oversee her and that generally the religious life of the Community was being sacrificed to the pressure of work and business. More sensational were their allegations, eagerly echoed by the press, that children were treated cruelly and kept in cages, though these in fact turned out to be dormitory cubicles.

When the Archbishop of Canterbury, who was a patron, wrote to Mother Emily to suggest that he conduct an enquiry, her response was to remove his name, with those of all other males, from the list of patrons.

On one of these issues a later generation may sympathize more with Mother Emily than with critics, who alleged that the Community's care of foundlings encouraged sin. She had many other causes. Her fiercest fight was for establishment of Church Schools instead of the Board Schools set up under the Education Act of 1870, which she regarded as a menace to the nation because they were non-sectarian. She campaigned for abolition of the rents charged for pews, which she considered as an affront to the poor.

She was remembered by her Sisters as 'literally on fire with enthusiasm' and for her wonderful way of imparting that enthusiasm: the Community in her time relieved much misery, at home and abroad. Their life became more tranquil however after Mother Emily's death when a Visitor was at last appointed in the person of the Bishop of London, and criticisms died down.[25]

Edith Langridge

If Lydia Sellon and Emily Ayckbowm were considered to be autocratic, this was not a criticism which could be made of Edith Langridge who founded a Sisterhood within the Oxford Mission to Calcutta. The Mission's original aim had been to convert the students of Calcutta University. When it extended its work to pastoral care of Indian Christians in a rural area of Bengal, women missionaries became essential. Edith Langridge had been Vice Principal of Lady Margaret Hall, Oxford and Warden of its settlement in London when she responded to Charles Gore's request to start a Sisterhood within the Oxford Mission. A brilliant scholar, to her contemporaries it seemed that there was nothing that she could not do better than anyone, and dismay was expressed that she should be 'sent to teach village women to wear chemises instead of letting her work in a college in a big city.' She shaped the Sisterhood as a family in the traditions of St Benedict and of Lady Margaret Hall in its early years. Its members were to be Sisters of Mercy rather than nuns, easily accessible, but with prayer as their first priority. After teaching the 'Esaus' of London slums, Mother Edith found the Indians to be 'Jacobs', capable of seeing visions and unveiling spiritual treasures to the West. She deplored the way in which

Anglo Saxon missionaries were so busy with good works that there was little room for prayer, and regretted the 'corporate pride' of the British. As Mother of the Community she preferred to 'arrange' than to 'organize'. Criticized for not giving a more vigorous lead, she replied 'I don't want a lot of little sheep running after me and feeling bad.' She believed in 'radiation' rather than direct evangelism. Her long silences in interviews and her difficulty in discussing spiritual things seem to have appeared less baffling to Indian women than to her European Sisters. On two occasions she failed to obtain the necessary two thirds majority for re-election as Mother of the Sisterhood.[26]

Frances Ball

Among Roman Catholic founders of Communities in the 19th century, perhaps the most remarkable was Frances Mary Teresa Ball. Her father was a wealthy silk manufacturer in Dublin where, strangely, at a dance at the age of 17 she heard the words 'Seek first the Kingdom of God and His justice, and all things else shall be added unto you.' Taking Mary Ward as a model, she entered a convent and eventually set up the Loreto Convent Schools for Girls in India, Africa and Australia. She was described as 'a woman born to rule, but childlike in submission.'[27]

Emma Cons and Lilian Baylis

There were spiritual women who moved in several worlds. Emma Cons (1838–1912) for example, whom Beatrice Webb described as one of the most saintly as well as farsighted of Victorian philanthropists, was involved in housing reform, set up crèches and clinics, and then leased the Old Vic to provide a music hall without drink. She in turn was succeeded by Lilian Baylis who continued the Christian tradition in the theatre. Women wrote some of the most popular and enduring hymns of the 19th century. Catherine Winckworth indeed, though

British, has her day in the American Lutheran Book of Festivals and Commemorations.

Pioneers in Education and Medicine

Of those who opened up higher education to women, though the sparkling, dynamic Barbara Bodichon was a Unitarian, Emily Davies, the first Principal of Girton College, Cambridge, was a clergyman's daughter, and Elizabeth Wordsworth, the first Principal of Lady Margaret Hall, was the daughter of a Bishop. Among the educationists, Dorothea Beale of Cheltenham, the 'Doctor Arnold' of Girls' Public Schools, might also deserve consideration. She was imaginative, compassionate and a fine organizer. The faith of the Church of England was her mainspring. She was however prone to fits of depression, as she brooded over the lists of her own faults which she compiled each day.

The first woman to practise as a medical doctor in Britain, after enormous difficulties, was Elizabeth Blackwell, who had qualified in America. She expressed the scientist's view that study of God's laws of human growth was a sacred task: 'The fevers of the poor, the hysteria of the luxurious, the indigestion of the learned, the devastation of our mining districts equally show contempt for the wonderful organization which God has made – indifference to the conditions which He had laid down as essential to its welfare ... It is only when we have learned to recognize that God's law for the human body is as sacred as, nay is at one with, God's law for the human soul that we shall begin to understand the religion of health.'[28] Elizabeth Garrett Anderson, the first woman to qualify as a doctor in Britain, attended F.D. Maurice's Church for a time. The almost superhuman patience which she showed in putting up with humiliations in the interests of the future of women in her profession was magnificent. Her ability to combine medicine with a successful family life was an encouragement to many. She was the first woman in England to become a Mayor and in her seventies became a militant suffragette. But there does not seem evidence that the inspiration for this splendid life was to any considerable extent religious.[29]

Eva Gore Booth

Sometimes British women have been distinguished both as activists and contemplatives. Such was Eva Gore Booth who has been overshadowed by her more famous sister Constance, Countess Marcievicz, Irish revolutionary and the first woman to be elected to the British Parliament. They were daughters of a well to do Anglican Irish landlord. Eva's enjoyment of a privileged youth was tempered by passionate sympathy for suffering and strong feeling of responsibility for life's inequalities. She was to lead two different lives. One was as a political and social reformer, organizing Trade Unions in Manchester for women textile workers, barmaids and even acrobats. The other was as a poet and mystic. H.W. Nevinson considered that her religious poems were the finest since the early 17th century. She deserves to be better known.[30]

From this survey, which is far from exhaustive, it will be seen how many women, in how many different ways, led lives in the 19th and 20th century which appear to meet the criterion of exciting others to holiness. The problem is not to find them but to choose between them.

Notes

1. F. Martin, *Elizabeth Gilbert and Her Work for the Blind*, London 1891.
2. R.M. Barrett, *Ellice Hopkins*, London 1907, p. 139.
3. *Ibid.*, p. 17
4. *Ibid.*, p. 153
5. *Ibid*, p. 172, p. viii.
6. *Ibid.*, pp. 236, 262.
7. *Ibid.*, p. 149.
8. *Ibid.*, p. 101.
9. *Ibid.*, p. 73.
10. *Ibid.*, p. 243.
11. Ellice Hopkins, *Autumn Swallows*, London 1883, p. 178.
12. L.F. O'Rorke, *The Life and Friendships of Catherine Marsh*, London 1917, p. 297.
13. *Ibid.*, pp. 168, 176.

14. *Ibid.*, p. 241, and Catherine Marsh, *English Hearts and English Hands.*, London, n.d.
15. M.A. Lloyd, *Susanna Meredith*, London 1903.
16. *Brief Sketch of the Life of Sarah Martin*, London Religious Tracts Society, 1847, pp. 2–5.
17. S.F. Harris, *The Yarmouth Prison Visitor*, London, 1904, p. 107.
18. D. Orton, *Made of Gold. A Biography of Angela Burdett Coutts.*, London, 1980.
19. Sarah Biller, *Memoir of the late Hannah Kilham*, London 1837.
20. J. Manton, *Mary Carpenter and the Children of the Streets*, London 1976.
21. L.R. Govan Stewart, *The Love that was Stronger, Lilias Trotter of Algiers*, London 1958, pp. 15–16.
22. C.E. Padwick, *The Master of the Possible, Sayings of Lilias Trotter of Algiers*, London, 1938, p. viii. See also B.A.F. Piggott, *I, Lilias Trotter*, London, 1930.
23. C.C. Rise, *Mary Bird in Persia*, London 1922.
24. T.J. Williams, *Priscilla Lydia Sellon*, London 1965.
25. Anon., *The Life and Times of Mother Emily Ayckbowm*, London 1964; also A.M. Allchin, *The Silent Rebellion*, London 1958, chapter 12.
26. Sister Gertrude, *Mother Edith*, Beaconsfield, 1984.
27. A Loreto Sister, *A Joyful Mother of Children, Mother Frances Mary Teresa Ball*, Dublin 1961.
28. Dr Elizabeth Blackwell, *The Religion of Health*, London, N.D.
29. Jo Manton, *Elizabeth Garrett Anderson*, London 1965.
30. Eva Gore Booth, *Selected Poems*, London 1929, Introduction by Esther Roper.

13

Reflections and Conclusions

And now though Paul forbids her sex to preach,
Yet may her life instruct and her death teach.
Epitaph on Lettice, Viscountess Falkland, 1649

A glance at the qualifications of the post-Reformation British men who were chosen for commemoration in the ASB helps to explain why women were so largely disqualified. Of the nineteen men, seventeen had studied at Oxford or Cambridge Universities, to which women only obtained limited access in the late 19th century and where they could not take degrees until well into the 20th century. Fourteen of the men were priests and one a deacon in the Church of England, positions which were not open to women when the ASB was approved. Poverty was not necessarily a bar to the education which could take a boy up the ladder to the University, ordination and promotion in Church or State: Richard Hooker and Lancelot Andrewes were rescued from becoming apprentices by schoolmasters who were impressed by their abilities and found patrons to pay for their education. This kind of patronage was seldom available to clever but poor girls. Of the women to whom chapters are devoted in this book only Mary Slessor, who was a Scottish Presbyterian, came from the working class.

After the Reformation had closed the convents and monasteries, opportunities for women to lead lives of sanctity depended far more than those of men on family circumstances. In societies where women have enjoyed no economic independence men have always exercised much greater rights of decision than women in selection of marriage partners. It has been possible for men to continue their work and maintain saintly reputations even when their marriages have proved unfortunate. Hooker's shrewish wife delighted to interrupt his conversations with scholarly visitors by overwhelming

273

him with domestic duties. According to some accounts John Wesley's wife pulled him round the floor by his hair; she certainly made noisy scenes and opened his correspondence; yet Hooker and Wesley have made their way into the ASB.

For a woman an unfortunate marriage could be a disaster; the restriction of her movements by a proprietary husband, limitless pregnancies, care of children and other domestic duties could be serious obstacles to the kind of life in which she wished to express her religious faith. There could on the other hand be advantages in marriage; pious divines indeed liked to point out the scope which bringing up children and running households gave for Christian virtues. Marriage to a generous and sympathetic husband could not only provide moral support but might open doors where single women could hardly penetrate. When Florence Nightingale declared that she wished to emulate Elizabeth Fry and Caroline Chisholm, her aunt pointed out that she lacked a Mr Fry or a Captain Chisholm. The life of a spinster, obliged to remain at home nursing aged parents, could be even more restrictive than marriage. It has been seen how Mary Bird and Mary Slessor were called back to Britain from important careers in the mission field to care for relatives. Florence Nightingale felt bitterly that her genius had nearly been stifled by her family before it had been expressed; but she too left her work to nurse her aged mother after the years of fame.

Who is known and honoured has depended to a great extent on the accident of what has been written about them in their lifetime or shortly afterwards to serve as the raw material for all subsequent biographies; the saintly life of Thomas More is only well known because his son-in-law, William Roper, lived in his house and kept verbatim notes. Izaak Walton's life of George Herbert was written some 40 years after the latter's death at the request of the Archbishop of Canterbury in order to provide a lesson for the Restoration clergy to lead less selfish lives. Nicholas Ferrar's fame is largely due to the discovery, 150 years after his death, of a manuscript account of his life by his brother, upon which a Victorian best selling novel was based.

Such fortunate chances seldom applied to Anglican women though the Roman Catholics continued to make women saints after the Reformation. The holy lives of English women were not so much regarded as insane, as ignored because they were not known. The early exceptions were the Anglo Saxon abbesses, whose lives were lovingly embellished by chroniclers because they came from royal families, and the very few medieval women, such as Julian of Norwich, who wrote devotional works.

The position in the 19th and early 20th century was very different; there never was a time before or since when it was so easy and inexpensive to have a book published, whether biographical or devotional or both. Of the women of this period who have been discussed, most wrote books about their ideas or work, and biographies of almost all of them appeared shortly after their deaths, often including their letters. Whilst Christina Rossetti was a major poet, even the poetry of those who were not, such as Evelyn Underhill, Eglantyne Jebb, and Ellice Hopkins, found publishers without difficulty. Girls too were encouraged to keep journals. With the penny post correspondence expanded vastly until the telephone age commenced. There exists therefore a large quarry of materials on 19th-century worthies.

A colleague of Eglantyne Jebb perceptively remarked that her character showed an integration which had distinguished many women saints. That integration was often hardly won. Josephine Butler and Caroline Chisholm struggled to avoid the disgusting tasks to which they felt that God was summoning them. Ellice Hopkins was miserable at being transformed from a singing bird into a sewer rat. There was bitterness before Christina Rossetti was changed from being 'a very melancholy girl' into 'a very cheerful old woman.' Out of the struggle came Josephine Butler's belief that suffering must precede success in any great cause which is God's. Mary Slessor went even further in saying that God cannot give success because we cannot bear it. Mother Cecile, from her own experience, told her Sisters that it is through the daily thwarting of our plans that we learn obedience.

Integration brought together love of God and love of the people who were His creation. As Mother Harriet Monsell put it, 'Sisters must always be prepared to leave God for God.' Sister Dora vividly advised her nurses to see Christ in their patients, and she herself emerged from incarceration with the smallpox patients 'having learned to love God more.' At times some of these women appeared to enjoy a mystical relationship with God. Yet Evelyn Underhill pointed out that mystics were not quietists but people remade in harmony with God's will. 'Your first prayer,' she told a correspondent, 'must not be to see Him first and always, but to be useful to Him first and always.' Octavia Hill wanted most of all to get near to people and help to bring their spirits into harmony with God's will and purpose. All work done without love, she said, was quite despicable. What is noticeable in all those whose lives have been described is an indomitable faith in human potential. As Eglantyne Jebb put it, 'Everyone is born to work for others; what is wanted is love.' The prison visitors, Elizabeth Fry and Sarah Martin, saw that everyone, however poor or depraved, needed to give as well as to receive, as they persuaded prisoners to make toys and baby clothes for the children of others.

Quiet acceptance of the divine will only came with self discipline. 'Christ was never in a hurry,' wrote Mary Slessor in the margin of her Bible. Octavia Hill noted that 'Restlessness and anxiety arise from a lingering doubt that God can really arrange His world without our help.' Mother Cecile explained 'God allows our environment. When we accept this humbly, and out of our failures learn to cry to God, our deeper life of prayer begins.'

It was prayer, of course, that sustained them all. This too sometimes did not come easily. Josephine Butler considered that it took more courage to be alone with God than to meet human opposition. Mary Slessor found prayer harder than doing, and yet recognized that her life was one long daily, hourly record of answered prayer. Mother Cecile gave practical advice to her novices, 'Bring each person, each difficulty to Him. Then really pray. Then get on with the next.'

Again and again we find thanks raised to God by these women for the privilege of the arduous, often apparently unrewarding work and the uncomfortable lives which they had been given. So the blind Elizabeth Gilbert delighted to praise God in the Psalms; Lilias Trotter, who converted hardly anybody, was thrilled by the Song of Solomon; Caroline Chisholm regarded the work for immigrants which exhausted

her means and ruined her health as 'a Godlike occupation'.
Mary Slessor, old and bald and covered with boils, looked
back on her life in the bush with joy. 'People will only understand vocation,' said Mother Cecile, 'when they see Sisters full
of humble, loving and unselfish joy.' Joy indeed was to out-
siders the most remarkable quality in these lives, and with it
was often linked a sense of fun and humour.

Integration seemed to carry a power of charm such as
Eglantyne Jebb exercised when she collected a £5 contribution from the prosecuting lawyer to the cause for whose
propagation she was on trial. Mary Slessor was perhaps
unconscious of it as she bent District Officers, tough contractors and obstinate tribal chiefs to her will. Mother Cecile,
on the other hand, was aware of the danger that her personality might exercise too much influence on her novices.

Perhaps the clearest sign that integration had been achieved
was seen in the quality of restfulness which it brought. As her
friends remembered Lilias Trotter, 'She was still and carried
a stillness. She was beautiful to feel near.' Evelyn Underhill
gave out a feeling of peacefulness. Visitors to Ramabai's huge
widows' home noticed that even when she did not know how
to pay for the next meal, her faith kept her unworried and
unharried. 'Tarry the Lord's will and be still,' Mother Cecile
told her Sisters. 'He cannot work on us if we are all in
a fuss.'

Along with the obvious qualities of courage, imagination
and energy came attention to detail and an interest in and
sympathy for the day to day problems of life. It was by small
graces that God would judge our lives, as Octavia Hill put it.
Caroline Chisholm was supremely observant of the cares and
needs of her individual immigrants and can been seen advising
them on every article which they should and should not take
with them. Sister Dora saw accurate observation as the first
duty of a Christian and a nurse. It was this concern for detail
which caused Harriet Monsell to be described as having a
degree of common sense amounting to genius.

The women whose lives we have considered were, on the
whole, remarkable for their tolerance of denominational differences. They tended to be ecumenical before their time. This
was the quality in Ramabai which distressed the Wantage

Sisters. Octavia Hill found great comfort in her Anglican faith, yet told a Quaker that she also felt herself to be a Friend. Caroline Chisholm was rebuked by her co-religionists for not working exclusively for Roman Catholics. Sister Dora was so sympathetic to all denominations that several of them claimed her after her death. They were tolerant even of agnostics and those with no faith; Christina Rossetti moved happily between her strict Anglo Catholic Church circle and the bohemian world of her brother Gabriel. Mary Slessor had a great rapport with sinners of all sorts. They were tolerant indeed of the faults of all except themselves.

At Oxford University in the late 19th century undergraduates were required to take an examination in Divinity which was so vestigial that it had become a formality. For many years the first question was 'List the Ten Commandments.' Eventually however a zealous examiner was appointed who decided that this would not do. Thus an examinee was unexpectedly faced, to his dismay, with a different first question – 'Distinguish between the major and minor Prophets of the Old Testament.' Undespairing, he began his answer 'Far be it from me to distinguish between the major and minor Prophets. Let it suffice to repeat the Ten Commandments ...'

At the end of this study, the writer has a somewhat similar feeling. It might seem acceptably pious for one who is neither a theologian nor a church historian to write in an earlier book about those who had already been chosen by the Church of England for commemoration: it could appear audacious on the other hand for him to proffer advice as to who else should be commemorated. It is hoped that the book will not be read in this sense. The names which are put forward as illustrative are one person's choice. Others may have different favourites. The purpose will be achieved if the book stimulates attention to righting a wrong, to redressing a balance, and doing justice to the memories of those like Mary Collett, who told the Little Gidding Academy, 'We may tread out the way to Heaven and we may lead with good works, though we cannot teach by words.'

Appendix
The Church of England's Commemoration
of Saints and Heroes of the Faith

The initiative for the Church of England's commemoration of its recent heroes came from Africa. In 1937 the Bishop of Nyasaland, Dr F.O. Thorne, wrote to the Archbishop of Canterbury, Dr Cosmo Lang, to seek his guidance on a request by the priest and elders of one of his parishes for the beatification of Archdeacon W.P. Johnson who had recently died after serving in Central Africa for 47 years. The Archbishop replied that whilst he had no objection to a special service being used to commemorate Johnson annually, 'beatification' was not in the vocabulary of the Church of England.

The Bishop remained persistent that the Church should have a recognized way of commemorating its departed members for their 'heroic sanctity'. ' The fact that at present a gap of hundreds of years separates the saints we commemorate from the life of today,' he wrote, 'does not help, to put it at its mildest, our Christians to realize that sanctity is a permanent possibility of the Christian life of all ages.' At his suggestion the question of commemoration was discussed at the Lambeth Conference of Bishops in 1948 and as a consequence the Archbishop of Canterbury (Dr Fisher) appointed a Commission in 1950 'to consider in relation to the Church of England questions concerning the recognition or commemoration of Anglican martyrs, doctors, confessors, bishops or the like in Church Calendars, diocesan or provincial, with special reference to missionary dioceses; and to report as to whether there should be some recognized procedure or any regulation in the matter both for missionary dioceses and dioceses in England.'[1]

The report of this Commission, of which the Dean of York, Eric Milner-White was Chairman, was published in 1957 as *The Commemoration of Saints and Heroes of the Faith of the Anglican Communion*. After a survey of the practice in the Roman Catholic and Orthodox Churches, the Commission described the historic and current position of the Church of England. It noted that while the prayer book prescribed a special Collect, Epistle and Gospel for the red-letter days of the Calendar, no liturgical provision was made for minor festivals on black letter days. Within the Church however universities, religious communities and some cathedrals had established their own calendars in which local saints or heroes of the community had been commemorated. In the twentieth century a few churches had been named after recent heroes of the faith such as John Keble and William Temple. The calendars of the Anglican Church overseas contained a considerable number of post-Reformation names.

The Commission recommended that the Church of England should add further names to its Calendar, but in response to local demands rather than to historical research; it offered little guidance as to the criteria for their selection.

In 1964 the Archbishops of Canterbury and York set up a smaller Commission to consider the question in more detail. This suggested that those commemorated should either have laid down their lives for the faith or have lived a life of such quality that to quite an exceptional and uncommon degree they had manifested something of the holiness of Christ. 'Modern saints' should be included because they lived in the devotion of the Church, not because they illustrated the life of the Church in a particular period.[2]

Such was the limited guidance which the Liturgical Commission of the Church of England received when between 1954 and 1980 it prepared the Alternative Service Book. The Commission in 1969 circulated a list of people who might be commemorated in the new Calendar,[3] and on the basis of the comments received in 1976 published another draft Calendar which included three Nonconformists, George Fox, Richard Baxter and Isaac Watts, as well as two women, Florence Nightingale and the Quaker Elizabeth Fry. All five were omitted by the Revision Committee which was appointed by the General Synod in 1977 to make final revisions in the ASB. This Committee altered the balance in favour of the Anglo Catholics and against Evangelicals and excluded all who had not been baptized into the Church of England or the Roman Catholic Church.

As has been seen in Chapter 1, a few women were finally added to the list by the General Synod, but of these only one, Josephine Butler, was British and lived since the Reformation. In the approved list of Lesser Festivals and Commemorations which appeared in the Alternative Service Book of 1980 the following are the British people who lived since the Reformation: Thomas More, William Tyndale, Thomas Cranmer, Richard Hooker, Lancelot Andrewes, George Herbert, Nicholas Ferrar, King Charles I, Jeremy Taylor, John Bunyan, Thomas Ken, William Law, John and Charles Wesley, William Wilberforce, Charles Simeon, John Keble, James Hannington, Josephine Butler and Edward King.

The post-Reformation people of other nationalities who are included are all Continental Roman Catholics, namely St Francis de Sales, St Vincent de Paul, St Francis Xavier, St Teresa of Avila and St John of the Cross.

A more detailed account is contained in the Introduction to the present writer's book *Alternative Saints*.

Notes

1. *The Commemoration of Saints and Heroes of the Faith in the Anglican Communion*, Report of a Commission appointed by the Archbishop of Canterbury, London 1957 p. 67 and passim.
2. Liturgical Commission Memoranda 75D and 75Q, 1957, unpublished.
3. *Calendar and Lessons for the Church's Year*, Report of the Church of England Liturgical Commission, London 1969. Report of the Church of England Liturgical Commission on Calendar Lectionary and Rules to Order the Service, London 1976, GS 292, 292B, 292C and 292X (Report of Revision Committee).

Index